The Origins and Growth of ARCHAEOLOGY

The Origins and Growth of

ARCHAEOLOGY

GLYN DANIEL

GALAHAD BOOKS · NEW YORK CITY

Library of Congress Catalog Card Number: 73-92828

ISBN: 0-88365-209-9

Published by arrangement with T. Y. Crowell Company

Manufactured in the United States of America

Acknowledgments are due to the following for the use of material from the publications stated:

Antiquity, E. D. Phillips, "The Greek Vision of Prehistory," 1964, and Professor Stuart Piggott, "Archaeological Draughtsmanship," 1965. Ernest Benn Ltd., Sir Leonard Woolley, *Digging Up the Past,* 1930. Ernest Benn Ltd. and W. W. Norton & Co., Inc., Sir Leonard Woolley, *Ur of the Chaldees,* 1929. A. & C. Black Ltd. and Harvard University Press, Professor Stuart Piggott, *Approach to Archaeology,* 1959. Cambridge University Press, Professor Grahame Clark, *The Study of Prehistory,* 1954; J. P. Droop, *Archaeological Excavation,* 1915. The Clarendon Press, Oxford, Gordon Childe, *The Danube in Prehistory,* 1929; O. G. S. Crawford and Alexander Keiller, *Wessex from the Air,* 1928; Sir Mortimer Wheeler, *Archaeology from the Earth,* 1954. Franklin Watts, Inc., Professor Grahame Clark and Gordon Childe, *Social Evolution,* 1951. Curtis Brown Ltd., Howard Carter and A. C. Mace, *The Tomb of Tut-ankh-Amen,* 1923. J. M. Dent & Sons Ltd., S. J. De Laet, *Archaeology and Its Problems,* 1957. Professor Robert J. Braidwood and Department of Anthropology, University of Chicago, "Terminology in Prehistory" from *Human Origins: An Introductory General Course in Anthropology,* 1946. Gerald Duckworth & Co. Ltd., Dr. Glyn Daniel, *A Hundred Years of Archaeology,* 1950. Hamish Hamilton Ltd., Professor R. J. C. Atkinson, *Stonehenge,* 1956. Lawrence & Wishart Ltd. and International Publishers, Inc., Frederick Engels, *The Origin of the Family, Private Property and the State,* trans. 1940, Joan Evans and Longmans Green & Co., *Time and Chance,* 1943. Lutterworth Press, Sir Leonard Woolley, *Spadework,* 1953. Methuen & Co. Ltd., Professor Grahame Clark, *Archaeology and Society,* 1939. Professor Christopher Hawkes and the Prehistoric Society, Presidential Address for 1951. Prentice-Hall, Inc., Robert F. Heizer (ed.), *Man's Discovery of His Past: Literary Landmarks in Archaeology,* © 1962. *Science,* W. F. Libby, E. C. Anderson, J. R. Arnold, "Age Determination by Radiocarbon Content: World Wide Assay of Natural Radiocarbon," Vol. 109, 4 March 1949, pp. 227–8. Thames & Hudson Ltd., C. W. Ceram (ed.), *The World of Archaeology.* Alfred A. Knopf, Inc., and Thames & Hudson Ltd., Jacquetta Hawkes (ed.), *The World of the Past* (trans. of *Les Caverne de Volp* by Abbe Breuil, Arts et Méliers Graphiques), 1963. Franklin Watts, Inc., Professor Robert J. Braidwood, *Archaeologists and What They Do,* 1960. Cambridge University Press, Glyn Daniel, *The Three Ages,* 1943. Joseph Déchelette, *Manuel d'Archéologie Préhistorique, Celtique, et Gallo-Romaine,* Paris, 1908, trans. Glyn Daniel.

For
Stuart Piggott

Preface

The purpose of this book is to illustrate by a series of extracts the way in which a particular discipline has come into existence and how it worked as it grew. No competent archaeologist interested in the history of his subject would agree with my selection: I have had to tailor my anthology to the space available, and my guide has been what I think is important and significant in the origins and growth of archaeology.

Professor Stuart Piggott has read through the book in typescript and made many helpful suggestions. This book is dedicated to him, one of the few archaeologists who are also historians of archaeology, and who realize that the present state of archaeology cannot be divorced from its past state. Archaeology studies the past in the present, but the archaeologist must never forget that the present is clouded and conditioned by past archaeologies, and that present archaeological scholarship will itself be one of the many past archaeologies in a decade or so.

GLYN DANIEL

Contents

Plates

The Origins and Growth of ARCHAEOLOGY

1 What Is Archaeology?

Before we set out on our collection of extracts from writers whose work illustrates the origins and growth of archaeology, it might be wise to get some agreement as to what archaeology is, or at least what the editor of this volume considers it to be. The word "archaeology" was first used in the English language to mean ancient history in general. Even in the year 1803 reference could be made (in *Archaeologia,* XIV, 211) to the fact that "the contents of the Archaeiology [*sic*] of Wales are derived from various collections of old manuscripts." But although these words were written in the first few years of the nineteenth century, it had already been established well before this that archaeology meant the systematic and descriptive study of antiquities. This was certainly what Alexander Gordon understood in the early eighteenth century, and the following passage from his *Itinerarium Septentrionale* (1726), with its clear view of what archaeology was and its charming reasons for the study of this subject, is a good beginning to our anthology.

> Seeing Reason and Knowledge are the Characteristicks which distinguish Mankind from the more ignoble Part of the Animal Creation, those Studies, which are the most improving, deserve our greatest application: In the number of which, *Antiquity* claims a great share, particularly *Archiology,* which consists of Monuments, or rather Inscriptions, still subsisting. . . .
>
> I know, that there are People to be found, and it is to be re-

gretted, some of them of Birth and Fortune, who expose their own Ignorance, in discountenancing this Kind of Knowledge, giving out, that Antiquity, and such like branches of Learning, are but the Chymeras of *Virtuosi,* dry and unpleasant Searches; So, because they themselves are blind, and uncapable to relish such Pleasures, they have the Imprudence to betray their own Weakness to the World. Hence we observe, That Things which are in their Nature rough, unpolish'd, vicious, and cruel, these fit their Genius the best; violent Hunting, Bear-Gardens, Gaming-tables, Quarrelling, and Midnight Revellings, are their Darling Delights.

Let us go directly from the early eighteenth century to the present day, and see what modern scholars in different countries think archaeology is about, what its methods and aims are or should be. We will quote the words of scholars from several countries, and first Sigfried J. De Laet, a Belgian who is Professor of Archaeology at the University of Ghent. The following extract comes from the English edition of his introduction to archaeology published in London in 1957 under the title of *Archaeology and Its Problems.*

For many people the word "archaeologist" immediately conjures up the memory of Labiche's character M. Poitrinas, solemn of speech, vulgar in appearance, puffed up with empty and pretentious learning; who passed for a harmless and amusing lunatic, without malice save at the expense of his colleagues. For other people, however, an archaeologist wears a romantic halo: he is the man who searches for cities lost in the jungle, or buried in the desert; who discovers, at one stroke of the pick, dazzling works of art or fabulous treasures. Both these conceptions are false. Doubtless such as M. Poitrinas, who would trace a safety match back to the Romans, still exist. . . . It also happens that an excavator, lighting by good fortune on some rare treasure, may find it glamourized by the press. But just as a bone setter is not representative of the medical profession, so the bearded and sententious dilettante has no right to be dubbed archaeologist. Sensational discoveries, such as that of the tomb of Tutankh-Amen, to cite only the most celebrated of them, are often but

2

the crowning achievement of long years of research and are not, for the archaeologist, an end in themselves. The task of archaeology lies on an entirely different plane. . . .

There are still many misconceptions as to the nature of archaeology, even among members of the profession. These may be partly explained by the origins of this discipline, in particular the assimilation of archaeology by art history in the time of the Renaissance and of the Humanistic Movement. At that time, scholars and men of letters, full of an unbounded enthusiasm for ancient Greece and Rome, confined their archaeological interests to works of art and buildings of aesthetic value. Archaeology, to their eyes, was identical with the history of ancient classical art. Other humanists regarded archaeology merely as an illustrative commentary on the texts which they were editing. This subordination of archaeology to philology, especially evident during the Renaissance, continued throughout the seventeenth and eighteenth centuries. It was not until the nineteenth century, and the birth of prehistory as a scientific discipline, that the archaeologist found at last his own sphere of research: the study and historical interpretation of *all* the material remains that vanished civilizations have left in the ground. These remains, from the magnificent Colosseum to the humble sherd of badly fired pottery, are studied from every aspect, as a means of reconstructing the life of past civilizations. Works of art are not, of course, excluded from the province of archaeology, if they can clarify in any way the history of former civilizations. They remain, however, for archaeology purely historical documents and archaeology should refrain, *as should the archaeologist,* from formulating a subjective judgement on their aesthetic value. The distance which separates archaeology from art history, moreover, increases every day. The art historian concerns himself exclusively with works of art as expressions of the aesthetic taste of a definite epoch. . . .

The archaeologist, on the contrary, takes pains to be scrupulously objective. Steady development in methods of reconnaissance and interpretation, especially notable during the last few years, has raised his profession to the level of a real scientific discipline. As an auxiliary science to history, its essential task is to reconstruct the different stages of the material civilization of mankind since earliest times.

And now a statement of the aims and purpose of archaeology from an American writer, Robert J. Braidwood, Professor of Old World Prehistory in the Oriental Institute, and Professor in the Department of Anthropology at the University of Chicago. It comes from his book *Archaeologists and What They Do,* published in New York in 1960 in a series deliberately planned and written to explain to the general interested public what various professions do, and how and why.

It has been said that the past is "flat" for most Americans. This undoubtedly means that Americans (and probably many other peoples, too) think of a generalized past, starting not too long ago and stretching back to the beginnings of time. In this range from not too long ago to the beginnings of time they evidently sense little of the depth or duration of time itself. They think little of the long succession of changes that took place in the ways in which men of the past lived their lives.

Except in some of the older communities along the Atlantic seaboard, few Americans live with the traces of their own cultural past. If the house they live in or the things they use are over fifty years old, these things are *old*—for them. The Indians may be of romantic interest, but their ancient ways are not part of the cultural heritage of most Americans. Because it is not very much a part of *their own* cultural past, the past of the American Indian has for them a sort of storybook unreality.

Few Americans know much about the actual way of life of their own earlier ancestors in Europe. . . .

The past is somewhat less flat for Europeans. . . . They live amid much older traces of their own past, and if they are interested they are able to work their way back much further in time. As Americans travel to Europe or elsewhere in the Old World, they too acquire more sense of depth of time and of the ways in which the lives of people have changed with time. For example, any American of Norwegian descent must, if he makes a tour of the old country, visit the great outdoor Folk Museum near

4

Oslo. The past of his own family line will then never again be as flat as it was. . . .

An archaeologist is interested in *things* and in the way they may be used to reconstruct the ways of life of past peoples. Unfortunately, most history books concentrate on political events and on accounts of wars, treaties, and the doings of kings and cardinals. History books usually say little enough of the way in which the ordinary family lived its life. This is because most "history," in the conventional sense, is taken from written sources. . . . Truly complete histories of the ways of life of peoples can only be made through study of what these peoples wrote of themselves, and also of what they made and did for themselves. And, for that long ninety-nine per cent of all human history before men learned to write, it is only by the archaeological study of the things men made and did that we can arrive at any understanding of their history whatsoever.

This is a pretty broad definition of archaeology: the study of the things men made and did, in order that their whole way of life may be understood. If you think of an archaeologist, what probably comes to your mind first is an image of a bearded professor who goes to Egypt to dig up the treasure-filled tomb of a long-dead Pharaoh. In the early days of archaeology, when museums were clamoring to be filled with spectacular antiquities, such archaeologists were fashionable. I believe it is fair to say today, however, that most archaeologists are as interested in the life of the common man as in the life of his ruler the Pharaoh . . .

I cannot tell you just where the interests and methods of an archaeologist should end, in time. The procedures and ways of thinking that a good detective uses in solving a crime, the way he studies the meaning of his clues (the *things* of the crime), are quite familiar to me as an archaeologist. I am trying to suggest to you that archaeology is the way in which the actions of human beings may be understood through the study of what human beings *did,* rather than simply through what they *said* of themselves. . . .

There are probably as many different kinds of archaeologists as there are different kinds of doctors or engineers. Since there

5

are far fewer archaeologists in total than there are doctors and engineers, the difference between one archaeologist and another may seem more extreme. Thus, one good friend and colleague of mine began as a geologist and gradually shifted his interest to the archaeology of early Ice Age prehistory. He feels most at home when talking with geologists, paleontologists, soil chemists, and climatologists.

Another good friend and colleague is a specialist on the stone or brass grave lids used in English churches late in the Middle Ages. These grave lids are engraved with the figures of the knights and ladies that the graves contain. This colleague feels most at home when talking with art historians, specialists in medieval dress or armor or heraldry, and with church historians.

Both of these colleagues deserve to be called archaeologists. They use things made by men in such a way as to gain understanding of the lives of people in the past. If we were to assume that these two persons represent two extremes of archaeology, then you may take it for granted that there are archaeologists of all possible kinds in between.

Some archaeologists who have written about the history of this branch of knowledge speak of two separate and distinct archaeologies. The first archaeology, they say, arose during the great rebirth of intellectual curiosity, the Renaissance, which spread from Italy into the rest of Europe following about A.D. 1400. This intellectual curiosity had as a particular focus of attention the antiquity of Greece, Rome, and the Bible lands. Johann Winckelmann, a German born in 1717, who spent most of his life as an art historian in Rome, is often called the "father of archaeology." Winckelmann wrote, for example, that "by no people has beauty been so highly esteemed as by the Greeks." The archaeologists who followed in the intellectual tradition of Winckelmann had, as a rule, little interest in any other past than that of Greece, Rome, or the Bible lands. Nor were these archaeologists much interested in the objects that the ordinary Greek or Roman or Near Easterner used daily. The archaeologists of the Winckelmann fine-arts tradition concentrated their

6

study on such things as vase painting, sculpture, and monumental architecture.

The second or alternate stream of archaeology is said to have arisen just over one hundred years ago, as a part of the great burst of interest in the natural sciences. The appearance of Charles Darwin's *Origin of Species* in 1859 and of Sir Charles Lyell's *The Antiquity of Man* in 1863 could perhaps be taken as the base line of serious archaeology in the tradition of the natural sciences. It was, however, the early sociologists and anthropologists, such as the American Lewis Henry Morgan and the Englishmen Herbert Spencer and Edward Burnett Tylor, who gave the archaeology of this tradition its particular slant. In effect, these men asked, If there was natural biological evolution, why might there not be social evolution as well? Are there, perhaps, still existing in out-of-the-way places in the world, living social fossils? Or, by excavating the remains of peoples who once lived in other parts of the world than in Greece, Rome, or the Bible lands, may we not find other fossils of social evolution?

I myself suspect that this strict separation of archaeology into two rigid intellectual streams is overdrawn. Other ideas entered into the growth of archaeology. Many Europeans took to the spade simply because of their curiosity about their own national origins: the French sought for traces of the Gauls, the English for ancient Britons, the Germans for the old Teutonic tribes, and so on. . . .

To the degree that such a pair of archaeologies actually ever existed as strictly separate fields of knowledge it may have been a good thing. The fine arts, or classical and Biblical, tradition threw much light on the origins and development of the whole Western cultural tradition. It gave scholars in the English-speaking lands, in France, in Germany, and so on, a common international interest and it clarified much of the history taken solely from written records. The archaeology of the natural and social sciences tradition, on the other hand, found its interests exactly with the so-called "exotic" or "peripheral" peoples who had lived outside the Western cultural tradition, and with the

7

more remote thousands of years of prehistoric time. There was international scholarly cooperation within this tradition of archaeology as well as within the fine-arts tradition.

Actually, I am convinced these two streams of knowledge were never completely separated. There was, and is, much overlap between the two in both field and laboratory techniques and in the ways in which the traces of peoples of the past are studied. . . . To the really good and thoughtful archaeologist in either tradition the important thing is that the ways of life of peoples of the past may be better understood. The clues to this understanding, in both traditions, are to be found in the things that men made and did and that we may discover through excavation or often simply through travel and acute observation either outdoors or in museum collections. The over-all goal of understanding is the same in either tradition.

We now turn to English scholars, and first to the late Sir Leonard Woolley (1880–1960), whose *Digging Up the Past,* from which the following extract is taken, was first published in 1930.

The prime duty of the field archaeologist is to collect and set in order material with not all of which he can himself deal at first hand. In no case will the last word be with him; and just because that is so his publication of the material must be minutely detailed, so that from it others may draw not only corroboration of his views but fresh conclusions and more light. Should he not then stop at this? It might be urged that the man who is admirably equipped to observe and record does not necessarily possess the powers of synthesis and interpretation, the creative spirit and the literary gift which will make of him a historian. But no record can ever be exhaustive. As his work in the field goes on, the excavator is constantly subject to impressions too subjective and too intangible to be communicated, and out of these, by no exact logical process, there arise theories which he can state, can perhaps support, but cannot prove: their truth will depend ultimately on his own calibre, but, in any case, they have their value as summing up experiences which no student of his objects and his notes can ever share. Granted that the excavator is adequate to his task, the conclusions which he draws from his own work ought to carry weight, and he is bound to put them forward; if they are palpably wrong then his observations also may justly be held suspect. Between archaeology and history there is no fenced frontier, and the digger who will best observe and record his discoveries is precisely he who sees them as historical material and rightly appraises them: if he has not the power of synthesis and interpretation he has mistaken his calling. It is true that he may not possess any literary gifts, and that, therefore, the formal presentation of results to the public may be better made by others; but it is the field archaeologist who, directly or indirectly, has opened up for the general reader new chapters in the history of civilized man; and by recovering from the earth such documented relics of the past as strike the imagination through the eye, he makes real and modern what otherwise might seem a far-off tale.

Now let us consider the views of another English archaeologist, Sir Mortimer Wheeler. The following statement comes from his *Archaeology from the Earth,* first published in 1954.

What in fact is Archaeology? I do not myself really know. Theses have been written to demonstrate that it is This or That or not the Other Thing. . . . I do not even know whether Archaeology is to be described as an art or as a science. . . . But it is at least abundantly clear that Archaeology is increasingly dependent on a multitude of sciences and is itself increasingly adopting the methodology of a natural science. It draws today upon physics, chemistry, geology, biology, economics, political science, sociology, climatology, botany, and I know not what else. As a science, it is pre-eminently a synthetic process; and if we prefer to regard it as an art, or even as a philosophy, we must still affirm that it is an integration of scientifically observed and dissected phenomena relating to man; it is still a synthesis. . . .

There is an analogy between archaeological and military field work that is recurrent and illuminating. The analogy rests—

9

strangely enough between the dead and the deadly—in the underlying *humanity* of both disciplines. The soldier, for his part, is fighting not against a block of coloured squares on a war map; he is fighting against a fellow being, with different but discoverable idiosyncrasies which must be understood and allowed for in every reaction and manoeuvre. . . . the archaeological excavator is not digging up *things,* he is digging up *people;* however much he may analyse and tabulate and desiccate his discoveries in the laboratory, the ultimate appeal across the ages, whether the time interval be 500 or 500,000 years, is from mind to intelligent mind, from man to sentient man. Our graphs and schedules mean nothing if they do not ultimately mean that. Of our scraps and pieces we may say, with Mark Antony in the market place, "You are not wood, you are not stones, but men." It is a truism of which I constantly find it necessary to remind the student and indeed myself: that the life of the past and the present are diverse but indivisible; that Archaeology, in so far as it is a science, is a science which must be extended into the living and must indeed itself be lived if it is to partake of a proper vitality. . . .

Year after year, individual after individual, learned society after learned society, we are prosaically revealing and cataloguing our discoveries. Too often we dig up mere things, unrepentantly forgetful that our proper aim is to dig up people.

For another view, let us turn to Grahame Clark, Professor of Archaeology at the University of Cambridge; this is what he wrote in his *Archaeology and Society,* first published in 1939 (taken from the third edition, 1957).

Archaeology may be simply defined as the systematic study of antiquities as a means of reconstructing the past. For his contributions to be fruitful the archaeologist has to possess a real feeling for history, even though he may not have to face what is perhaps the keenest challenge of historical scholarship, the subtle interplay of human personality, and circumstance. Yet he is likely to be involved even more deeply in the flow of time. The prehistoric archaeologist, in particular, is confronted by historical changes of altogether greater dimensions than those with which the historian of literate civilizations is concerned, and has to face demands on his historical imagination of a commensurate order; further, at a purely technical level he is likely to be met with much greater difficulties of decipherment, difficulties which can as a rule only be surmounted by calling on scientists and scholars practiced in highly specialized branches of knowledge.

And the last of our four passages in which English archaeologists define their subject is from Professor Stuart Piggott's *Approach to Archaeology* (1959).

What is popularly called "archaeology" has at the present time a widespread appeal to many people to whom "history" (if you used that word to them) would seem something different, and without much interest. What I want to make clear is that archaeology is in fact a branch of historical study, and that far from being something that can be easily understood without much mental effort, it is a real discipline in both senses of the word. . . .

There has been much confusion in many people's minds between some of the techniques and process of archaeology (such as excavation or air photography), and the study itself which they serve. This is to confuse means with ends. Again, it is frequently thought that archaeologists are only concerned with prehistoric peoples and their remains, whereas the techniques of archaeology can be used equally well (perhaps even better) in the study of communities with a written record. If we are to understand what archaeology is about, and what archaeologists are trying to do, we must begin by looking for a definition.

If we are going to study individuals, societies, communities, or other groupings of people in the past, we have got to use various techniques which will get round the fact that just because it *is* the past, the people we are studying are dead, and we cannot go and ask them questions or watch their daily life. In its wider sense, the word "history" covers all inquiry into the human past, from the earliest times to a few generations ago; in a more restricted use, it covers the study of those periods or communities in the past who used some sort of written record. If we use it for a moment in the wide sense, then archaeology comes within its scope as a set of techniques for investigating the human past by means other than those of history in the narrow sense—in other words, by means which are not those provided by written records. It is concerned with material objects of human origin, whether they are great works of art or masterpieces of architecture, or whether they are broken pots and pans or the remains of the hut of a stone-using savage. Archaeologists are students of material evidence surviving from the past, of the tangible and visible products and achievements of extinct communities.

For societies which existed before the art of writing was invented in the Near East some five thousand years ago, or those which continued to be illiterate side by side with the higher civilizations (as for instance the British Isles until the coming of the Romans in the first century A.D.), this material evidence is all we have to testify to their very existence. For prehistoric, nonliterate peoples, outside the range of written history, the archaeological approach is the only one that can be used to obtain direct information. . . . there are other means which can sometimes provide indirect information, but that is another thing, and is not the application of strictly archaeological techniques.

The sources used by archaeologists in default of written records form what we might call unconscious evidence, provided by the things made in the extinct communities they are studying, and surviving into the present. It is unconscious evidence because prehistoric flint implements, or Roman pottery, or medieval churches were not thought of as historical evidence by the men who made them, but they acquire the character of evidence when the archaeologist discovers, examines, and interprets them. The archaeologist is really always making the best of a bad job, and trying to reconstruct some sort of history from material that sometimes looks very unpromising, but is all he has to work with.

We should now be reasonably clear, despite Sir Mortimer Wheeler's disclaimer, that we know what archaeology is: the study and practice of writing the history of man from material sources. In medieval and modern times the material source is not so important as written sources, and the further we go back the more important the material source is, until in times before there was any writing archaeology is the paramount source. This is prehistory, and here prehistory and prehistoric archaeology mean almost the same thing. It is usually stated that the word prehistory was introduced to a general reading public by Sir John Lubbock in his *Prehistoric Times* (in 1865). Tylor used the word in his *Primitive Culture* (1871), Gladstone was using it in 1878, *The Times* in 1888, and *Nature* in 1902. Many of us thought that the first person to use the word was Daniel Wilson in the title of his book *The Archaeology and Prehistoric Annals of Scotland,* first published in 1851; and indeed Daniel Wilson thought so himself, because in his Preface to the second edition, published twelve years later, he says "the application of the term prehistoric introduced—if I mistake not—for the first time in this work." But he was mistaken, as Professor Heizer has shown us; the word was being used by M. Tournal twenty years before Wilson, as can be seen from the following extract from a paper published in the *Annales de chimie et de physique* for 1833, in the translation by R. F. Heizer in his *Man's Discovery of His Past: Literary Landmarks in Archaeology* (1962).

The only division that should be adopted, and which has been, I believe, already proposed, is the following:

Ancient Geological Period

This includes (1) the immense stretch of time which preceded the appearance of man on the surface of the globe, during which an infinity of generations have succeeded each other, and (2) the modern geological period or "Age of Man." This period perhaps divided into:

Prehistoric Period

This started with the appearance of man on the surface of the globe, and extends to the beginning of the most ancient traditions. It is probable that during this period sea level rose to 150 feet above its present level. M. Reboul is to publish on this subject a very important work, which will remove doubts and will settle many irresolutions.

Historic Period

This hardly dates beyond seven thousand years ago, i.e., to the epoch of the construction of Thebes, during the nineteenth Egyptian Dynasty (Josephus cites the kings of this dynasty month by month and day by day). This period could be extended farther back, following new historic observations.

But while the name and notion of prehistory became well established in the nineteenth century, as did the discipline of archaeology, those who gave thought to problems of nomenclature and classification were not all certain that human history could now be divided into four great phases, namely prehistory, ancient history, medieval history, and modern history. The French invented, in addition to *préhistoire, protohistoire*. The following extract is from the presidential address to the Prehistoric Society given in 1951 by Professor Christopher Hawkes.[1] It discusses the development of these names and suggests some additional ones.

To the Frenchman, *la préhistoire* means (roughly) what we call the Stone Ages. He adopted it, very logically, to denote the ages before there was any *histoire,* or History in the documentary sense, anywhere in the world; in the nineteenth century those were assumed to include both the Old and the New Stone Ages, and, though today the beginnings of a Metal Age in the Middle East are known to go back before the earliest written documents, it still appears reasonable to Frenchmen to call the Old, Middle, and New Stone Ages together *préhistoriques,* and to distinguish the Metal Ages, so long as they produce written documents here and there but not yet everywhere, by a fresh word, the adjective *protohistorique*—of which the substantive is *la protohistoire,* the Italian *protostoria.* The corresponding German word is *Frühgeschichte,* which really means only "early history," in contrast to *Vorgeschichte* or prehistory in a stricter

[1] *Proceedings of the Prehistoric Society,* 1951, 1ff.

sense; German usage is complicated by the presence of a third word, *Urgeschichte,* but the shades of meaning involved, though they may arouse strong partisanship, can be toned down by the convenient German habit of using *Vor- und Frühgeschichte,* or *Ur- und Frühgeschichte* (whichever you adhere to), as a single composite expression for the whole run of prehistoric and non-Classical cultures down to the Carolingian or Saxon emperors. No such convenience is open to English speakers. Standard English can adopt expressions from any language under the sun, but only on its own terms; and I do not think those are likely ever to be such as to admit the locution "Pre- and Proto-History" to our language as an everyday portmanteau phrase. In these things it is use and wont that are rightly all-important. The Englishman, except by concession to foreign usage, will not call his Anglo-Saxon period "protohistory"; he calls it "early history," and has as much right to keep the phrase as the Germans have to keep their *Frühgeschichte.* "Prehistoric," on the other hand, is his standard broad term for everything in his country that is generally or generically Pre-Roman, from Eoliths to Druids. . . .

Terminology is of two kinds: common or everyday, and learned or scientific. . . . The word "Norman," for the style of architecture, was at first used only by the learned, but with the spread of education it has been adopted into common speech. All of us know a Norman church; and if the more refined specialist of today were to tell us we ought only to call it Post-Conquest Romanesque, we should say he had forgotten the difference between his specialist vocabulary and our everyday one. It is the same with "prehistoric." The word, denoting everything in pre-Roman Britain from Eoliths to Druids, has passed into common speech; we can today only accept the situation, and be thankful for the spread of education that has caused it.

But when we who are prehistorians assemble in our capacity as specialists, the case is altered. . . . We have seen that the word *protohistorique* in French—*protohistórico* in Spanish, in Italian *protostorico*—is used to denote those ages whence written documents for history are forthcoming here and there but are not yet universal, as opposed to the ages *préhistoriques,* which lack them altogether. It was logical enough when it was invented in the nineteenth century, for evolutionary thought then held that the whole ancient world had progressed through a single series of stages, broad enough for regional time lags in their incidence to be no great matter. Today, discovery in the Near and Middle East—often by the French themselves—has made it logical no longer. When the first use of metal on the west of the Mediterranean appears a full thousand years after the emergence of literate civilization on the east of it, such a use of the word is almost meaningless.

Yet should not "protohistoric" now be given a revised and corrected meaning. . . . "Protohistoric" must denote an age, or stage, in which the first rudiments . . . of historical documentation are already present, not thousands of miles away, but *in the denoted culture itself,* where they will be followed, in the next stage after, by the fully formed documents of history proper . . . the most, I think that can properly be called *protohistoric:* the final stage of a country's prehistory when history is already beginning to glimmer visibly within it, and is not merely reflected from outside.

But history will, before that, have been often so reflected; and the reflection may come from near at hand. When the southerly lands of Mediterranean Europe were already historic, with only some areas still protohistoric among the main focuses of Greek, Etruscan, Roman, and Carthaginian history, there were great stretches of [the European] Continent (to go no farther afield) whose peoples were very close to history, and whose cultures, for that reason, can be studied and dated at close range. If we want to subdivide what we loosely call Prehistory *according to how much our knowledge of it owes to reflected historical light,* we should have a word for this stage of it, which is not yet protohistory, and yet is almost historic but not quite. What is almost an island, almost insular but not quite, we call a peninsula; a brooch that is almost an annular or ring brooch but not quite, we call penannular. It would convey the same meaning if we gave the name *penehistoric* to these almost but not quite historic times. In Britain, their beginning would lie

in the fifty years centred on 300 B.C. . . . [the] island was visited by the renowned Mediterranean explorer Pytheas, the
Greek of Marseilles, who made his voyage most probably about
325–320. The surviving scraps of his description bring us almost into history, but, since they are only scraps, not quite.

However, both the ways [to Britain] from the Mediterranean
by the Western sea, and by Central Europe and across the North
Sea, had been travelled long before Pytheas' time. . . . We can
be sure that in Britain . . . the Wessex Culture begins at 1500.

That is twelve centuries short of [European] penehistoric
times. The reflected light of history that helps us through shines
from far off, and on the way it may turn dim and blue, or even
for a space go out. Barbarian Europe is moving alongside history, but not yet nearly inside: *parahistoric* is the most now we
can call it. . . . For Britain, then, taken in its place in this
great whole, the round date of 1500 can be marked with a line
across the page, which sets an anterior limit to everything, no
matter how obscure within itself, that follows after.

From about 1500 to the half-century around 300, then, I call
the *parahistoric* period of our prehistory; the *penehistoric* follows and the *protohistoric* last of all, on the margins of Roman
history. Each of the three in turn . . . brings us one step
nearer to the *historic* plane of knowledge.

Turn back beyond 1500, and at once you are a big step farther from it. . . . We want a brave new word which will embrace in one sweep everything from the "Mycenaean horizon"
in Britain and similarly placed countries back to the first appearance in them, or the first direct and drastic influence, of
Neolithic colonization. . . . What we want to have is a new
word; not meaning "far-off voice," which of course is what
"telephone" means, but "far-off history" . . . the study of *telehistoric* times.

The telehistoric period, then, and the ensuing sequence of
parahistoric, penehistoric, and protohistoric, which connect it
serially with full historic times, make a scheme whereby prehistory from the Neolithic colonizations onward is classified according to *the degree,* as we ascend the scale, *in which our
knowledge of it stands indebted to historical material* . . . .

17

It is time we considered "pure" prehistory. . . . There is no question here of History, except in the universal sense in which most of it, reckoned by duration, is our Prehistory. . . . If we need a name . . . which shall relate it to our names for the later stages when history has begun emerging, we can embrace the Stone Age sequence in one big curly bracket and write against it, above telehistoric and parahistoric, and the rest, the old name *antehistoric,* because it is all anterior to history. . . .

I call this the *Cognitional System of Nomenclature for Prehistory;* and I offer it as a modest, but I hope durable, birthday present to the second half of the twentieth century. [See diagram.]

	Cognition	*"Ages" and Specimen Dates (Britain)*
PREHISTORIC	ANTEHISTORIC (before all history)	Palaeolithic
		Mesolithic
		Neolithic, primary
	TELEHISTORIC (far-off from history)	Neolithic, secondary or diffusive
		EARLY METAL AGES:
		±1500 B.C. *in Britain*
	PARAHISTORIC (alongside history)	±300 B.C. *in Britain*
	PENEHISTORIC (almost history)	50 B.C. *(often later) in Britain*
	PROTOHISTORIC (beginning to be history)	
	HISTORIC	*Opening dates in Britain vary regionally: Roman, Celtic, Saxon, Viking*

In his inaugural lecture as Disney Professor of Archaeology at the University of Cambridge, Grahame Clark comments on this cognitional system of nomenclature and proposes the use of the phrases "primary prehistory" and "secondary prehistory." The following extract is from this lecture, entitled *The Study of Prehistory,* published in 1954.

Of one thing I am convinced, and that is the value of prehistory as a basic training-ground for archaeologists. The lack of written sources and the relative poverty of prehistoric remains alike compel the prehistorian both to develop the techniques of archaeology to their uttermost and to explore to the fullest the possibilities of cooperation with natural scientists. Moreover, prehistory underlies the history of all civilizations alike: it forms the one essential preface to the libraries of literate humanity.

It is often, and I think rightly, held that archeology should not be counted a separate field of study so much as a method of reconstructing the past from surviving traces of former societies. . . .

When the Abbé Breuil assumed the Chair of Prehistory at the Collège de France he declared it to be consecrated to the science of humanity before history. In our English usage we include under the heading prehistory much of *la protohistoire* as well as *la préhistoire* of our French colleagues. We prefer to include under a single head the history of all societies incapable of recording their own history. Yet no one conversant with the literature or who attends international congresses can fail to be aware of a marked difference in outlook between many of those who devote themselves primarily to one or other of the fields distinguished by the French terminology. Professor Christopher Hawkes, indeed, went so far, a few years ago, as to present to the second half of the twentieth century a cognitional nomenclature, in which he assigned the Stone Age, the French *la préhistoire,* to a kind of antehistoric limbo, and divided *la protohistoire* into proto-, pene-, para-, and telehistoric stages according as they were near to or far from the effulgence of recorded history. Now although it may be that we meditate on these fine shades of meaning in the recesses of our studies, my impression is that in public utterance we have not all testified to our regard for the donor by making the freest use of his gift.

Our remissness in this matter should not lead us into disregarding what from both a practical and theoretical point of view is a distinction of substance, between what one might term primary or basic prehistory, the prehistory that precedes all history and underlies literate civilizations the world over, and secondary or marginal prehistory, which in more or less remote territories ran parallel to the literary history of more favoured regions and indeed survived over extensive areas down to the time when these were first penetrated by Western explorers and subjected to the scrutiny of anthropologists. The contemporaneous existence of literate civilization introduces a new dimension into the study of secondary prehistory. It is not merely that we have the possibility of extending historic dates to prehistoric lands, the importance of which has been greatly diminished if not extinguished by the introduction of radiocarbon techniques: we now recognize that influences radiating from the potent and dynamic centres of ancient civilization were capable of transforming the economic life of relatively remote territories. . . . Thus, whereas primary prehistory is autonomous, secondary prehistory needs to be studied with reference to the history of contemporary civilizations.

Having now got clear, we hope, what is meant by archaeology and prehistory, and an idea of what the archaeologist is endeavoring to do, namely to write history from the surviving material sources, we can go on to see how the subject came into existence. The next four chapters deal with the origins of archaeology from its very beginnings until the time when, in the sixties of the nineteenth century, it could be said that archaeology existed as a recognized branch of learning. But there is one additional thing that should be said here and now. The purpose of archaeology is to extract history from the monuments and artifacts of the past, to write history from the often inadequate relics that time has spared. But to write and read history is also to appreciate and enjoy the past. Archaeologists are often mealymouthed about their profession, insisting on the one hand that they are creating history, which is a fine aim, but often enough spending their lives on the minutiae of flint arrowheads and bronze swords and the varying plans of megalithic tombs, which are arduous and highly technical and dull practices. Practice and aim should sometimes confess that the archaeologist is not always making and extracting the past. He is often enjoying it—the paintings at Lascaux, the great stone tombs and temples of France and the British Isles, the metalwork of the Celts, the pyramids and ziggurats of the ancient Near East, the goldwork from Mycenae, the Shang bronzes, the giant heads of the Olmecs of Mexico, the monastic cells of Skellig Michael, the temple at Sunion, and the bronze dancing girl from Mohenjo-daro. Perhaps the dichotomy between art history and archaeology, which Professor De Laet described, has left a legacy behind. The past that archaeology provides for us in the present is to be enjoyed as our common heritage, as well as tortured into typologies and transmuted into history. Through archaeology we own the pleasures of past time, as well as its historical witness.

2 Antiquaries and Travelers

While it is true that in the sixth century B.C. the princess Belshalti-Nanner, sister of Belshazzar, had a special room in her house for her collection of local antiquities, and that her father, Nabonidus, the last king of Babylon, engaged in antiquarian research and dug at Ur, there was no archaeology, properly speaking, in the ancient world. Greeks like Herodotus made ethnographical observations of great value, and indeed could be called, in a way, anthropologists: and some of their travels brought them into contact with barbarians surviving from prehistory. But there was no Greek archaeology. The following passage is from E. D. Phillips' article on "The Greek Vision of Prehistory," which appeared in *Antiquity* (1964, 171ff.).

No more than the rest of mankind before Europeans of the last two centuries did the Greeks practise archaeology, though they did occasionally make discoveries of archaeological interest and even drew correct conclusions. Thus the Athenians in the fifth century, carrying out a religious purification of Delos, opened some graves. These they judged from the make of arms buried with the bodies and from the fashion of the burial to be those of Carians, who still used arms and burial of the same kind. But such discoveries were accidental and never made in deliberate search for knowledge of former ages. Still less were they compared and classified, and no chronology could result from them.

The only field where the Greeks did find evidence which some of them used for inference concerning the remote past was that which we should now call anthropology and ethnography. For example, Hecataeus of Miletus, Herodotus, and, much later, Posidonius were all travellers who knew barbarous peoples, but though they left much information, the search for more was never organized, not even by the physicians, scholars, and geographers of Alexandria. In geography a wider acquaintance with primitive peoples of the tropics might have suggested that this was the original home of man, where he could have survived before he could make fire or clothes, or store food for winter. In Diodorus' time some Egyptians or Graeco-Egyptians did indeed maintain that mankind spread from Egypt, and in later ages civilization as well, but this is local pride rather than anticipation of Perry or Elliot Smith.

None the less, the Greek thinkers alone of their time had reached the stage of rational reflection on primitive man which needed to be reached before positive gains of knowledge could begin. It is odd that even this state of mind did not recur until very recent times, but fortunate that when this happened the relevant sciences had already made great strides.

It is also true that a Chinese compilation of A.D. 52 set out a sequence of Stone, Bronze, and Iron Age; of this Lowie wrote, ". . . this is not a case of genius forestalling science by two thousand years; an alert intelligence is simply juggling possibilities without any basis of facts or any attempt to test them." [1] We do not agree with Lowie's view: the Chinese scheme probably preserved a folk memory of the technological succession of stone, bronze, and iron. But, whether in China or in Greece, there was no archaeology until, as Phillips said in the extract we have quoted, "the Europeans of the last two centuries." Archaeology is the product of the last two hundred years. Its beginnings came in a formal way when the antiquity of man was established and the Three-Age system was developed by the Scandinavians, as recorded in chapters 3 and 4 of this book. But there was a groping toward archaeology in the antiquarianism of the previous two

[1] R. H. Lowie, *The History of Ethnological Theory*, 1937, p. 13.

hundred years, and it is these prearchaeological beginnings that are our concern in this chapter.

As far as we are concerned in Western Europe—and it is here, in France, Britain, and Scandinavia, that archaeology was born —the beginnings are of two kinds. There are first the antiquaries who worked in their own country, hoping by studying the visible remains of the past and the stray objects found by accident, to understand the past. We might perhaps call these people the local antiquaries. In the second place, there are the antiquaries and collectors who brought back from the Mediterranean and the Near East the visible remains of the past. There were Italian collectors from the fourteenth century onward; in Britain there were many distinguished collectors in the sixteenth, seventeenth, and eighteenth centuries, and in 1714, "some Gentlemen who had travelled in Italy, desirous of encouraging, *at home,* a taste for those objects which had contributed so much to their entertainment *abroad,"* founded the Society of Dilettanti. Our purpose in this chapter is to show by quotations the work of local antiquaries and of the traveled dilettanti. We begin with five British antiquaries, namely Camden, Aubrey, Lhwyd, Rowlands, and Stukeley.

William Camden (1551–1623) was first a master at Westminster School, then headmaster, and Clarenceux King of Arms in the College of Heralds, which, as Stuart Piggott has said, "came as near to being an Institute of Antiquarian Research as could have been conceived in Elizabethan England." [2] He traveled extensively in Britain studying its visible antiquities, and indeed defended what he described as the "back looking curiosity": he recognized that there were some "which wholly contemne and avile this study of Antiquity," but he was of quite another view. "In the study of Antiquity (which is always accompanied with dignity and hathe a certaine resemblance with eternity)," he wrote, "there is a sweet food of the mind well befitting such as are of honest and noble disposition." In 1586, when he was thirty-five, he produced his *Britannia,* the first general guide to the antiquities of Britain. It went through many editions, of which the most famous are Gibson's of 1695 and Gough's of 1789; what other archaeological work has been reproduced and revised during two hundred years? In the first (1586) edition there was an illustration, and this, as Sir

[2] *Proceedings of the British Academy,* 1951, p. 202.

Thomas Kendrick has said,[3] was the first illustration in an English archaeological work. It was of the reused Saxon chancel arch in the church of St. John-sub-Castro at Lewes in Sussex. In 1600, when Camden himself produced a new edition of the *Britannia,* he added to it illustrations of Roman coins and of Stonehenge, and we include in this book one of these illustrations (plate 3), the first step toward real archaeological illustration.

Here are two extracts from Camden, the first dealing with Silbury Hill in Wiltshire.

Here *Selbury,* a round hill, riseth to a considerable height, and seemeth by the fashion of it, and by the sliding down of the earth about it, to be cast up by men's hands. Of this sort there are many to be seen in this County, round and copped, which are call'd *Burrows* or *Barrows,* perhaps raised in memory of the Soldiers there slain. For bones are found in them; and I have read that it was a custom among the Northern People, that every soldier escaping alive out of Battel, was to bring his Helmet full of earth toward the raising of Monuments for their slain Fellows. Tho' I rather think this *Selbury-hill* to be placed instead of a boundary, if not by the Romans, yet by the Saxons, as well as the ditch call'd *Wodensdike,* seeing there were frequent battels in this country between the Mercians and the *West Saxons* about their limits; and *Boetius,* and the Writers that treat about Surveying, tell us, that such heaps were often raised for Landmarks.

Camden was a careful observer and in the second passage we quote from the *Britannia* he has observed in the sixteenth century what we now call crop marks: in a word he has, as a ground observer, noticed one of the essential elements in the development of air photography, but over three centuries before crop marks were appreciated as one of the main features in archaeological air reconnaissance.

But now age has eras'd the very tracks of it; and to teach us that Cities dye as well as men, it is at this day a corn-field,

---

[3] *British Antiquity,* 1950, p. 151. Kendrick says, "Camden, following the Continental example, was certainly the pioneer in antiquarian book illustration in this country."

wherein when the corn is grown up, one may observe the draughts of streets crossing one another, (for where they have gone the corn is thinner) and such *crossings* they commonly call *St. Augustine's cross*. Nothing now remains, but some ruinous walls of a tower, of a square form, and cemented with a sort of sand extremely binding. One would imagine this had been the *Acropolis*, it looks down from so great a height upon the wet plains in *Thanet*, which the Ocean, withdrawing itself by little and little, has quite left. But the plot of the City, now plow'd, has often cast up the marks of it's Antiquity, gold and silver coyns of the Romans.

John Aubrey (1626–97), the "Wiltshire Squire fallen on evil days," as Anthony Powell described him, was an antiquary full of the delights of field work. He was the first person to bring Avebury and Stonehenge into a context of archaeology and prehistory when he said, "The celebrated antiquity of Stonehenge, as also that stupendious but unheeded antiquity at Aubury, &c, I affirme to have been temples, and built by the Britons." His *Monumenta Britannica* still lies unpublished in the Bodleian Library in Oxford, but here is a passage from his *An Essay towards the Description of the North Division of Wiltshire,* written between 1659 and 1670.

Let us imagine then what kind of countrie this was in the time of the Ancient Britons. By the nature of the soil, which is a sour woodsere land, very natural for the production of oakes especially, one may conclude that this North Divison was a shady dismal wood; and the inhabitants almost as savage as the Beasts whose skins were their only rayment. The language British, which for the honour of it was in those days spoken from Orcades to Italie and Spain. The Boats of the Avon (which signifies River) were basketts of twigges covered with an oxe skin; which the poore people in Wales use to this day. They call them curricles. Within this Shire I believe that there were several Reguli which often made war upon another; and the great ditches which run on the Plaines and elsewhere so many miles (not unlikely) their boundaries; and withall served for defence against the incursions of their enemies, as the Pict's wall, Offa's Ditch; and that in China, to compare things small to great. Their religion is at large described by Caesar. Their priests were Druids some of their temples I pretend to have restored, as Avbury, Stonehenge, etc as also British sepulchres. Their way of fighting is lively sett down by Caesar. Their camps with their way of meeting I have sett down in another place. They knew the use of iron. . . . They were two or three degrees I suppose less savage than the Americans. . . . The Romans subdued and civilized them.

Edward Lhwyd (1660–1708) is a fine example of the late-seventeenth-century polymaths and antiquaries. A friend and correspondent of John Aubrey's, he was at first assistant to his old tutor Dr. Robert Plot, the first Keeper of the newly founded Ashmolean Museum in Oxford. When Plot went away to London to become secretary of the Royal Society, Lhwyd succeeded him as Keeper, and died, in the museum itself, at the early age of forty-eight. By then he had published the first figured catalogue of fossils, traveled extensively studying and recording natural history, languages, antiquities, customs, and published the first volume of his *Archaeologia Britannica* in 1707; it was subtitled as "giving some account additional to what has been hitherto Publish'd of the Languages, Histories and Customs of the Original Inhabitants of Great Britain from Collections and Observations in Travels through Wales, Cornwal, Bas-Bretagne, Ireland and Scotland." His study of fossils constantly brought him up against chipped stone implements, and this is what he had to say about the elf-shot theory of their origin, in a letter to Dr. Richard Richardson written from Linlithgow December 17, 1699, and printed in the *Philosophical Transactions of the Royal Society* (1713, p. 97).

In the High-lands we found the people every where civil enough. . . . We met with several inscriptions, but none of them Roman, nor indeed ancient: however, we copied all we met of two hundred years standing etc. . . . But what we were most diverted with, was their variety of Amulets; many of which (if not all) were certainly used by the Druids, and so

27

have been handed down from parents to children ever since. Some of these may be render'd in English, 1. Snake-button 2. Cock-knee stone 3. Toad-stone 4. Snail-stone 5. Mole-stone 6. Shower-stone; and 7. Elf-arrow. . . .

As to this *elf-stricking,* their opinion is, that the fairies (having not much power themselves to hurt animal bodies) do sometimes carry away men in the air, and furnishing them with bows and arrows, employ them to shoot men, cattle, &c. I doubt not but you have often seen of these Arrow-heads they ascribe to elfs or fairies: they are just the same chip'd flints the natives of New England head their arrows with at this day; and there are also several stone hatchets found in this kingdom, not unlike those of the Americans. . . . These elf arrow-heads have not been used as amulets above thirty or forty years; but the use of the rest is immemorial: whence I gather they were not invented for charms, but were once used in shooting here, as they are still in America. The most curious as well as the vulgar throughout this country, are satisfied they often drop out of the air, being shot by fairies, and relate many instances of it; but for my part I must crave leave to suspend my faith, untill I see one of them descend.

Edward Lhwyd traveled to Ireland in 1699 as part of his scheme to write an account of the archaeology and natural history of the Celtic parts of the British Islands and of France. He visited the great prehistoric tomb of New Grange, north of Dublin, which had only been discovered shortly before his visit. He writes the following account of it in a letter from Bathgate near Linlithgow in Scotland, dated December 15, 1699, and written to his friend Dr. Tancred Robinson. It is published in the *Philosophical Transactions of the Royal Society,* XXVII, 1712, p. 503, in a communication entitled "Several Observations relating to the Antiquities and Natural History of Ireland, made by Mr. EDW. LHWYD, in his Travels thro' that Kingdom."

We continued not above three days at Dublin, when we steer'd our course towards the Giants Causway. The most remarkable curiosity we saw by the way, was a stately Mount at a place called New Grange near Drogheda; having a number of huge stones pitch'd on end round about it, and a single one on the top. The gentleman of the village (one Mr. Charles Campbel) observing that under the green turf this mount was wholly composed of stones, and having occasion for some, employ'd his servants to carry off a considerable parcel of them; till they came at last to a very broad flat stone, rudely carved, and placed edgewise at the bottom of the mount. This they discover'd to be the door of a cave, which had a long entry leading into it. At the first entering we were forced to creep; but still as we went on, the pillars on each side of us were higher and higher; and coming into the cave, we found it about 20 foot high. In this cave, on each hand of us was a cell or apartment, and an other went on streight forward opposite to the entry. In those on each hand was a very broad shallow bason of stone, situated at the edge. The bason in the right hand apartment stood in another; that on the left hand was single; and in the apartment straight forward there was none at all. We observed that water dropt into the right hand bason, tho' it had rained but little in many days; and suspected that the lower bason was intended to preserve the superfluous liquor of the upper (whether this water were sacred, or whether it was for Blood in Sacrifice) that none might come to the ground. The great pillars round this cave, supporting the mount, were not at all hewn or wrought; but were such rude stones as those of Abury in Wiltshire, and rather more rude than those of stonehenge: but those about the basons, and some elsewhere, had such barbarous sculpture (viz. spiral like a snake, but without distinction of head and tail) as the fore-mentioned stone at the entry of the cave. . . . They found several bones in the cave, and part of a Stags (or else Elks) head, and some other things, which I omit, because the labourers differ'd in their account of them. A gold coin of the Emperor Valentinian, being found near the top of this mount, might bespeak it Roman; but that the rude carving at the entry and in the cave seems to denote it a barbarous monument. So, the coin proving it ancienter than any Invasion of the Ostmans or Danes; and the carving and rude sculpture, barbarous; it should follow, that it was some place of sacrifice or burial of the ancient Irish.

Although Lhwyd in this passage shows his romantic attachment to Druids and sacrifice, the argument in his last few sentences is one of the earliest examples of clear archaeological reasoning. He makes the same point in writing to his friend Henry Rowlands and giving him a description of New Grange; the letter is dated Sligo, March 12, 1699–1700, and begins by saying that for some while his time had "been spent in places quite remote from all correspondence, amongst the Hebrides, and other Highlands of Scotland with whom their neighbours seem to have less commerce than they have with either of the Indies." And adds, "They are nothing so barbarous as the Lowlanders and English commonly represent them. . . ." He then goes on to describe New Grange.

> I also met with one monument in this kingdom very singular: it stands at a place called New-Grange near Drogheda. . . . This mount is all the work of hands, and consists almost wholly of stones, but is cover'd with gravel and greenswerd, and has within it a remarkable cave. . . . Near the top of this Mount they found a gold coin of the Emperor Valentinian; but notwithstanding this, the rude carving . . . makes me conclude this monument was never Roman, not to mention that we want History to prove that ever the Romans were at all in Ireland. [See plate 4.]

The Reverend Henry Rowlands (1655–1723) was Vicar of Llanidan on the island of Anglesey, and a close friend and correspondent of Edward Lhwyd. He himself wrote a book, first published in Dublin in 1723, entitled *Mona Antiqua Restaurata; an Archaeological Discourse on the Antiquities, Natural and Historical, of the Isles of Anglesey, the Ancient Seat of the British Druids,* from which the following passage comes.

> Archaeology, or an account of the Origin of Nations after the Universal Deluge, admits of two ways of inquiry—either beginning at Babel, the place of man's dispersion, and tracing

them downwards to our own times by the light of records, which is History, and of natural reason, which is Inference and Conjecture; or else beginning from our own time, and winding them upwards, by the same helps, to the first place and origin of their progression—both which ways are usually taken by Historians and Genealogists, and are equally to be allowed in their manner of proceeding. By the former of these methods I have in the following Sections adventured through some of the darkest tracks of time, to calculate the Archaeology, and to fetch out and put together some rude strokes and lineaments of the AN-TIQUITIES of the ISLE OF ANGLESEY, from its first planting to the time of the Roman Conquest, mostly in an hypothetical way, or a rational scheme of inquiry.

A method, I confess, very unusual; viz. to trace the footsteps of historical actions any other way, than by that of ancient memoirs and records. But where those lights are wanting, what shall we do? Shall we lie down with our forefathers in the general slumber, blaming the past ages for leaving us in the dark? . . . No; that were to act unfaithfully with the designs of nature: Knowledge is her gift from God to us; and we ought to employ all the means and helps she affords, to improve and enlarge it.

The main and principal helps to guide us through the dark recesses of time, are the testimonies of unexceptionable records, and such consequences as are naturally deducible from them. These are like the solar rays; where-ever they shine, there is pure and perfect light; and the motion guided by them is even, steady and regular. . . .

Antiquity recordeth, and the consent of nations celebrateth, the sons of Japhet to have been the first planters of Europe. Our commonly received stories make our Britain to be peopled by these men, very soon after the flood. But it is not easy to imagine, how so large and remote a territory should become thoroughly planted and peopled in so short a time. . . .

But probable it is, and we have nothing but probabilities and conjectures to guide us in things of that remoteness and obscurity, I say, probable it is, that when those people, who moved to the westward, had extended their colonies to the Belgic or Gallic shores, and had thence taken a view of the great *Albion* or isle of *Britain,* they soon wafted over; and being entered into, and possessed of that rich and spacious land, their multiplied families proceeded on in the like manner, hewing and hunting (the work of that time) until they came to the end or utmost corner of the land, which, on the western side of it, was this island I am accounting for. . . .

The first beginnings of nations having so little footsteps in history, no wonder if that of this little spot of earth in so obscure a corner, as to true matter of fact, be as dark as we can imagine then the island. But in these inextricable recesses of antiquity we must borrow other lights to guide us through, or content ourselves to be without any. Analogy of ancient names and words, a rational coherence and congruity of things, and plain natural inferences and deductions grounded thereon, are the best authorities we can rely upon in this subject, when more warrantable relations and records are altogether silent in the matter.

What language was first spoken in the western parts of Europe, it is not easy to determine; neither doth antiquity decide the point. All that it tells us is, that the ancientest names in several parts of the kingdom of France, and throughout the isle of Great Britain, are by the best congruity of sound and reason of the thing . . . resolved to our present Welsh and British etymons. . . .

We the Celtae came to call our first masters of knowledge Druids, from the Celtic word *Derw,* as is generally thought; and that because these men seemed passionately fond of that tree, under which it is certain they frequently appeared in every solemn and public transaction.

It is indeed acknowledged on all hands, that the ancient druids had their name from *Derw.* . . . But that their custom of celebrating the oak and using formed groves for their public ministrations and solemn performances, proceeded from the example and imitation of Abraham . . . though it be the general opinion, yet I shall take the liberty to differ from it and to suppose farther, that both Abraham and they took up this custom from a more ancient pattern, viz. the antediluvian practice.

There could be no better example of the eighteenth-century antiquary than William Stukeley (1687–1765), described by Stuart Piggott, in his biography of him, as "one of the most curious and complex of the English eccentrics, pathetic, charming, admirable, and laughable by turns." [4] He is perhaps mainly remembered because of his Druidomania, but this would be unfair. Like many other antiquaries and protoarchaeologists of the seventeenth and eighteenth centuries, he had in the end to interpret the past in terms of written sources, and the writings of Classical authors about the barbarian past of Europe said little; but that little did include the Druids, and this romantic, exciting priesthood seized the imagination of all, or almost all. But because Stukeley attributed Avebury and Stonehenge to the Druids and indeed peopled the world of the past (and sometimes the eighteenth century A.D.) with them, we must not forget that he was an accurate field archaeologist, and like Lhwyd, had made observations of a basic archaeological character. (See plates 6 and 7). Let us quote Piggott's view of Stukeley as an archaeologist.

> Stukeley's ideas are, I think, in no way discreditable, and contain, in their muddled way, a perception of certain basic archaeological principles. The first . . . is the recognition of a long pre-Roman period over which the field antiquities could be distributed, a second is the appreciation of the possibility that various prehistoric cultures might arrive in southern England by means of invasions or immigrations from the Continent, and a third is the application of the geographical and topographical method to the study of a group of related structures (the linear earthworks) in order to interpret them as a coherent whole in the light of such historical knowledge as was available. The observation of the relative dating of two contiguous earthworks such as the barrows and the Roman road is, of course, as fundamental to archaeological field work today as it was in the eighteenth century.

And here are Stukeley's own comments on monuments and other archaeological matters.

[4] S. Piggott, *William Stukeley: An Eighteenth Century Archaeologist*, 1950, xi.

[*On the Rollright Stones*]

. . . the greatest Antiquity we have yet seen . . . corroded like wormeaten wood by the harsh Jaws of Time . . . a very noble, rustic, sight and strike an odd terror upon the spectators and admiration at the design of 'em. I cannot but suppose 'em to have been an heathen temple of our Ancestors, perhaps in the Druids' times.

[*On crop marks at Great Chesterford in Essex*]

Thither I summoned some of the country people, and over a pot and a pipe, fished out what I could from their discourse, as we sat surveying the corn growing upon the spot . . . the most charming sight that can be imagined is the perfect vestigia of a temple, as easily discernible in the corn as upon paper. . . . The people say, let the year come as it will, this place is ever visible, and that it has been so ever since the memory of man, and fancy the fairies dancing there causes the appearance.

[*On the prehistoric hill fort of Maiden Bower, near Dunstable in Hertfordshire, which had been claimed to be Roman*]

I am persuaded it is a British work, like that at Ashwell, at like distance from the Chiltern and of like form, but more circular. . . . Between here and the town is a long barrow called the Millhill, no doubt from a mill which was afterwards set upon it: it stands east and west; the ends of it ploughed somewhat: I have no scruple in supposing it Celtic. A high prominence of the Chiltern overlooks all, called the Five Knolls, from that number of barrows, or Celtic *tumuli*, round, pretty large, and ditched upon the very *apex* of the hill.

[*On prehistoric fields, later called Celtic fields by O. G. S. Crawford, first describing the hill fort of Ogbury, between Amesbury and Salisbury*]

. . . within it are many little banks, carried strait and meeting one another at right angles, square, oblong parallels and some oblique, as the meres and divisions between ploughed lands; yet it seems never to have been ploughed.

[*And then writing about Cranborne Chase*]

I frequently observed on the sides of hills long divisions, very strait, crossing one another with all kind of angles; they look like the baulks or meres of ploughed lands, and are really made of flint overgrown with turf; they are too small for ploughed lands, unless of the most ancient Britons, who dealt little that way.

[*And as a final quotation from Stukeley, his passage on the Roman Wall in his* Itinerarium Curiosum]

The amazing scene of Roman grandeur in Britain which I beheld this journey, the more it occurred with pleasure to my own imagination, the more I despaired of conveying it to the reader in a proper light by a rehearsal. It is easy for some nations to magnify trifles and in words gild over inconsiderable transactions till they swell to the appearance of an history; and some moderns have gone great lengths that way; but if in any people action has outdone the capacity of rhetoric, or in any place they have left historians far behind in their valour and military performances, it was in our own country; and we are as much surprised in finding such infinite reliques of theirs here, as that we have no history of them that speaks with any particularity of the last 300 years that the Romans dwelt in Britain, and rendered it perfectly provincial. The learned memoirs are very short; and it is well they were guided with such a spirit, as left monuments sufficient to supply that defect, when handled as they deserve; though I have no hope of coming up to that yet I hold myself obliged to preserve, as well as I can, the memory of such things as I saw; which, added to what future times will discover, will revive the Roman glory among us, and may serve to invite noble minds to endeavour to that merit and public-spiritedness which shine through all their actions. This tribute at least we owe them, and they deserve it at our hands, to preserve their remains.

So much, as we can see in a few extracts from the writings of five men, for our local antiquaries. Now let us turn to the dilettanti, the travelers to distant lands in search of antiquities, beauty, and knowledge. From the many writings of antiquarian travelers and excavators in the eighteenth and early nineteenth centuries we select two only—Giovanni Belzoni and Edward Daniel Clarke.

Giovanni Belzoni (1778–1823) was one of the most eccentric and remarkable characters operating in archaeology in the early nineteenth century. A native of Padua, he made a living in England by performing prodigious feats of strength at circuses, went to Egypt to sell hydraulic machinery for irrigation purposes, and stayed on to rob tombs. He gave an account of his adventures in his *Narrative of the Operations and Recent Discoveries within the Pyramids, Temples, Tombs and Excavations in Egypt and Nubia,* first published in 1820. The entries in the summary of contents are in themselves a foretaste of the fascination of the book and of Belzoni himself: "Danger in proceeding to Cairo—confined to the house in consequence of the revolution—description of it," "Shot at by soldier—A young lady shot by a soldier," "Frighten away the natives," "Difficulties encountered from the natives," "Attempt to rob the boat," "Surprised by a hyena," and so on. In the following extract we learn of the way in which Belzoni proceeded as he tottered in and out of the ancient Egyptian tombs. It should be remembered what he says at the end of this extract, namely that "The purpose of my researches was to rob the Egyptians of their papyri."

It took us three days to reach Thebes, when we moored our bark at Luxor, and I recommenced my operations with what Fellahs I could obtain. . . . Could it but be accurately known, with what a wretched set of people in these tribes travellers have to deal, their mean and rapacious dispositions, and the various occurrences that render the collection of antiquities difficult, whatever came from thence would be the more prized, from the consideration of these circumstances. . . .

Gournou is a tract of rocks, about two miles in length, at the foot of the Libyan mountains, on the west of Thebes, and was the burial-place of the great city of a hundred gates. Every part

36

of these rocks is cut out by art, in the form of large and small chambers, each of which has its separate entrance; and, though they are very close to each other, it is seldom that there is any interior communication from one to another. I can truly say, it is impossible to give any description sufficient to convey the smallest idea of these subterranean abodes, and their inhabitants. There are no sepulchres in any part of the world like them; there are no excavations, or mines, that can be compared to these truly astonishing places; and no exact description can be given of their interior, owing to the difficulty of visiting these recesses. The inconveniency of entering into them is such that it is not everyone who can support the exertion. . . .

Of some of these tombs many persons could not withstand the suffocating air, which often causes fainting. A vast quantity of dust rises, so fine that it enters into the throat and nostrils, and chokes the nose and mouth to such a degree that it requires great power of lungs to resist it and the strong effluvia of the mummies. . . . In some places there is not more than a vacancy of a foot left, which you must contrive to pass through in a creeping posture like a snail, on pointed and keen stones that cut like glass. After getting through these passages, some of them two or three hundred yards long, you generally find a more commodious place, perhaps high enough to sit. But what a place of rest! surrounded by bodies, by heaps of mummies in all directions; which, previous to my being accustomed to the sight, impressed me with horror. The blackness of the wall, the faint light given by the candles or torches for want of air, the different objects that surrounded me, seeming to converse with each other, and the Arabs with the candles or torches in their hands, naked and covered with dust, themselves resembling living mummies, absolutely formed a scene that cannot be described. In such a situation I found myself several times, and often returned exhausted and fainting, till at last I became inured to it, and indifferent to what I suffered, except from the dust, which never failed to choke my throat and nose; and though, fortunately, I am destitute of the sense of smelling, I could taste that the mummies were rather unpleasant to swallow. After the exertion of entering into such a place, through a passage of fifty, a hundred, three hundred, or perhaps six hundred yards, nearly overcome, I sought a resting place, found one and contrived to sit; but when my weight bore on the body of an Egyptian, it crushed it like a bandbox. I naturally had recourse to my hands to sustain my weight, but they found no better support; so that I sunk altogether among the broken mummies, with a crash of bones, rags, and wooden cases, which raised such a dust as kept me motionless for a quarter of an hour, waiting till it subsided again. I could not remove from the place, however, without increasing it, and every step I took I crushed a mummy in some part or other. Once I was conducted from such a place to another resembling it, through a passage of about twenty feet in length, and no wider than that a body could be forced through. It was choked with mummies, and I could not pass without putting my face in contact with that of some decayed Egyptian; but as the passage inclined downwards, my own weight helped me on: however I could not avoid being covered with bones, legs, arms, and heads rolling from above. Thus I proceeded from one cave to another, all full of mummies piled up in various ways, some standing, some lying, and some on their heads. The purpose of my researches was to rob the Egyptians of their papyri; of which I found a few hidden in their breasts, under their arms, in the space above the knees, or on the legs, and covered by the numerous folds of cloth that envelop the mummy. The people of Gournou, who make a trade of antiquities of this sort, are very jealous of strangers, and keep them as secret as possible, deceiving travellers by pretending that they have arrived at the end of the pits, when they are scarcely at the entrance.

There was one particularly arresting entry in Belzoni's summary of contents: "Assaulted by a band of Arabs, led on by two Piedmontese in Mr. Drouetti's employ." Belzoni was working on behalf of the British consul-general in Egypt, as well as on his own account; he had as an enemy Drouetti, who was working on behalf of the French consul. Belzoni thought he had secured the obelisk at Philae for his side but had adventures in its securing. As Howard Carter wrote, "Those were the great days of excavation.

Anything to which a fancy was taken, from a scarab to an obelisk, was just appropriated, and if there was a difference with a brother excavator, one laid for him with a gun" (*The Tomb of Tut-ankh-Amen,* 1, p. 68). One might perhaps cavil at the phrase "the great days of excavation": perhaps it should be "the heroic days of excavation"? Anyway it was an age of heroes and scoundrels, as the following extract from Belzoni's *Narrative* shows only too clearly.

About this time Mr. Drouetti arrived in Thebes, and, by the medium of Mr. Bankes, made an offer to purchase the celebrated sarcophagus of alabaster, but his offer was not accepted. At this period Mr. Bankes solicited me to ascend the Nile as far as the island of Philoe, to remove the obelisk I had taken possession of before in the name of the British consul. The consul then informed me that he had ceded the said obelisk to Mr. Bankes, who intended to send it to England on his own account. I gladly accepted the undertaking, as I was pleased to have the opportunity of seeing another piece of antiquity on its way to England, and of obliging a gentleman for whom I had great regard. . . . On our landing at Luxor we met Mr. Drouetti, who offered to accompany us to Carnak, to be witness of the various spots of ground which were to be allotted to me for excavation. On the way, Mr. Drouetti told us a pleasant story of a man who was dressed like myself, and who was hidden among the ruins of the temple; whom he, Mr. Drouetti, had great reasons to believe was a person who wished to do him some injury.

. . . Mr. Drouetti, with all the complaisance possible, invited the consul and myself into his habitation among the ruins of Carnak. We were regaled with sherbet and lemonade. . . . The discourse turned on our next expedition to the Isle of Philoe; when I happened to say that, as I had to take the obelisk from that island down the cataract, I feared it was too late in the season, as the water would not serve at the cataract to float and launch down a boat adequate to support such a weight. On hearing this, Mr. Drouetti said that those rogues at the Shellal, meaning at Assouan, had deceived him; that they promised many times to bring down the said obelisk for him, but that they only promised to do it to extort money from him. I then informed

Mr. Drouetti that those people knew they could not take away that obelisk; as, since my first voyage up the Nile, I took possession of it in consequence of a firman which the consul, Mr. Salt, who was there present, had obtained from the Bashaw. . . .

. . . we visited Edfu, and took a minute survey of these truly magnificent ruins, which are so covered with a profusion of objects that if a traveller was to repeat his visits every day of his life, he might still find something new to be observed. This place was at that time under the researches of Mr. Drouetti's agents: one of whom, we understood, had received a despatch from his master, by an extra courier, and had immediately set off for the island of Philoe. . . . I was anxious to reach Assouan, as I expected no good from the early journey of Lebulo, the agent of Mr. Drouetti. . . . On my arrival at Assouan, I found that the said Lebulo had suggested to the Aga of Assouan, and to the natives of the island of Philoe, not to let the English party, who were coming up, carry away the obelisk. The Aga remonstrated with him that the obelisk had been taken possession of by me three years before, and a guard had been paid for it on that account. In consequence of this refusal, Mr. Lebulo proceeded to the island of Philoe; and having heard from all the natives that I had taken possession so long before, he adopted the method of a trick to seduce those simple people; he pretended he could read the hieroglyphics on the obelisk, and said it was written that the obelisk belonged to Mr. Drouetti's ancestors; consequently he had a right to it. . . .

[*Then Belzoni outwits the Drouetti-Lebulo party and sets off with the obelisk*]

On the eve of Christmas, the boat with the obelisk on board arrived, and stopped at Luxor, waiting for a few small articles to be loaded and then to proceed to Rosetta. It will be recollected that, previous to our last departure for the cataract, I entered into an arrangement with Mr. Salt, settling where I was to excavate on several spots among the ruins of Carnak. On St. Stephen's day I passed the Nile to that place, with the intention of examining the spots of ground which were allotted to our party. . . . At Luxor I was mounted on a very high donkey, the only mode of travelling short journeys in those countries, as horses are scarce, and it is too inconvenient to mount a camel for a small distance. I was followed by my Greek servant and two Arab drivers. I was unarmed: my servant had two pistols as usual. Our opponents, with their commander, Mr. Drouetti, were lodged in some mud houses among the ruins of Carnak. The boat with the obelisk, which I had just brought down and put up at Luxor, was rather too close under their noses. . . . I was at about three hundred yards from the great propylaeon when I saw a group of people running toward us; there were about thirty Arabs, headed by two Europeans, agents of Mr. Drouetti. On their approaching, Mr. Lebulo was first, and the renegade Rossignano second, both Piedmontese, and country-men of Mr. Drouetti. Lebulo began his address to me, by asking what business I had to take away an obelisk that did not belong to me; and that I had done so many things of this kind to him that I should not do any more. Meanwhile he seized the bridle of my donkey with one hand, and with the other he laid hold of my waistcoat, and stopped me from proceeding any far-ther: he had also a large stick hung to his wrist by a string. By this time my servant was assailed by a number of Arabs, two of whom were constantly in the service of Mr. Drouetti. At the same moment the renegade Rossignano reached within four yards of me, and with all the rage of a ruffian, levelled a double-barrelled gun at my breast, loading me with all the imprecations that a villain could invent; by this time my servant was dis-armed, and overpowered by numbers, and in spite of his efforts, they took his pistols from his belt. The two gallant knights be-fore me, I mean Lebulo and Rossignano, escorted by the two other Arab servants of Mr. Drouetti, both armed with pistols, and many others armed with sticks, continued their clamourous imprecations against me, and the brave Rossignano, still keep-ing the gun pointed at my breast, said that it was time that I should pay for all I had done to them. The courageous Lebulo said, with all the emphasis of an enraged man, that he was to have one-third of the profit derived from the selling of that obelisk. . . . My situation was not pleasant, surrounded by a band of ruffians like those, and I have no doubt that if I had attempted to dismount, the cowards would have despatched me on the ground, and said that they did it in defence of their lives, as I had been the aggressor. I thought the best way was to keep on my donkey, and look at the villains with contempt. . . . I told Lebulo to let me proceed on my way, and that if I had done any thing wrong, I should be ready to account for it; but all was to no purpose. Their rage had blinded them out of their senses.

While this was going on, I observed another band of Arabs running towards us. When they came nearer, I saw Mr. Drouetti himself among them, and close to him a servant of his, armed with pistols. . . . In an authoritative tone he desired I should dismount, which I refused to do. At this moment a pistol was fired behind me, but I could not tell by whom. I was determined to bear much, sooner than come to blows with such people, who did not blush to assail me all in a mass: but when I heard the pistol fired behind my back, I thought it was high time to sell my life as dear as I could. I dismounted, but then the kind Mr. Drouetti assured me that I was not in danger while he was there; and Mr. Lebulo, who had before acted the part of a ruffian, now contrived to play that of a neutral gentleman. By this time many other Arabs of the village of Carnak had reached this place, and seeing me thus surrounded, would any one suppose it! for the honour of Christendom and civilization, those wild Arabs, as we call them, were disgusted at the conduct of Europeans, and interfered in my behalf. . . .

I then informed Mr. Drouetti that I had resisted many and various sorts of attacks by his agents, but I did not expect they would come to such a pitch, and that it was high time for me to quit the country; so I returned to Beban-el-Malook, and immediately commenced my preparations to depart for Europe, as I could not live any longer in a country where I had become the object of revenge, of a set of people who could take the basest means to accomplish their purpose . . . as the boat with the obelisk was not set off, I availed myself of the opportunity of descending the Nile in it.

Giovanni Belzoni was a splendid, colorful adventurer. The Reverend Doctor Edward Clarke (1769–1821) was a sober, quiet character who was Professor of Mineralogy at the University of Cambridge and Librarian to the University.[5] This extract, characteristic of what went on in the Aegean and the Near East at this time, is from his own account of his travels.

The difficulties to be encountered were not trivial; we carried with us from Athens but few implements: a rope of twisted herbs, and some large nails, were all that the city afforded, as likely to aid the operation. Neither a wheeled carriage, nor blocks, nor pulleys, nor even a saw, could be procured. Fortunately, we found at *Eleusis* several large poles, an axe, and a small saw about six inches in length, such as cutlers sometimes adopt to the handle of a pocket knife. With these we began to work. The stoutest of the poles were cut, and pieces were nailed in a triangular form, having transverse beams at the vertex and base. Weak as our machine was, it acquired considerable strength by the weight of the *Statue,* when placed up upon the transverse beams. With the remainder of the poles were made rollers, over which the triangular frame might move. The rope was then fastened to each extremity of the transverse beams. This simple contrivance succeeded, when perhaps more complicated machinery might have failed: and an amass of marble weighing near two tons was moved over the brow of the hill or *Acropolis of Eleusis,* and from thence to the sea in about nine hours.

An hundred peasants were collected from the village and neighbourhood of *Eleusis* and near fifty boys. The peasants were ranged, forty on each side, to work at the ropes; some being employed, with levers, to raise the machine, when rocks or large stones opposed its progress. The boys who were not strong enough to work at the ropes and levers were engaged in taking up the rollers as fast as the machine left them and in placing these again in the front.

But the superstition of the inhabitants of *Eleusis,* respecting an idol which they all regarded as the protectress of their fields, was not the least obstacle to be overcome. In the evening, soon after our arrival with the firman, an accident happened which

[5] William Otter, *The Life and Remains of the Reverend Edward Daniel Clarke,* 1824.

43

had nearly put an end to the undertaking. While the inhabitants were conversing with the *Tchohadar,* as to the means of its removal, an ox, loosed from its yoke, came and placed itself before the *Statue,* and after butting with its horns for some time against the marble, ran off with considerable speed, bellowing, into the Plain of *Eleusis.* Instantly a general murmur prevailed; and several women joining in the clamour, it was with difficulty any proposal could be made. *They had been always,* they said, *famous for their corn and the fertility of the land would cease when the Statue was removed.* . . .

The people had assembled and stood around the *Statue;* but no one among them ventured to begin the work. They believed that the arm of any person would fall off who should dare to touch the marble, or to disturb its position. . . . Presently however the Priest of *Eleusis,* partly induced by entreaty and partly terrified by the menaces of the *Tchohadar,* put on his canonical vestments, as for a ceremony of high mass, and descending into the hollow where the *Statue* remained upright . . . gave the first blow with a pickaxe for the removal of the soil, that the people might be convinced no calamity could befall the labourers.

When Napoleon I invaded Egypt in 1789 he transported with his army a large body of scholars—artists, antiquaries, and scientists—and their mission was to complete a record of the land of the Nile and its monuments and curiosities. The French Institute in Cairo was founded by and for these scholars, and the many volumes of the *Description de l'Égypte* were published between 1809 and 1813. One member of this team was D. V. Denon, whose *Travels in Upper and Lower Egypt during the Campaigns of General Bonaparte,* first published in French, appeared in an English translation in London in 1802. Here is an account of one of Denon's adventures.

I could not help flattering myself that I was the first to make so important a discovery, . . . but was much more delighted, when, some hours after, I was assured of the proof of my discovery, by the possession of a manuscript itself which I found in the hand of a fine mummy. . . . One must have the passion of curiosity, and be a traveller and collector, to appreciate the full extent of such delight. . . . I felt that I turned pale with anxiety; I was just going to scold those who, in spite of my urgent requests, had violated the integrity of this mummy, when I perceived in his right hand and under his left arm the manuscript of a papyrus roll, which perhaps I should never have seen without this violation: my voice failed me; I blessed the avarice of the Arabs, and above all the chance which had arranged this good luck for me. I did not know what to make of my treasure; so much was I frightened lest I should destroy it, I dared not touch the book, the most ancient book so far known; I neither dared to entrust it to anyone, nor to lay it down anywhere; all the cotton of my bed quilt seemed to me insufficient to make a soft-enough wrapping for it. Was it the story of this person? Did it tell the period of his life? Was the reign of the sovereign under whom he had lived inscribed there? Or did the roll contain theological dogmas, prayers, or the dedication of some discovery? Without realizing that the script of my book was not known, any more than the language in which it was written, I imagined for a moment that I held in my hand the *compendium* of Egyptian literature. . . .

Men like Denon, and the staff of the French Institute in Cairo as a whole, showed that a serious and organized approach to the study of the past through archaeology was beginning, and the antiquaries and dilettanti, the travelers and the tomb robbers, were soon to give way to professional archaeologists.

3 Geology and the Antiquity of Man

Antiquarians like Lhwyd and Stukeley, and travelers and dilettanti like Belzoni and Clarke could not create the discipline of archaeology. They had, and they stimulated, an interest in the remote past of man, and they hoped to know about that past, but for all their efforts they did not get very far. Two things were necessary: first, an appreciation of the depth of the human past, and secondly, some system of relative chronology within that defined depth. The system of relative chronology that became the main classificatory system of nineteenth-century archaeology was the so-called Three-Age system, and the origins and development of this system are discussed in the succeeding chapter. Here, we deal with the first problem, namely the appreciation of the great antiquity of man. This major advance in thinking about man's past involved three things: first, the recognition as human artifacts of stones hitherto described as elf shot or thunderbolts; secondly, a change in geological thinking from the catastrophism of Buckland and others to the diluvialism of men like Buckland's pupil Lyell; and thirdly, the finding of artifacts and remains of human beings in undisturbed contexts which, according to the new geology, must be very old indeed.

One man in England at the end of the eighteenth century had the courage to make the right deductions from what he observed in a gravel pit. This was John Frere (1740–1807), a Fellow of the Royal Society living at Roydon Hall, Norfolk. He set out the nature of his discoveries and his views of their meaning in this celebrated letter to the secretary of the Society of Antiquaries of London. The letter is dated 1797, and it is published in the twelfth volume of the society's periodical *Archaeologia* (1800, p. 204).

Sir,

I take the liberty to request you to lay before the Society some flints found in the parish of Hoxne, in the county of Suffolk, which, if not particularly objects of curiosity in themselves, must, I think, be considered in that light from the situation in which they were found.

They are, I think, evidently weapons of war, fabricated and used by a people who had not the use of metals. They lay in great numbers at the depth of about twelve feet, in a stratified soil, which was dug into for the purpose of raising clay for bricks.

The strata are as follows:

1. Vegetable earth 1½ feet
2. Argill 7½ feet
3. Sand mixed with shells and other marine substances 1 foot
4. A gravelly soil, in which the flints are found, generally at the rate of five or six in a square yard, 2 feet.

In the same stratum are frequently found small fragments of wood, very perfect when first dug up, but which soon decompose on being exposed to the air; and in the stratum of sand were found some extraordinary bones, particularly a jawbone of enormous size, of some unknown animal, with the teeth remaining in it. I was very eager to obtain a sight of this; and finding it had been carried to a neighbouring gentleman, I inquired of him, but learned that he had presented it, together with a huge thighbone, found in the same place, to Sir Ashton Lever, and it therefore is probably now in Parkinson's Museum.

The situation in which these weapons were found may tempt us to refer them to a very remote period indeed, even beyond that of the present world; but, whatever our conjectures on that head may be, it will be difficult to account for the stratum in which they lie being covered with another stratum, which, on that supposition, may be conjectured to have been once the bottom, or at least the shore, of the sea. The manner in which they lie would lead to the persuasion that it was a place of their manufacture and not of their accidental deposit; and the numbers of them were so great that the man who carried on the brickwork told me that, before he was aware of their being objects of curiosity, he had emptied baskets full of them into the ruts of the adjoining road. It may be conjectured that the different strata were formed by inundations happening at distant periods, and bringing down in succession the different materials of which they consist: to which I can only say that the ground in question does not lie at the foot of any higher ground, but does itself overhang a tract of boggy earth, which extends under the fourth stratum; so that it should rather seem that torrents had washed away the incumbent strata and left the bog earth bare, than that the bog earth was covered by them, especially as the strata appear to be disposed horizontally, and present their edges to the abrupt termination of the high ground.

If you think the above worthy the notice of the Society, you will please to lay it before them.

I am, Sir,

with great respect,

Your faithful humble Servant, *John Frere*.

John Frere's letter attracted little attention, and it was not for nearly half a century that people looked back to what he said in view of the discoveries that were being made by Boucher de Perthes in the Somme Valley and by MacEnery, Pengelly, and others in south Devon. MacEnery was dissuaded from carrying on his work in Kent's Cavern, Torquay, by Dean Buckland of Oxford, who told him that the artifacts he found could not be contemporary with the remains of extinct animals. He suggested to MacEnery that they were the remains of feasts of the ancient Britons, who scooped out ovens in the stalactite, and thus the artifacts got down into apparently undisturbed strata. When MacEnery replied that there was no evidence of such ovens, Buckland replied that if he went on looking he would find them. This had a discouraging effect on MacEnery, and thus it is that it is the Frenchman Boucher de Perthes who was really the key figure in the recognition of the antiquity of man. Here is a passage from De Perthes's work, *De l'homme antédiluvien et ses oeuvres,* published in Paris in 1860.[1]

Gentlemen,

Nearly a quarter of a century has gone by since I addressed you here on the antiquity of man and his probable contemporaneity with the giant mammals, which species, destroyed in the great diluvial catastrophe, have not reappeared on earth.

This theory which I submitted for your consideration was new: that man who prior to the flood lived among the giants who were his predecessors in creation was never given recognition by science.

Rejected by science, this theory was also rejected by opinion; one century before, this view, which accepted the human giants without question, did not want to believe in the giant animals, and in each elephant bone science saw the bone of a human.

Today science believes in the elephants but no longer believes in the giants. In this respect science is right, but its skepticism was too far afield when it denied that man had lived during the period which preceded the diluvian formation or the cataclysm which gave the terrestrial surface its present configuration. It is this lacuna in our history, this ignorance of ours of the first steps of man on earth, to which I draw your attention; it is on these primitive peoples, their customs, their habits, their monuments, or the vestiges they must have left, that I desire to shed some light.

Your advice has not failed me; I had used it amply when in our meetings of 1836 to 1840 I brought out this theory as a complement to my book *De la création,* adding that this fossil man or his artifacts should be found in the diluvium or the deposits called tertiary. If you did not follow all my ideas, you did not deny them either; you heard them, not with the intention of

[1] Translated by Stephen Heizer in R. F. Heizer (ed.), *Man's Discovery of His Past* (1962).

condemning them but with that of judging them; you agreed with the principle but you wished proof.

Alas! I had none to give you; I was still dealing with probabilities and theories. In a word, my science was nothing but an anticipation. But this anticipation of mine had become certitude; though I had not analyzed a single stratum, I believed my discovery to be fact.

I was quite young when this thought first engrossed me. In 1805, when I was in Marseilles at the home of M. Brack, brother-in-law of Georges Cuvier and a friend of my father, I went to see a rock shelter called the Grotte de Roland, in the vicinity. My main purpose was to look there for the bones about which I had often heard Cuvier speak. I collected several specimens. Were they fossils? I did not dare say.

Later, in 1810, I visited another rock shelter. . . . They claimed to have found there some human skeletons. It was possible, but we did not see any. We collected, as I did at Marseilles, animal bones, and I collected several stones which seemed to me to be worked. . . .

When in 1836 I spoke to you on worked stones of the diluvial age, stones which had yet to be discovered, I had formed a collection of these from rock shelters, tombs, peat bogs, and similar areas. While collecting these stones which evidently were no longer in their primitive deposits, the idea came to me that I should find out what could have been their origin or the composition of this deposit. The yellow coloring of a few was the first indication. Only on the exterior, this coloring was not that of the patina of the flint. I concluded that it must be due to the ferruginous nature of the soil with which it was originally in contact. A certain stratum of the soil of the diluvium fulfilled this condition; the shade was surely that of my axes. They had definitely lain there; but was this location the effect of a recent occurrence and of a secondary altering, or did it date from the formation of the layer? There was the question.

In the affirmative case, that is, if the ax had been in the layer since its origin, the problem was resolved: the man who had made the instrument had existed prior to the cataclysm which formed the layer. Here there is no further possible doubt since the diluvial deposits do not present, as do the peat bogs, an elastic and permeable mass; nor like the bone caves, an inconcealable cavern, open to all who come, and which from century to century served as a sanctuary and then as a tomb to so many diverse beings. . . .

In the diluvial formations . . . each period is clearly divided. The horizontally superimposed layers, these strata of different shades and materials, show us in capital letters the history of the past: the great convulsions of nature seem to be delineated there by the finger of God.

Though united in a single group today like the foundation of a wall, all these levels are not brothers; centuries may separate them, and the generations which saw the birth of one did not always see the formation of the next. But since the day when each bed was laid and solidified, it remained integrally the same; in being compressed, it neither lost nor gained anything. Nothing was introduced from above, nor was there any secondary infiltration: each stratum is exempt from the influence of that which followed it and that which preceded it; homogeneous and compact, its modification required an influence no less powerful than that which created it. As one now sees it, so it was on the day of its formation. If a landslide or some type of action altered its regularity, an oblique or perpendicular line, cutting the horizontal line, would tell you so.

Here, gentlemen, the proofs start. They will be unanswerable: this human work for which we search, this work about which I tell you, *it is there* and has been there since the day that it was brought there. No less immobile than the layer itself, it came with the layer; it was held there as was the layer; and because it contributed to the layer's formation, it existed before it.

These shellfish, this elephant, this ax or the person who made it, were, therefore, witnesses to the cataclysm that gave our country its present configuration. Perhaps the shell, the elephant, and the ax were already fossilized at this time; could they be the debris surviving from an earlier deluge, the souvenirs of another age? Who can put limits on the past? Is it not infinite, as is the future? Where, then, is the man who has seen the beginning of any one thing? Where is he who will see it end? Let us not bargain over the duration of ages; let us believe that the days of the creation, those days that began before our sun, were the days of God, the interminable days of the world. Let us remember, finally, that for this eternal God a thousand centuries are no more than one second, and that He put on earth causes and effects which these thousands of centuries have not made any less young than they were at the time that His hand created them.

But all these foundations of the earth, all these schistose, chalky, clayey, and sandy layers which cover its core, are not the result of a sudden cause—of a convulsion or of a deluge. If the power of one torrent could have lifted in a day these beds torn away from other beds, there are also forces that are the consequence of slow action and of successive deposits from still water which, accomplishing their work, made hills and built mountains, not with masses thrown on masses, but with grains of sand scattered on grains of sand. Now, if we agree that the layers at Menchecourt and others were raised by an imperceptible accumulation, by a succession of deposits and sediments, the antiquity of these bones and these axes which lie under several meters of slowly accumulated sand, covered by a layer of lime or of clay, then covered again by a bed of varied chalk and of broken stones, and the whole covered by a thick layer of vegetal soil— this antiquity, I say, will be much greater than that which the rapid formation of diluvial beds appears to be.

After having reminded you of the configuration of the terrain and the nature of the elements of which it was composed, I will repeat to you on which principles, in 1836 and 1837, I established the probability of the presence of man and his works, and the type of certitude that I had of finding them there. I based this certitude:

1st, upon the tradition of a race of men destroyed by the flood;

2nd, upon the geological proofs of this flood;

3rd, upon the existence in this era of mammals closely related to man and unable to live except within the same atmospheric conditions;

4th, on the proof, thereby acquired, that the earth was habitable for man;

5th, on the basis [that] in all the regions, islands, or continents where one found these large mammals, man lived or had lived, from which one might conclude that if the animals appeared on earth before the human species, man followed closely, and at the era of the flood was already sufficiently numerous to leave signs of his presence;

6th, and finally, that these human remains had been able to escape the notice of geologists and naturalists because the difference of structure which exists between the fossil types and their living analogues could have existed between antediluvial man and those of today so that one might have confused them with other mammals; that physical probabilities, present and past experience, geology as well as history, and finally universal belief come to the support of tradition; that evidently a race of men, prior to the last cataclysm that had changed the surface of the earth, had lived there at the same time and probably in the same area as the quadrupeds whose bones have been discovered.

You recognize the truth of this reasoning, but you ask of me, why were these terrains rather than others the burial place of primitive man or the repository of his artifacts?

I answer that the diluvial torrent, while sweeping the terrestrial surface, had done that which, daily, on a lesser scale, our rainstorms do when, collecting objects in the ground which are not solidly enough fixed by their weight or their appendages, they carry articles along and throw them in some sewer; or, when the rains do not find anything but flatlands, spread them there in more or less thick layers. Then, if you examine these layers, their analysis will indicate with certainty the areas which the flood had crossed; you will know if it had crossed a populated or desert country, a town or fields, a prairie or forest, a cultivated field or stony or arid ground; you will see also whether the area had been populated by men or by animals. In brief, in this residue of a storm you cannot only follow its course, but can describe occurrences along the way.

Without doubt, as the days pass, this analysis will become less easy; all the soluble bodies will have changed shape or will dissolve in the earthy mass, but the solid objects will still be there.

So does the torrent proceed, upsetting things, carrying off and piling up all that it seizes, forming enormous masses composed of objects belonging to every kingdom and works produced by every intelligence. There also the soft or perishable parts have disappeared; there is nothing left but that which survived the trial of time.

It is, therefore, within these ruins of the ancient world, in these deposits which have become their archives, that one must look for these traditions and, for want of medallions and inscriptions, to defend these rough stones which, in their imperfection, prove no less surely the existence of man than if he had made an entire Louvre.

Thus, strongly convinced of your approbation, I carried on my work. Circumstances favored me: immense works undertaken for the fortifications at Abbeville, the digging of a canal, the railroad tracks that were being built, revealed from 1830 to 1840 numerous strata of diluvium on top of which rests a part of our valley; the chalk which forms its base rises thirty-three meters above the sea level, an immense bench which from the basin of the Somme goes to rejoin that of Paris, and thus advances toward the center of France.

A vast field was therefore open to my studies. The number of days I passed bending over these terraces which had become for me the arena of science and my promised land! The thousands of flint chips, let us say the millions, that had not been revealed to my eyes. I did my work conscientiously; all that by color or by a special cleft were distinguished from others I collected; I examined all the facets, the least broken edge did not escape me; several times I believed I had found this painfully sought evidence: it may have been, but so meager! I found there an indication, but it was not proof.

Finally, this proof came: it was at the end of 1838 that I submitted to you my first diluvial axes. It was also about this time, or in the course of the year 1839, that I brought them to Paris and showed them to several members of the Institute, notably to my respected friend M. A. Brongniart, who was perhaps more interested in the fact that my discovery was only illusory since, with Cuvier, he had established as a principle that man, new on the earth, was not contemporary with the great antediluvian pachyderms. However, M. Brongniart, far from discouraging me, strongly encouraged me to continue.

Meanwhile, I swear to you that he could not, sirs, see the hand of man in these rude efforts. I saw axes, and I saw correctly, but the working was vague and the angles blunt; their flattened forms differed from those of the polished axes, the only axes which were then known; finally, if the traces of working were revealed there, it was necessary to see them with eyes that believed. I had them, but I alone had them; my belief had little influence; I had not one disciple.

I needed other proofs, as well as more research, and to attain them I took some associates. I did not choose them from among the geologists. I would not have found any; at the least mention of axes and of diluvium I saw them smile. It was, therefore, among the [quarry] workers that I looked for my helpers. I showed them my stones, and also drawings which represented that which they were supposed to have been before the diluvial abrasion.

In spite of this care, it took me several months to organize my students, but with patience, with rewards distributed opportunely, and above all with the discovery of several well-shaped bits that I found under their eyes in some layers, I tried to mold them as skillful as myself, and before the end of 1840 I was able to offer you, and to submit to the examination of the Institute, twenty flints in which the human hand was detectable.

M. Brongniart no longer doubted me; M. Dumas, his son-in-law, adopted his opinion. From this moment on I had proselytes. Their number was small in comparison with the opposition. My collection, which grew rapidly and which, from the start, I left open to the curious, attracted a few, but practical men disdained to come and see. Let us say, they were afraid; they feared to make themselves accomplices to that which they called a heresy, almost humbug; they did not question my good faith, but they doubted my good sense.

I hoped that the publication of my book on the antediluvian antiquities, which appeared first under the title of *De l'industrie primitive* would disperse these doubts; but on the contrary. Except yourselves, sirs, with whom I found constant support, nobody believed me. In 1837 the theory was accepted without too many difficulties; when, realizing this theory had become a fact that everyone could verify, no one wished to believe it any more, and they confronted me with an obstacle larger than objection, than criticism, than satire, than persecution: *disdain.* They no longer discussed the theory; they did not even bother to deny it; they forgot it.

Thus my theory slept peacefully until 1854. Then Doctor Rigollot, who, according to hearsay, had been for ten years my constant adversary, deciding to judge the question for himself, visited the exposures of Abbeville, and subsequently those of Saint-Acheul and of Amiens. His conversion was prompt; he saw that I was correct. Honest man that he was, he declared it loudly in a brochure that you all know.

Boucher de Perthes's discoveries were at first greeted with incredulity by his French colleagues, and it was English geologists and archaeologists like Sir Joseph Prestwich and Sir John Evans (1823–1908) who were converted to his views and who then converted the learned world to accepting the great antiquity of man. Here are some passages from John Evans' letters and diaries in 1859; they are taken from the book *Time and Chance: The Story of Arthur Evans and His Forebears,* written by his daughter (and Arthur Evans' stepsister), Joan Evans, and published in 1943.

Think of their finding flint axes and arrowheads at Abbeville in conjunction with bones of Elephants and Rhinoceroses forty feet below the surface in a bed of drift. In this bone cave in Devonshire, now being excavated by the Geological Society, they say they have found flint arrowheads among the bones, and the same is reported of a cave in Sicily. I can hardly believe it. It will make my ancient Britons quite modern if man is carried back in England to the days when Elephants, Rhinoceroses, Hippopotamuses, and Tigers were also inhabitants of the country. . . .

Easter Sunday. . . . Prestwich has altered his plans about

Abbeville and seeing M. Boucher de Perthes's collections and investigating the gravel pits where the flint weapons are found in conjunction with the bones, and has got up a party of some of the best men in the Geological Society for the purpose. As it has been deferred till after Easter I could not resist accepting his invitation to join in. . . . I have accordingly arranged to go to Abbeville on *Tuesday* and return on Thursday to London. . . . I shall miss seeing the collection of M. Boucher de Perthes but be in time I hope for the Gravel Pit. . . .

May 1st 1859. I crossed from Folkestone to Boulogne and had as rough a passage as the strongest stomach could desire. . . . I had about an hour and a half in Boulogne and at nine took the train to Abbeville, where I found Prestwich waiting for me at the Station, and very glad to see me, as of all the party he had asked to meet him there I was the only one who came. We went straight to bed and soon after seven the next morning M. Boucher de Perthes, the first discoverer of the stone axes we were in pursuit of, came to take us to some of the gravel pits from whence his collection had been derived. A M. Marotte, the curator of the Museum, accompanied us but we did not succeed in finding anything. We then adjourned to the house of M. de Perthes, which is a complete museum from top to bottom, full of paintings, old carvings, pottery, etc., and with a wonderful collection of flint axes and implements found among the beds of gravel and evidently deposited at the same time with them—in fact the remains of a race of men who existed at the same time when the deluge or whatever was the origin of these gravel beds took place. One of the most remarkable features of the case is that nearly all if not quite all of the animals whose bones are found in the same beds as the axes are extinct. There is the mammoth, the rhinoceros, the Urus—a tiger, etc., etc. After the examination of his Museum M. de Perthes gave us a most sumptuous *déjeuner à la fourchette* and we then set off for Amiens. Of course our object was if possible to ascertain that these axes had been actually deposited with the gravel, and not subsequently introduced; and we had received intelligence from Amiens that in one of the gravel pits an axe was to be seen in its original position, which made us set off at once. At Amiens we

were met by the President of their Society of Antiquaries and
the public Librarian, MM. Dufour and Garnier, and with them a
M. Pinsard, an architect. We proceeded to the pit, where sure
enough the edge of an axe was visible in an entirely undisturbed
bed of gravel and eleven feet from the surface. We had a photographer with us to take a view of it so as to corroborate our
testimony and had only time to get that done and collect some
twelve or fifteen axes from the workmen in the Pit when we
were forced to take the train again to Abbeville. The early part
of Friday we spent in and about Abbeville and returned to London in the afternoon reaching home or rather the Euston Hotel
about midnight. All together I enjoyed the trip very much, and
am now only troubled to find time to write an account of our
investigations for the Antiquaries, as Prestwich is going to do
for the Royal Society.

Joseph Prestwich (1812–96) read his paper to the Royal Society on May 26, 1859. It was entitled "On the Occurrence of Flint
Implements associated with the remains of animals of extinct species in beds of a late geological period at Amiens and Abbeville
and in England at Hoxne." This abstract of it was published in the
Proceedings of the Royal Society of London, X, 1860, p. 50.

The author commences by noticing how comparatively rare
are the cases even of the alleged discovery of the remains of
man or of his works in the various superficial drifts, notwithstanding the extent to which these deposits are worked; and of
these few cases so many have been disproved, that man's non-ex-
istence on the earth until after the latest geological changes, and
the extinction of the mammoth, tichorhine rhinoceros, and other
great mammals, had come to be considered almost in the light of
an established fact. Instances, however, have from time to time
occurred to throw some doubt on this view, as the well-known
cases of the human bones found by Dr. Schmerling in a cavern
near Liège, the remains of man instanced by M. Marcel de
Serres and others in several caverns in France, the flint implements in Kent's Cave, and many more. Some uncertainty, however, has always attached to cave evidence, from the circum-

stance that man has often inhabited such places at a comparatively late period, and may have disturbed the original cave deposit; or, after the period of his residence, the stalagmitic floor may have been broken up by natural causes, and the remains above and below it may have thus become mixed together, and afterward sealed up by a second floor of stalagmite. Such instances of an imbedded broken stalagmitic floor are in fact known to occur; at the same time the author does not pretend to say that this will explain all cases of intermixture in caves, but that it lessens the value of the evidence from such sources.

The subject has, however, been latterly revived, and the evidence more carefully sifted by Dr. Falconer; and his preliminary reports on the Brixham Cave, presented last year to the Royal Society, announcing the carefully determined occurrence of worked flints mixed indiscriminately with the bones of the extinct Cave Bear and the Rhinoceros, attracted great and general attention amongst geologists. This remarkable discovery, and a letter written to him by Dr. Falconer on the occasion of his subsequent visit to Abbeville last autumn, instigated the author to turn his attention to other ground, which, from the interest of its later geological phenomena alone, as described by M. Buteux in his *Esquisse Géologique du Départment de la Somme,* he had long wished and intended to visit.

In 1849 M. Boucher de Perthes, President of the *Société d'Émulation* of Abbeville, published the first volume of a work entitled *Antiquités Celtiques et antédiluviennes,* in which he announced the important discovery of worked flints in beds of undisturbed sand and gravel containing the remains of extinct mammalia. Although treated from an antiquarian point of view, still the statement of the geological facts by this gentleman, with good sections by M. Ravin, is perfectly clear and consistent. Nevertheless, both in France and in England, his conclusions were generally considered erroneous; nor has he since obtained such verification of the phenomena as to cause so unexpected a fact to be accepted by men of science. There have, however, been some few exceptions to the general incredulity. The late Dr. Rigollot, of Amiens, urged by M. Boucher de Perthes, not only satisfied himself of the truth of the fact, but corroborated it, in 1855, by his *Mémoire sur des Instruments en Silex Trouvés à Saint-Acheul*. Some few geologists suggested further inquiry; whilst Dr. Falconer himself, convinced by M. de Perthes's explanations and specimens, warmly engaged Mr. Prestwich to examine the sections.

The author, who confesses that he undertook the inquiry full of doubt, went last Easter, first to Amiens, where he found, as described by Dr. Rigollot, the gravel beds of Saint-Acheul capping a low chalk hill a mile southeast of the city, about 100 feet above the level of the Somme, and not commanded by any higher ground. The following is the succession of the beds in descending order:

	Average thickness in ft.
1. Brown brick-earth (*many old tombs and some coins*) with an irregular bed of flint-gravel. No organic remains. *Divisional plane between 1 and 2a very uneven and indented*	10-15
2a. Whitish marl and sand with small chalk debris. Land and freshwater shells (*Lymanea, Succinea, Helix, Bithynia, Planorbis, Pupa, Pisidium* and *Ancylus,* all of recent species) are common, and mammalian bones and teeth are occasionally found	2-8
2b. Coarse subangular flint-gravel—white with irregular ochreous and ferruginous seams—with tertiary flint pebbles and small sandstone blocks. Remains of shells as above, in patches of sand. Teeth and bones of the elephant, and of a species of horse, ox, and deer—generally near base. This bed is further remarkable for containing worked flints (*haches* of M. de Perthes, and *langues de chat* of the workmen)	6-12

Uneven surface of chalk.

The flint implements are found in considerable number in [stratum] 2b. On his first visit, the author obtained several

specimens from the workmen, but he was not successful in finding any himself. On his arrival, however, at Abbeville, he received a message from M. Pinsard of Amiens, to whose cooperation he expresses himself much indebted, to inform him that
one had been discovered the following day, and was left *in situ*
for his inspection. On returning to the spot, this time with his
friend Mr. Evans, he satisfied himself that it was truly *in situ,*
seventeen feet from the surface, in undisturbed ground, and he
had a photographic sketch of the section taken.

Dr. Rigollot also mentions the occurrence in the gravel of
round pieces of hard chalk, pierced through with a hole, which
he considers were used as beads. The author found several, and
recognized in them a small fossil sponge, the *Coscinopora globu-
laris,* D'Orb., from the chalk, but does not feel quite satisfied
about their artificial dressing. Some specimens do certainly appear as though the hole had been enlarged and completed.

The only mammalian remains the author here obtained were
some specimens of the teeth of a horse, but whether recent or
extinct, the specimens were too imperfect to determine; and part
of the tooth of an elephant (*Elephas primigenius?*). In the
gravel pit of Saint-Roch, $1\frac{1}{2}$ miles distant, and on a lower level,
mammalian remains are far more abundant, and include *Ele-
phas primigenius, Rhinoceros tichorhinus, Cervus somonensis,
Bos priscus,* and *Equus* (to this list the author has to add the
Hippopotamus, of which creature four fine tusks were obtained
on this last visit), but the workmen said that no worked flints
were found there, although they are mentioned by Dr. Rigollot.

At Abbeville the author was much struck with the extent and
beauty of M. Boucher de Perthes's collection. There were many
forms of flints, in which he, however, failed to see traces of design or work, and which he should only consider as accidental;
but with regard to those flint instruments termed "axes" (*haches*)
by M. de Perthes, he entertains not the slightest doubt of their
artificial make. They are of two forms, generally from four to
ten inches long. . . . They are very rudely made, without any
ground surface, and were the work of a people probably unac-
quainted with the use of metals. These implements are much
rarer at Abbeville than at Amiens. . . . The author was not

fortunate enough to find any specimens himself; but from the experience of M. de Perthes, and the evidence of the workmen, as well as from the condition of the specimens themselves, he is fully satisfied of the correctness of that gentleman's opinion, that they there also occur in beds of undisturbed sand and gravel.

At Moulin Quignon, and at Saint-Gilles, to the southeast of Abbeville, the deposit occurs, as at Saint-Acheul, on the top of a low hill, and consists of a subangular, ochreous and ferruginous flint-gravel, with a few irregular seams of sand, twelve to fifteen feet thick, reposing upon an uneven surface of chalk. It contains no shells, and very few bones. M. de Perthes states that he has found fragments of the teeth of the elephant here. The worked flints and the bones occur generally in the lower part of the gravel.

In the bed of gravel also on which Abbeville stands, a number of flint implements have been found, together with several teeth of the *Elephas primigenius,* and, at places, fragments of fresh-water shells.

The section, however, of greatest interest is that at Menche-court, a suburb to the northwest of Abbeville. The deposit there is very distinct in its character; it occurs patched on the slopes down under the peat beds of the valley of the Somme to the southward. The deposit consists, in descending order, of:

	Average thickness in ft.
1. A mass of brown sandy clay, with angular fragments of flints and chalk rubble. No organic remains. Base very irregular and indented into bed No. 2.	2-12
2. A light-coloured sandy clay (*sable gras* of the workmen), analogous to the loess, containing land shells, *Pupa, Helix, Clausilia,* of recent species. Flint axes and mammalian remains are said to occur occasionally in this bed.	8-25

62

3. White sand (*sable aigre*), with 1 to 2 feet of subangular flint gravel at base. This bed abounds in
   land and freshwater shells of recent species of the
   genera *Helix, Succinea, Cyclas, Pisidium, Valvata,
   Bithynia,* and *Planorbis,* together with the marine
   *Buccinum undatum, Cardium edule, Tellina soli-
   dula,* and *Purpura lapillus.* The author has also
   found the *Cyrena consobrina* and *Littorina rudis.*
   With them are associated numerous mammalian
   remains, and, it is said, flint implements.   2-6
4. Light-colored sandy marl, in places very hard,
   with *Helix, Zonites, Succinea,* and *Pupa.* Not
   traversed.   3+

   The Mammalian remains enumerated by M. Buteux from
this pit are—*Elephas primigenius, Rhinoceros tichorhinus, Cervus somonensis?, Cervus tarandus priscus, Ursus spelaeus,
Hyaena spelaea, Bos primigenius, Equus adamaticus,* and a
Felis. It would be essential to determine how these fossils are
distributed—which occur in bed No. 2, and which in bed No. 3.
This has not hitherto been done. The few marine shells occur
mixed indiscriminately with the freshwater species, chiefly
amongst the flints at the base of No. 3. They are very friable
and somewhat scarce. It is on the top of this bed of flints that
the greater number of bones are found, and also, it is said, the
greater number of flint implements. The author, however, only
saw some long flint flakes (considered by M. de Perthes as flint
knives) turned out of this bed in his presence, but the workmanship was not very clear or apparent; still it was as much so as in
some of the so-called flint knives from the peat beds and barrows. There are specimens, however, of true implements
(*haches*) in M. de Perthes's collection from Menchecourt; one
noticed by the author was from a depth of five, and another of
seven metres. This would take them out from bed No. 1, but

63

would leave it uncertain whether they came from No. 2 or No. 3. From their general appearance, and traces of the matrix, the author would be disposed to place them in bed No. 2, but M. de Perthes believes them to be from No. 3; if so, it must have been in some of the subordinate clay seams occasionally intercalated in the white sand.

Besides the concurrent testimony of all the workmen at the different pits, which the author after careful examination saw no reason to doubt, the flint implements (*haches*) bear upon themselves internal evidence of the truth of M. de Perthes's opinion. It is a peculiarity of fractured chalk flints to become deeply and permanently stained and coloured, or to be left unchanged, according to the nature of the matrix in which they are embedded. In most clay beds they become [on the] outside . . . a bright opaque white or porcelainic; in white calcareous or siliceous sand their fractured black surfaces remain almost unchanged; whilst in beds of ochreous and ferruginous sands, the flints are stained the light yellow and deep brown colours so well exhibited in the common ochreous gravel of the neighbourhood of London. This change is the work of very long time, and of moisture before the opening out of the beds. Now in looking over the large series of flint implements in M. de Perthes's collection, it cannot fail to strike the most casual observer that those from Menchecourt are almost always white and bright, whilst those from Moulin Quignon have a dull yellow and brown surface; and it may be noticed that whenever (as is often the case) any of the matrix adheres to the flint, it is invariably of the same nature, texture, and colour as that of the respective beds themselves. In the same way at Saint-Acheul, where there are beds of white and others of ochreous gravel, the flint implements exhibit corresponding variations in colour and adhering matrix; added to which, as the white gravel contains chalk debris, there are portions of the gravel in which the flints are more or less coated with a film of deposited carbonate of lime; and so it is with the flint implements which occur in those portions of the gravel. Further, the surface of many specimens is covered with fine dendritic markings. Some few implements also show, like the fractured flints, traces of wear, their sharp edges being blunted.

64

In fact, the flint implements form just as much a constituent part of the gravel itself—exhibiting the action of the same later influences and in the same force and degree—as the rough mass of flint fragments with which they are associated.

With regard to the geological age of these beds, the author refers them to those usually designated as post-Pliocene, and notices their agreement with many beds of that age in England. The Menchecourt deposit much resembles that of Fisherton near Salisbury; the gravel of Saint-Acheul is like some on the Sussex coast; and that of Moulin Quignon resembles the gravel at East Croydon, Wandsworth Common, and many places near London. The author even sees reason, from the general physical phenomena, to question whether the beds of Saint-Acheul and Moulin Quignon may not possibly be of an age one stage older than those of Menchecourt and Saint-Roch; but before that point can be determined a more extended knowledge of all the organic remains of the several deposits is indispensable.

The author next proceeds to inquire into the causes which led to the rejection of this and the cases before mentioned, and shows that in the case of M. de Perthes's discovery, it was in a great degree the small size and indifferent execution of the figures and the introduction of many forms about which there might reasonably be a difference of opinion; in the case of the arrow-heads in Kent's Cave a hidden error was merely suspected; and in the case of the Liège cavern he considers that the question was discussed on a false issue. He therefore is of opinion that these and many similar cases require reconsideration; and that not only may some of these prove true, but that many others, kept back by doubt or supposed error, will be forthcoming.

One very remarkable instance has already been brought under the author's notice by Mr. Evans since their return from France. In the thirteenth volume of the *Archaeologia,* published in 1800, is a paper by Mr. John Frere, F.R.S., and F.S.A., entitled "An Account of Flint-Weapons Discovered at Hoxne in Suffolk," wherein that gentleman gives a section of a brick pit in which numerous flint implements had been found, at a depth of eleven feet, in a bed of gravel containing bones of some un-

known animal; and concludes from the ground being undisturbed and above the valley, that the specimens must be of very
great antiquity, and anterior to the last changes of the surface
of the country—a very remarkable announcement, hitherto
overlooked.

The author at once proceeded in search of this interesting
locality, and found a section now exposed to consist of ten.

The weapons referred to by Mr. Frere are described by him
as being found abundantly in bed No. 4; but at the spot where
the work has now arrived, this bed is much thinner, and is not
worked. In the small trench which the author caused to be dug,
he found no remains either of weapons or of bones. He saw,
however, in the collection of Mr. T. E. Amyot, of Diss, specimens of the weapons, also an astragalus of the elephant from, it
was supposed, this bed, and, from bed No. 3, the teeth of a
horse, closely resembling those from the elephant bed of Brigh-
ton.

The specimens of the weapons figured by Mr. Frere, and
those now in the British Museum and elsewhere, present a
singular similarity in work and shape to the more pointed forms
from Saint-Acheul.

One very important fact connected with this section, is that it
shows the relative age of the bone and implement-bearing beds.

Feet

1. Earth and a few flints   2
2. Brown brick-earth, a carbonaceous seam in middle and
   one of gravel at base; no organic remains. The workmen stated that two flint implements (one of which
   they shortly picked up in the author's presence) had
   been found about 10 feet from the surface during the
   last winter.   12
3. Grey clay, in places carbonaceous and in others sandy,
   with recent land and freshwater shells (*Planorbis, Valvata, Succinea, Pisidium, Helix,* and *Cyclas*) and bones
   of Mammalia   4
4. Small subangular flint-gravel and chalk pebbles   2 ½
5. Carbonaceous clay (stopped by water)   ½ +

They form a thin lacustrine deposit, which seems to be superimposed on the Boulder Clay, and to pass under a bed of the ochreous sand and flint gravel belonging to the great and latest drift beds of the district.

The author purposely abstains for the present from all theoretical considerations, confining himself to the corroboration of the facts:

1. That the flint implements are the work of man.

2. That they were found in undisturbed ground.

3. That they are associated with the remains of extinct Mammalia.

4. That the period was a late geological one, and anterior to the surface assuming its present outline, so far as some of its minor features are concerned.

He does not, however, consider that the facts, as they at present stand, of necessity carry back Man in past time more than they bring forward the great extinct Mammals toward our own time, the evidence having reference only to relative and not to absolute time; and he is of opinion that many of the later geological changes may have been sudden or of shorter duration than generally considered. In fact, from the evidence here exhibited, and from all that he knows regarding drift phenomena generally, the author sees no reason against the conclusion that this period of Man and the extinct Mammals—supposing their contemporaneity to be proved—was brought to a sudden end by a temporary inundation of the land; on the contrary, he sees much to support such a view on purely geological considerations.

The paper concludes with a letter from Mr. John Evans, F.S.A. and F.G.S., regarding these implements from an antiquarian rather than a geological point of view, and dividing them into three classes:

1. Flint flakes—arrowheads or knives.

2. Pointed weapons truncated at one end, and probably lance or spear heads.

3. Oval or almond-shaped implements with a cutting edge all round, possibly used as sling stones or as axes.

Mr. Evans points out that in form and workmanship those of

the two last classes differed essentially from the implements of the so-called Celtic period, which are usually more or less ground and polished, and cut at the wide and not the narrow end; and that had they been found under any circumstances, they must have been regarded as the work of some other race than the Celts, or known aboriginal tribes. He fully concurs with Mr. Prestwich that the beds of drift in which they were found were entirely undisturbed.

Édouard Lartet (1801–71), a magistrate in the south of France who gave up the pursuit of the law to study fossil animals, and then through paleontology came to the study of the cultural fossils of man, was one of the great nineteenth-century French pioneers of archaeology. His work followed on and supplemented that of Boucher de Perthes. It was Lartet, assisted by the Englishman Henry Christy (1810–65), who began the systematic exploration of rock shelters and was responsible for the discovery and appreciation of Upper Paleolithic mobiliary art. The following extract is from a paper by Lartet communicated to the Geological Society of London and printed in their *Quarterly Journal* (XVI, 1860, p. 471). It was entitled "On the Coexistence of Man with certain Extinct Quadrupeds, proved by Fossil Bones, from various Pleistocene deposits bearing incisions made by sharp instruments."

You have been good enough to offer to communicate to the Geological Society of London the observations which I have for some time past made upon fossil bones exhibiting evident impressions of human agency. The specimens of them which I showed to you yesterday were those only whose origin is authentic, and which were obtained from deposits well defined in regard to geological relations. Thus the fragments of the Aurochs exhibiting very deep incisions, apparently made by an instrument having a waved edge, and the portion of the skull of the *Megaceros Hibernicus,* in which I thought I recognized significant marks of the mutilation and flaying of a recently slain animal, were obtained from the lowest layer in the cutting of the Canal de l'Ourcq, near Paris. These very specimens are figured or mentioned by Cuvier, . . . and Alex. Brongniart . . . has given a detailed description of the deposit, consisting of distinct layers, which he considers to be of higher antiquity than those of the valleys. The bones of the Aurochs and the *Megaceros* were found in the same layer as the remains of the Elephant (*Elephas primigenius*) of which Cuvier had given figures of two molars, which, according to that author, had not been rolled, and were found under circumstances which showed that they were in an original and not in a *remanié* deposit. I have said that the deep incisions on the bone of an Aurochs from the cutting of the Canal de l'Ourcq (which you may remember I showed you in the Gallery of the Jardin des Plantes) appear to have been made by an instrument with a waved edge. By this I meant an instrument having an edge with slight transverse inflections, so as to produce, by cutting obliquely through the bone, a plane of section somewhat undulated. The cut seems to have been made by a hatchet not entirely finished—a state in which the greatest part of the flint implements from Saint-Acheul, near Amiens, seem to be; but in the marked bones of Abbeville and other ancient localities the incisions must have been made by rectilinear edges. These considerations would lead us to think that, independently of the case of the hatchets simply chipped and roughed out, the place for the manufacture of which might be near that where they are now found, those primitive people must have been provided with more perfect instruments, such as would be more suited to their ordinary wants. I should therefore hesitate to adopt the system (too absolute, in my opinion) of Mr. Worsaae, who distinguishes the first subdivision of the Stone Period by hatchets that are merely chipped, to the exclusion of those that are polished, which he assigns to the second subdivision. It is to be presumed that the want of instruments with polished surfaces and having a fine cutting edge must have been felt from the earliest time, when the people had learned to fix, by a much more difficult process, to flints and other rocks intentional forms so well defined.

Among the bones with incisions obtained from the sands of Abbeville, there is a large antler of an extinct Stag, referred to the *Cervus Somonensis,* or the *grand Daim de la Somme* of Cuvier, together with several horns of our common Deer, which

I was not able to show you. The bones of the Rhinoceros (*Rh. tichorhinus*) which I laid before you were found at Menchecourt, a suburb of Abbeville, where there are gravel pits which formerly afforded many fossil bones of Elephants, etc., and where M. Boucher de Perthes, at a later period, obtained the flints worked by human hands. The incisions that may be observed on those bones are neither so deep, nor do they afford evidence so striking, as those in the bones of the Aurochs from the Canal de l'Ourcq; but the shallow cuts and the incisions of the bony surfaces which may be observed on them, especially in the articulations, have in my eyes not less value; for I have satisfied myself, by comparative trials on homologous portions of existing animals, that incisions presenting such appearances could be only made in fresh bones still retaining their cartilage. As to the fragment of the horn of the *Megaceros Hibernicus,* which Cuvier had received from England without any indication as to where it came from, you may have observed that it bears the marks of several blows, which have made incisions of a depth that would be impossible to produce in the present state of mineralization of that fragment; further, the blow which detached that piece from the rest of the horn must have been given before that immersion in the sea which caused its fossilized condition; for in the internal cavity of this fragment there was found the valve of an *Anomia* (preserved with the specimen), which could not have found its way there except at the place of fracture. I have observed very significant marks, evidently produced by a sharp tool, on the horn of a young *Megaceros* which the late M. Alcide d'Orbigny had received from Ireland some years ago.

I would call to your recollection that the Rev. John Cumming, in his geological description of the Isle of Man (*Quarterly Journal of the Geological Society,* vol. ii, p. 345), notices the occurrence of the remains of the *Megaceros* imbedded in blue marl "with implements of human art and industry, though of an uncouth and ancient character"; and in a note at the foot of page 344, alluding to a submarine forest, to which he is inclined to assign a more ancient date, he says, "It is singular that the trunk of an oak tree, which has been removed from the submerged forest at Standhall, exhibits upon its surface the marks of a hatchet." With regard to the historical existence of the *Megaceros,* after referring to what is to be found in the works of Oppian, of Julius Capitolinus, and S. Münster, I have found nothing which appears to me to justify in this respect the opinion put forth by Dr. Hibbert, and since then accepted by other palaeontologists, except Professor Owen, who, speaking of the *Megaceros* of the British Isles, entirely dissents from the opinion of Dr. Hibbert. All the remains of that animal found on this side of the Channel, which I have examined, belong to deposits of greater antiquity than that of the peat bogs.

M. Delesse has shown you fragments of bone that have been sawn, which he recently obtained from a deposit in the neighbourhood of Paris, where he had previously collected remains of the Beaver, the Ox, and the Horse. From an examination of these fragments, I have satisfied myself, by experiments on recent bones, that the action of a metallic saw would not produce the transversally striated plane of section which you must have observed on those ancient bones collected by M. Delesse; but I have obtained analogous results by employing as a saw those flint knives, or splinters with a sharp chisel edge, found in the sands of Abbeville.

If, therefore, the presence of worked flints in the diluvial banks of the Somme, long since brought to light by M. Boucher de Perthes, and more recently confirmed by the rigorous verifications of several of your learned fellow countrymen, have established the certainty of the existence of man at the time when those ancient erratic deposits were formed, the traces of an *intentional operation* on the bones of the Rhinoceros, the Aurochs, the *Megaceros,* the *Cervus Somonensis,* etc., supply equally the inductive demonstration of the contemporaneity of those species with the human race.

It is true that certain of those species, the *Cervus elephus* of Linnaeus (the same as your Red deer or Stag) and the Aurochs, are still represented in existing nature: but although it be exactly the bones of the Aurochs which exhibit the most evident proof of human action, the fact is not of less value as regards the relative antiquity; for the remains of the Aurochs have been found associated in the same beds with those of *Elephas* and

Megaceros, not, as I have already said, by the effect of a *remaniément,* but in an original inhumation. Moreover, fossil remains of the same Aurochs have been found in England, in France, and in Italy, in preglacial deposits (that is, in deposits anterior to the most ancient pleistocene formations imbedding bones of *Elephas primigenius* and *Rhinoceros tichorhinus*). I would add, that the more rigorous observation of facts tends clearly to demonstrate that a great proportion of our living Mammifers have been contemporaneous with those two great extinct species, the first appearance of which in Western Europe must have been preceded by that of several of our still existing quadrupeds.

In endeavouring to connect those proofs of the antiquity of the human race with the geological and geographical changes which have since taken place, I have not met with any more precise induction than that offered by M. d'Archiac, viz., the relative epoch of the separation of England from the Continent. The former connection of the two is a fact generally admitted: it is proved by the similarity in structure of the opposite sides of the Channel, by the identity of species of terrestrial animals, the original intermigration of which could only have been effected by the existence of *terra firma.* M. d'Archiac (*Bull. de la soc. géol. de France,* 1 ère série, t. x, p. 220, and *Histoire des progrès,* etc., t. ii, pp. 127 and 170) has been led, by a series of well-weighed inductions from stratigraphical considerations, to consider the epoch of the separation of the British Islands as occurring after the deposition of the diluvial rolled pebbles, and before that of the ancient alluvium, the Loess of the North of France, of Belgium, the Valley of the Rhine, etc. The inference to be drawn from that hypothesis is self-evident; it is this, that the primitive people to whom we attribute the hatchets and other worked flints of Amiens and Abbeville might have communicated with the existing land of England by dry land, inasmuch as the separation did not take place until after the deposit of the rolled diluvial pebbles, from among which the hatchets and worked flints have been collected. On the other hand, M. Élie de Beaumont having assigned the production of the erratic phenomena existing in our valleys to the last dislocation of the Alps, we should be authorized to conclude from this second hypothesis that the worked flints carried along with the pebbles in that erratic deposit in the bottom of the valleys afford a proof of the existence of Man at an epoch when Central Europe had not yet reached the completion of its present great orographic relief.

While it has been held that no change has taken place in the great lines of level since the formation of the erratic deposits in the lower parts of our valleys, and although such changes cannot be distinctly traced in the central parts of the continents, from the absence of standards of comparison, they are not the less easy to be recognized as having occurred, even since the existence of Man, throughout the whole extent of the European coasts, from the Gulf of Bothnia to the very eastern extremity of the Mediterranean. They have been observed by different authors on a considerable number of points of the coast, where they have verified the existence of objects of human industry in deposits of marine origin, raised up at different elevations above the sea level. Such changes, be they the result of action more or less violent, of movements more or less sudden, have not amounted to catastrophes so general as to affect to a sensible degree the regular succession of organized beings.

We find incontestable proof of this in the British Islands, whither the most considerable number of terrestrial species must necessarily have immigrated prior to the separation of those islands from the Continent, and where they have established themselves and have continued by successive generations to the present day. The same thing has occurred on the Continent, where the same terrestrial fauna has continued without any other modifications than the geographical displacement of certain species and the final disappearance of some others—disappearances that have resulted not from a simultaneous destruction, but rather from a series of successive extinctions which appear to have been equally gradual as regards space and time.

I may add to what I have stated above that the finding of worked flints in the diluvium of Amiens and Abbeville is by no means an isolated fact. M. Gosse of Geneva, a young medical student in Paris, has recently discovered in the sands of the Parisian suburb of Grenelle, of the same age as those of Abbeville and of other parts of Europe, a flint hatchet of a most distinct form, together with knives or thin plates split in a longitudinal direction. I myself have had an opportunity of verifying these facts in the collection formed by that skilful explorer. He has shown me an Elephant's tooth, a canine tooth of a large Feline animal, and bones of the Aurochs, Horse, etc., all obtained from the same sands and from the same bed in which the flint hatchet was found.

I may add that, among the bones obtained in Switzerland under the lacustrine habitations of the Stone Period (in the lakes of Moosdorf, Bienne, and others), there never have been found any remains of the *Megaceros,* although the remains of the Elk, the Aurochs, and the *Bos primigenius* are by no means rare. In Denmark, where still more ancient stations have been carefully examined with the same object, Prof. Steenstrup has assured me that he has never discovered the smallest fragment of the *Megaceros* in the midst of the most abundant remains of the Reindeer, Elk, Aurochs, and other species of animals which from time immemorial have not existed in that region. Nevertheless these primitive stations in Denmark are referred back to a period when no other domestic animal existed in that country except the Dog. No remains have been found either of the Horse, Sheep, or Goat—not even any kind of dwarf Ox.

If, Sir, you are of opinion that the above notes, drawn up in haste, are likely to prove interesting to the Geological Society of London, I should be happy if you would submit them to the enlightened judgement of your learned associates, and if they will receive them at the same time as a mark of my deference, and as feeble expression of the profound gratitude I feel for the honour conferred upon me by my name having been inscribed among the Foreign Members of that Society.

We may appropriately bring this chapter to an end with a passage from Lyell's *The Geological Evidences of the Antiquity of Man with Remarks on Theories of the Origin of Species by Variation,* which was published in 1863. Sir Charles Lyell (1797–1875) had been one of the pioneers of the new geology. Himself a pupil of Dean Buckland at Oxford, he had broken away from the catastrophic and diluvialist geology of Buckland and Conybeare, and, when he went to London as Professor of Geology, taught the doctrines of uniformitarianism and the new fluviatilist geology. He taught that no processes could be admitted in the past which did not happen at the present, and that it was changes in land and sea level and the work of rivers that were mainly responsible for the strata—not universal disasters and great floods. Lyell's *Principles of Geology* was published in three volumes between 1830 and 1833, and these volumes were a primer of the new geology. The implication of Lyell's theory for the archaeologists was that artifacts deposited in undisturbed gravel many feet below the present ground level were very old, and indeed belonged to a time which John Frere had described in his letter to the Society of Antiquaries of London as "beyond that of the present world."

Artifacts—the cultural fossils of man—were only one of the evidences of man's antiquity. Actual skeletal remains of man himself in similar geological circumstances were more exciting and more readily understood by the average person. In 1857, two years before Prestwich had lectured to the Royal Society and Darwin had published the *Origin of Species,* the long bones and the skull cap of a manlike being had been discovered in a limestone cave at Neanderthal in Rhenish Prussia. In his *The Geological Evidences of the Antiquity of Man* (1863), Lyell discusses the problem of Neanderthal man in these words.

Before I speak more particularly of the opinions which anatomists have expressed respecting the osteological characters of the human skull from Engis, near Liège, mentioned in the last chapter and described by Dr. Schmerling, it will be desirable to say something of the geological position of another skull, or rather skeleton, which, on account of its peculiar conformation, has excited no small sensation in the last few years. I allude to the skull found in 1857, in a cave situated in that part of the valley of the Düssel, near Düsseldorf, which is called the Neanderthal. The spot is a deep and narrow ravine about seventy English miles northeast of the region of the Liège caverns treated of in the last chapter, and close to the village and railway station of Hochdal between Düsseldorf and Elberfeld. The

cave occurs in the precipitous southern or left side of the winding ravine, about sixty feet above the stream, and a hundred
feet below the top of the cliff.

When Dr. Fuhlrott of Elberfeld first examined the cave, he
found it to be high enough to allow a man to enter. The width
was seven or eight feet, and the length or depth fifteen. I visited
the spot in 1860, in company with Dr. Fuhlrott, who had the
kindness to come expressly from Elberfeld to be my guide, and
who brought with him the original fossil skull, and a cast of the
same, which he presented to me. In the interval of three years,
between 1857 and 1860, the ledge of rock on which the cave
opened, and which was originally twenty feet wide, had been almost entirely quarried away, and, at the rate at which the work
of dilapidation was proceeding, its complete destruction seemed
near at hand.

In the limestone are many fissures, one of which, still partially
filled with mud and stones, is continuous from the cave to the
upper surface of the country. Through this passage the loam,
and possibly the human body to which the bones belonged, may
have been washed into the cave below. The loam, which covered
the uneven bottom of the cave, was sparingly mixed with
rounded fragments of chert, and was very similar in composition to that covering the general surface of that region.

There was no crust of stalagmite overlying the mud in which
the human skeleton was found, and no bones of other animals in
the mud with the skeleton; but just before our visit in 1860 the
tusk of a bear had been met with in some mud in a lateral em-
branchment of the cave, on a level corresponding with that of
the human skeleton. This tusk, shown us by the proprietor of
the cave, was two and a half inches long and quite perfect; but
whether it was referable to a recent or extinct species of bear, I
could not determine.

From a printed letter of Dr. Fuhlrott we learn that on removing the loam, which was five feet thick, from the cave, the
human skull was first noticed near the entrance, and, further in,
the other bones lying in the same horizontal plane. It is supposed that the skeleton was complete, but the workmen, ig-

norant of its value, scattered and lost most of the bones, preserving only the larger ones.

The cranium, which Dr. Fuhlrott showed me, was covered both on its outer and inner surface, and especially on the latter, with a profusion of dendritical crystallizations, and some other bones of the skeleton were ornamented in the same way. These markings, as Dr. Hermann von Meyer observes, afford no sure criterion of antiquity, for they have been observed on Roman bones. Nevertheless, they are more common in bones that have been long embedded in the earth. The skull and bones, moreover, of the Neanderthal skeleton had lost so much of their animal matter as to adhere strongly to the tongue, agreeing in this respect with the ordinary condition of fossil remains of the post-Pliocene period. On the whole, I think it probable that this fossil may be of about the same age as those found by Schmerling in the Liège caverns; but, as no other animal remains were found with it, there is no proof that it may not be newer. Its position lends no countenance whatever to the supposition of its being more ancient.

When the skull and other parts of the skeleton were first exhibited at a German scientific meeting at Bonn, in 1857, some doubts were expressed by several naturalists, whether it was truly human. Professor Schaaffhausen, who, with the other experienced zoologists, did not share these doubts, observed that the cranium, which included the frontal bone, both parietals, part of the squamous, and the upper third of the occipital, was of unusual size and thickness, the forehead narrow and very low, and the projection of the supraorbital ridges enormously great. He also stated that the absolute and relative lengths of the thigh bone, humerus, radius, and ulna agreed well with the dimensions of a European individual of like stature at the present day; but that the thickness of the bones was very extraordinary, and the elevation and depression for the attachment of muscles were developed in an unusual degree. Some of the ribs, also, were of a singularly rounded shape and abrupt curvature, which was supposed to indicate great power in the thoracic muscles.

In the same memoir, the Prussian anatomist remarks that the

depression of the forehead is not due to any artificial flattening, such as is practised in various modes by barbarous nations in the Old and New Worlds, the skull being quite symmetrical, and showing no indication of counter-pressure at the occiput; whereas, according to Morton, in the Flatheads of the Columbia, the frontal and parietal bones are always unsymmetrical. On the whole, Professor Schaaffhausen concluded that the individual to whom the Neanderthal skull belonged must have been distinguished by small cerebral development and uncommon strength of corporeal frame.

When on my return to England I showed the cast of the cranium to Professor Huxley, he remarked at once that it was the most ape-like skull he had ever beheld. Mr. Busk, after giving a translation of Professor Schaaffhausen's memoir in the *Natural History Review,* added some valuable comments of his own on the characters in which this skull approached that of the gorilla and chimpanzee.

Professor Huxley afterward studied the cast with the object of assisting me to give illustrations of it in this work, and in doing so discovered what had not previously been observed, that it was quite as abnormal in the shape of its occipital as in that of its frontal or superciliary region.

4   The Three-Age System

Although the idea of an age of stone existed in the writings of Greek philosophers and historians, and the recognition of stone implements as such by antiquaries and geologists in the sixteenth, seventeenth, and eighteenth centuries had prepared the way for the recognition as a historical fact of a stone age in the human past, it was the writings of Scandinavian historians and archaeologists, and their work in museums and in excavation, that established not only the idea of a stone age, but a sequence of three ages in the prehistoric past—Stone, Bronze, and Iron. The Three-Age system has very properly been described by Joseph Déchelette as "the basis of prehistory," and by R. A. S. Macalister as "the corner-stone of modern archaeology."

P. F. Suhm in his *History of Denmark, Norway and Holstein* (1776) stated that in that area tools and weapons were first of stone, then of copper, and then of iron. Skuli Thorlacius, in his *Concerning Thor and his Hammer, and the earliest Weapons that are related to it, and also the so-called Battle-Hammers, Sacrificing Knives and Thunder-Wedges, which are found in Burial Mounds* (1802), refers all through to three successive ages of stone, copper, and iron.

The clearest statement of this concept was in the writings of L. S. Vedel Simonsen, particularly in his *Udsigt over Nationalhistoriens aeldste og maerkeligste Perioder*, published in 1813–16.

At first the tools and weapons of the earliest inhabitants of Scandinavia were made of stone or wood. Then the Scandinavians learnt to work copper and then to smelt it and harden it . . . and then latterly to work iron. From this point of view the development of their culture can be divided into a Stone Age, a Copper Age, and an Iron Age. These three ages cannot be separated from each other by exact limits, for they encroach on each other. Without any doubt the use of stone implements continued among the more impoverished groups after the introduction of copper, and similarly objects of copper were used after the introduction of iron. . . . Artifacts of wood have naturally decomposed, those of iron are rusted in the ground; it is those of stone and copper which are the best preserved.

Professor Rasmus Nyerup (1759–1829), of the University of Copenhagen, published in 1806 his *Oversyn over Faedrelandets Mindesmaerker fra Oldtiden,* in which he advocated the formation of a National Danish Museum of Antiquities. For many years Nyerup had been collecting antiquities privately and had formed them into a small museum at the University of Copenhagen, of which he was librarian. But he had no idea of how to classify them; in urging the formation of a national museum he thought that only by means of a comprehensive collection and careful study could any definite information be found out about the prehistoric past. In his book he confessed that

everything which has come down to us from heathendom is wrapped in a thick fog; it belongs to a space of time which we cannot measure. We know that it is older than Christendom, but whether by a couple of years or a couple of centuries, or even by more than a millennium, we can do no more than guess.

A year after the publication of Nyerup's book with this despairing confession of failure, the Danish Government set up a Royal Committee for the Preservation and Collection of National Antiquities. This committee was charged with the job of forming a national museum of Danish antiquities, seeing to the preservation of the ancient and historic monuments of Denmark, and also of making known to the general public the importance and value of antiquities. Nyerup himself was the first secretary of this committee. The collections which he and his staff made in the peat bogs, burial chambers, and kitchen middens of Denmark formed the nucleus of the National Museum in Copenhagen. Christian Jurgensen Thomsen (1788–1865) succeeded Nyerup as secretary of the committee in 1816; at the same time he was appointed the first curator of the National Museum, a post which he held until his death. Thomsen arranged the collections by classifying them into three ages of Stone, Bronze, and Iron on the basis of the material used in making weapons and implements. He claimed that the classification represented three chronologically successive ages. In 1819 the Danish National Museum was open to the public. They found it organized on the Three-Age system: it was the first museum or, for that matter, private collection to be so organized. Thomsen was always there to expound the collections and the basis of classification to the public. He paid very special attention in his guide lectures to peasants, "because," he said, "it is by them that we shall have our collections enlarged."

In 1836 a guidebook to the National Museum was published entitled *Ledetraad til Nordisk Oldkyndighed* (Copenhagen, 1836). An English edition of this guide appeared in 1848, translated by Lord Ellesmere and called *A Guide to Northern Antiquities*. Thomsen was responsible for the section in the guide on the early monuments and antiquities of the north, although some parts of his essay were elaborated by other members of the Archaeological Committee of the Royal Society of Northern Antiquaries. The following extract is from Thomsen's section of the *Guide*.

OF THE DIFFERENT PERIODS TO WHICH THE HEATHEN
ANTIQUITIES MAY BE REFERRED

Our collections are . . . still too recent and our facts too few for the drawing of conclusions with full degree of confidence in the greatest number of cases. The remarks which we now proceed to offer must therefore be viewed merely in the light of conjectures, destined to be confirmed or rectified in proportion as a more general attention is devoted to the subject. To facilitate the view, we shall give to each of the different periods, whose limits, however, cannot be accurately defined, a separate appellation.

The Age of Stone, or that period when weapons and implements were made of stone, wood, bone, or some such material, and during which very little or nothing at all was known of metals. Even if we suppose that some of the stone articles were in a later age used either on account of the costliness of metal, or from their being dedicated to the celebration of sacred rites, and that they continued in consequence to be of the same shape and material as in the remoter periods of antiquity, still they are so frequently found in the North, and moreover in such multitude of instances with obvious traces of being worn by use and several times ground afresh, that there can be no question of a time having existed when these articles were in common use in the North. That the Stone Age is the earliest in which we find our regions to have been inhabited by human beings seems established beyond all doubt, as is also the fact that the people must have borne a resemblance to savages. It is very natural that in different regions, that particular species of stone should have been employed which was of most common occurrence and at the same time suited to the fabrication of stone implements; accordingly, flint was most frequently employed in Denmark; in those parts of Sweden and Norway where flint is not met with, they made a partial use of other species of stone, which sometimes had an influence on the shape of the implement. In the most northern parts of Sweden and Norway stone objects seldom or never occur, and it would seem as if those regions in earlier times were but thinly inhabited, or not at all.

It was about the period when metals first came, gradually and no doubt sparingly, to be used in the North, that the large sepulchral chambers of the North would seem to have been constructed. In these, as has been before remarked, the bodies have been most frequently found unburnt, in many instances with rudely fashioned urns beside them; articles of metal being very rarely met with, and at all events but little of bronze or gold; of silver or iron nothing whatever, but almost exclusively objects of stone and bone; the ornaments chiefly of amber. Articles of clothing seem to have been made chiefly of the skins of animals. The succeeding period, we are of opinion, ought to be called:

The Age of Bronze, in which weapons and cutting implements were made of copper or bronze, and nothing at all or but very little was known of iron or silver. Not in the North only but also in the countries of the South, it will be found that the metal of which mention is first made, and which first came into use was copper, either pure, or, as it was frequently used in ancient times, with a small addition of tin for the purpose of hardening it, to which alloy the name of bronze had been given. It was not till a much later period that they became acquainted with iron, the reason of which seems to be that copper is found in such a state as to be far more easily distinguishable as a metal than iron, which, before it can be wrought, must first undergo the process of smelting and purifying by a strong heat, an operation of which in the earliest ages they must have been ignorant. We should assuredly commit a great mistake in supposing the bronze articles to be imitations of those from the palmy days of the Romans, or that they were fabricated at that period in southern countries and thence conveyed through the channel of traffic to Germany and the North. It is to be remarked that by far the greatest number of antiquities of this description are found precisely in the more distant countries, for instance in the North and in Ireland, where it may reasonably be supposed that contact with the Romans was slightest. Moreover it was not before the conquest of Gaul by Julius Caesar and his advance to the Rhine that a firm and permanent connexion was formed with the interior of Germany, but long before that time the Romans had their weapons and cutting implements of iron. It would seem that an earlier culture, long before iron came into general use, was diffused over the greater part of Europe, the produce of which was in a great measure alike in regions very far apart. On a close examination of the cutting implements and weapons of bronze and of the connexions in which they are found in the North, the conviction will be forced upon us more and more that they originated and are derived from that earlier culture, and that they are also of very remote antiquity in the countries of the South. If we assume that articles were obtained from other countries, or that they were imitated, it follows as a matter of course that they must at that time have been in use in those countries, and it would be absurd to suppose that the Germans should have adopted anything after the Romans, or received anything from them, the use of which had been long discontinued by the latter. On the other hand later discoveries and improvements might, when international connexions were dissevered, or when these were only the result of migrations, easily have continued to be unknown to a people who had indeed been acquainted with the earlier culture, but had themselves made no great progress in civilisation, and who by reason of their remoteness and of the length of the period of their separation, had remained ignorant of the subsequent improvements and discoveries of other cultivated nations. Such specimens as are found in those countries will accordingly tend to elucidate the nature and appearance of similar objects of very remote antiquity in regions where the arts made a comparatively considerable progress at a much earlier period than in the North. . . . No instance is known to us of writing being found on any specimen belonging to the Bronze Age, although the workmanship in other respects evinces such a degree of skill as would lead us to suppose that the art of writing could not have been unknown at that period. It does not by any means follow that because they had metal, they should have entirely ceased to employ stone, and that so much the less, since metal was doubtless expensive at first, for which reason they strove to avoid using it in the fabrication of heavy articles. Most articles of metal were at this period fabricated by the process of casting, but when they were hammered we can scarcely err in supposing that operation to have been performed with a stone hammer on a stone anvil.

The Age of Iron is the third and last period of the heathen times, in which iron was used for those articles to which that metal is eminently suited, and in the fabrication of which it came to be employed as a substitute for bronze. To such articles as they would especially endeavour to procure of hardened iron, belong of course all sorts of cutting weapons and implements. On the other hand bronze was at this period fully as much used for ornaments, handles, and some sorts of domestic utensils, such as spoons and the like. From such specimens of bronze it cannot therefore by any means be inferred that an article belongs to the previous age unless that should be indicated by the shape and ornaments and the altered proportion of alloy.

1. Italian engraving of pyramids and tombs from Ciampini's *Vetera monumenta,* published in 1640.

2. A gathering of Dilettanti around the Medici Venus.
(Painting by Thomas Patch)

3. Drawings of ancient British coins from William Camden's *Britannia* (1600 edition), the first general guide to the antiquities of England.

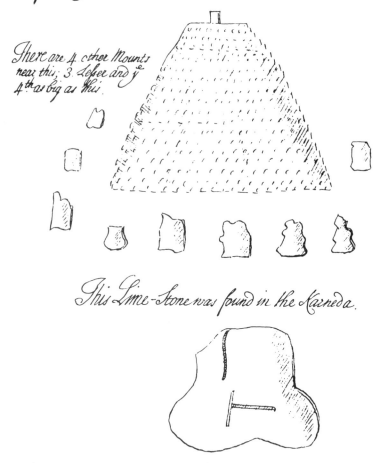

The Mount of New-Grange in the County of East Meath, not far from Drogheda

There are 4 other Mounts near this; 3 lesser and ỹ 4ᵗʰ as big as this.

This Lime-Stone was found in the Karneda.

4. A drawing of the mount at New Grange, north of Dublin, from the manuscript collection of John Anstis (1669–1745) in the British Museum. This drawing has been attributed to Anstis but it was most probably done by Edward Lhwyd, who visited the site in 1699.

A British Druid

5. A British Druid, member of the mysterious priesthood
of ancient times. Drawing by William Stukeley, 1723.

6. Drawing of Stonehenge by William Stukeley (1687–
1765), from his *Stonehenge, a Temple Restored to the
British Druids* (*1740*).

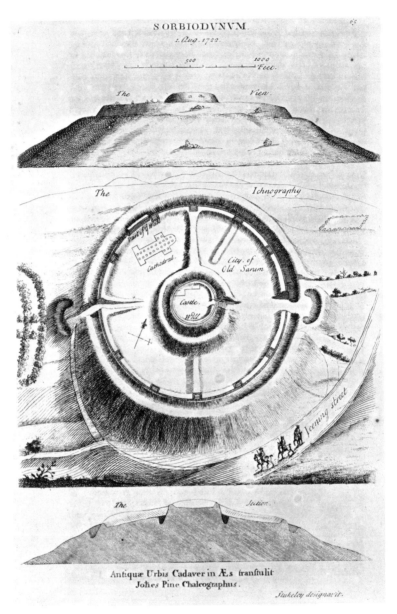

7. Stukeley's drawing of Sorbiodunum (Old Sarum),
from his *Itinerarium Curiosum*, Centuria I (1725).

G. BELZONI

8. Portrait of Italian tomb robber Giovanni Belzoni (1778–1823), a colorful adventurer who supplied the British Museum with treasures from Egypt.

9. Tomb breaking from Belzoni's *Narrative of the Operations and Recent Discoveries within the Pyramids, Temples, Tombs, and Excavations in Egypt and Nubia* (1820), the author's account of his adventures.

10. Illustration from Belzoni's book of statue being removed from a tomb.

12. Papyrus manuscript which D. V. Denon found in the hand of an Egyptian mummy. Denon described this find in his *Travels in Upper and Lower Egypt during the campaigns of General Bonaparte.*

11. Temple Apollinopolis. View of the interior of the temple.

13. Flint weapons discovered at Hoxne in Suffolk by John Frere (1740–1807), who identified his find as instruments used by ancient people who had no metals.

14. Portrait of Frenchman J. C. Boucher de Perthes, key figure in the recognition of the antiquity of man.

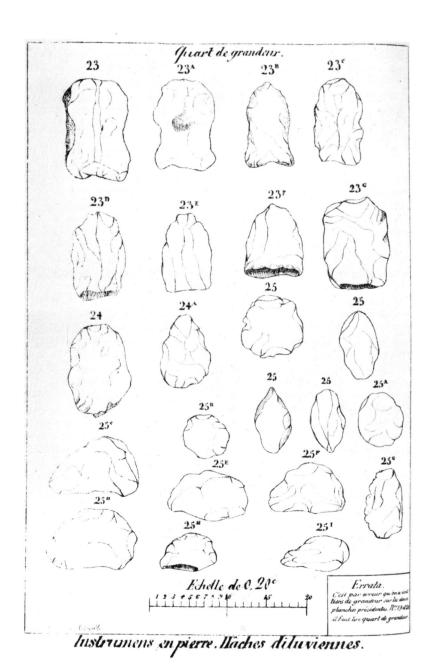

Quart de grandeur.

Échelle de 0.20c

Instrumens en pierre. Haches diluviennes.

Errata.
C'est par erreur qu'on a mis
tiers de grandeur sur les deux
planches précédentes. N°19 etc.
il faut lire quart de grandeur.

15. These primitive stone weapons of Abbeville, France, were discovered by Boucher de Perthes, and are reproduced in his book, *De l'homme antédiluvien et ses oeuvres,* published in Paris in 1860.

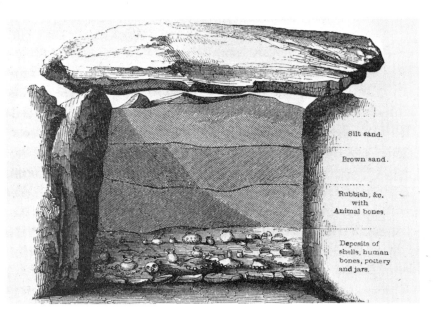

Silt sand.

Brown sand.

Rubbish, &c.
with
Animal bones.

Deposits of
shells, human
bones, pottery
and jars.

16. Illustration by W. C. Lukis showing a section through a megalithic tomb in the Channel Isles. (From the tomb of L'Ancresse, Guernsey)

N   S

17. Lukis's illustration of two skeletons in a megalithic tomb in the Channel Isles. (From the tomb of Le Déhus, Guernsey)

19. Great mound in Marietta, Ohio, as described by Squier and Davis in their *Ancient Monuments of the Mississippi Valley.*

18. Piles of the lake dwelling of Möringen (Bronze Age). Dr. Ferdinand Keller examined various finds from the Swiss lake dwellings. His book *The Lake Dwellings of Switzerland and Other Parts of Europe* was translated into English and published in 1866.

20. Artifacts from the mounds in Marietta, Ohio. Finds in the Mississippi Valley point to the existence of a Copper Age between the Stone and Bronze Ages in America.

21. Silbury Hill from *The Celtic Druids* by Godfrey Higgens (1827). John Lubbock (1834–1913) first discovered that this hill is older than a Roman road running close by it. The purpose of Silbury Hill is not yet known, but it was the largest man-made mound in Europe before the Industrial Revolution.

22. An early archaeological photograph of Ptolemaeion
frieze from Alexander Conze, *Archaeologische unter-
suchungen auf Samothrake.* Conze's excavation report
from Samothrace was illustrated by photographs, and this
is probably the first time photographs were used in such a
way.

If we suppose an emigration to the North of the people from the shores of the Black Sea, about the time of Julius Caesar or somewhat later, it is likely that the immigrants who were acquainted with iron, which at that period was in common use in the South, may have brought it hither along with them to the North. It has been believed that there was a period of transition in which iron was more precious than copper and when it was used very sparingly; axes, for instance, were then made partly of copper to which was added an edge of iron; daggers were made of bronze, likewise with an edge on both sides of iron. On one specimen of an ax which is believed to be from this transition period, consequently from the very earliest times of the Iron Age, an inscription has been found in Runic characters. Such specimens being however extremely rare, this period was not in all probability of long duration. That the transition to iron should have proceeded in this way, however, is a point not yet fully established, this combination of metals not having been unknown at later periods when it was employed for ornaments. When people's attention was once attracted to iron ore and the purposes to which it might be applied, that metal which is found in such abundance in Norway and Sweden must soon have superseded the one previously in use.

Thomsen was helped in the museum by a young law student of Copenhagen who, in his home in Jutland, had been collecting antiquities and excavating barrows for some while. This was Jens Jacob Asmussen Worsaae (1821–85). In due course he succeeded Thomsen as director of the National Museum, was Inspector General of Antiquities in Denmark, Riksantiqvariet, and Professor of Archaeology at the University of Copenhagen. He was, in the words of Professor Brøndsted, "the first professional archaeologist." He is to be remembered for that alone, but he was far in advance of his times. In 1843, when he was only twenty-two years old, he published *Danmarks Oldtid oplyst ved Oldsager og Gravhøje,* which was translated into English by William J. Thoms and published by Parkers in Oxford in 1849 as *The Primeval Antiquities of Denmark.* It is a most remarkable work. Here we have the clear understanding of the need for the Three-Age system, the

85

first exposition of the principles of excavation, the awareness of the comparative method and of the need to interest the public in archaeological matters. No words are too lavish in trying to estimate Worsaae's contribution. Thomsen called him a "heaven stormer," and so he was. When he was penniless and determined to give up law and pursue the study of the antiquities of his country, he sought an audience with the king, Christian VIII, and it was the encouragement of this monarch, and of his successor, Frederick VII, that kept Worsaae an archaeologist and made him the real father of modern archaeology. The extracts from his *Danmarks Oldtid* reproduced here should be read remembering the date of publication (1843), alongside the accounts of what was going on in Egypt and Great Britain at the time; and always keeping in mind that Worsaae was writing fifteen years before the publication of Darwin's *Origin of Species,* which, to some people, represents the beginning of modern archaeology. Archaeology had grown up long before, however: it was in existence when Thomsen opened the Danish National Museum in 1819, and when he wrote his part in the *Ledetraad.* And when Worsaae wrote his *Danmarks Oldtid* in 1843 a mature discipline was in existence in Denmark; it took half a century for it to develop in Western Europe. The whole process from Thomsen to Montelius and De Mortillet is an interesting period. It represents the growth of archaeology in the nineteenth century.

A nation which respects itself and its independence cannot possibly rest satisfied with the consideration of its present situation alone. It must of necessity direct its attention to bygone times, with the view of inquiring to what original stock it belongs, in what relations it stands to other nations, whether it has inhabited the country from primeval times or immigrated thither at a later period, to what fate it has been exposed; so as to ascertain by what means it has arrived at its present character and condition. For it is not until these facts are thoroughly understood, that the people acquire a clear perception of their own character, that they are in a situation to defend their independence with energy, and to labour with success at the progressive development, and thus to promote the honour and well-being of their country. . . .

If we now consider the most ancient accounts of Denmark and its inhabitants, we shall find that they are enveloped in obscurity and darkness. We know that the Gothic race who now occupy this land, and who are nearly allied to the inhabitants of Norway and Sweden, were not the aboriginal inhabitants of the country . . . it may be asked, how can we then ever hope to arrive, in some degree, at a clear knowledge of the early history of our native land. Such a result . . . can be effected only in part, by means of the existing records. It becomes therefore necessary to look to other sources. . . . Recognizing this principle, attention has recently been directed to the indisputable memorials of antiquity which we possess in the Cromlechs, Cairns, Barrows or Grave-Hills, Stone-circles, etc., which lie scattered over the country, as well as in the many and diversified objects of antiquarian interest which have been discovered in them. . . .

It is well known that stones shaped by art into the form of wedges, hammers, chisels, knives, etc., are frequently exhumed from the earth. These, in the opinion of many, could certainly never have served as tools or implements, since it was impossible either to carve or cut with a stone; hence it was concluded that they had formerly been employed by our forefathers in those sacrifices which were offered to idols, during the prevalence of heathenism. Thus it was said the hammers of stone were used to strike the sacrifice on the forehead; and after the sacrificing priest with a chisel, likewise formed of stone, had stripped off the skin, the flesh was cut to pieces with knives of stone, etc. The Cromlechs, Cairns, and Barrows in which such objects are found were conceived to have been partly places of sacrifice, partly temples and seats of justice. But when, amidst the vast mass of antiquities of stone which had been gradually collected, several shewed obvious marks of having been much used and worn, doubts began to be entertained whether they really had been employed as instruments of sacrifice. At length attention was directed to the fact that even at the present day, in several of the islands of the South Seas and in other parts, there exist races of savages who, without knowing the use of metals, employ implements of stone which have the same shape and adaptation as those which are discovered in the earth in such

87

quantities in Denmark, and further, it was shown in what manner those savages make use of such simple and apparently such useless implements. No one after this could longer remain in doubt that our antiquities of stone were also actually used as tools in times when metals were either unknown, or were so rare and costly that they were only in the possession of very few individuals. That this could not have been the case in this country while inhabited by our forefathers the Goths is evident from all historical records; we must therefore seek for the origin of the antiquities of stone in an earlier time, in fact, as we shall soon perceive, among the first inhabitants of our native land.

Thomsen had concerned himself with the material in the National Museum of Danish Antiquities in Copenhagen that he had to order. Worsaae was concerning himself with all antiquities ever found in Denmark and the wider problem of their arrangement in some form of chronological sequence. In one sentence he says what Cunnington and Colt-Hoare and their contemporaries in France and elsewhere could not appreciate, and it is the most telling sentence: "As soon as it was once pointed out that the whole of these antiquities could by no means be referred to one and the same period, people began to see more clearly the difference between them." But the people so blandly referred to were only a small group of scholars in northern Europe; scholars in Britain and France and elsewhere did not see anything more clearly at the time: they were still worried by the fog that disturbed Nyerup. The extract quoted from Worsaae is particularly important in that he shows how the existence of stone-age communities in other parts of the world in the nineteenth century was an important factor in persuading himself and others of the possibility, and indeed the actuality, of a stone age in man's past. He first argued from artifacts, and then, boldly, from monuments.

We are now enabled to pronounce with certainty that our antiquities belonging to the times of paganism may be referred to three chief classes, referable to three distinct periods. The first class includes all antiquarian objects formed of stone, respecting which we must assume that they appertain to the stone-period,

88

as it is called, that is, to a period when the use of metals was in a great measure unknown. The second class comprises the oldest metallic objects; these however were not as yet composed of iron, but of a peculiar mixture of metals, copper and a small portion of tin melted together, to which the name of "bronze" has been given; from which circumstance the period in which this substance was commonly used has been named the bronze-period. Finally, all objects appertaining to the period when iron was generally known and employed are included in the third class, and belong to the iron-period. . . .

To obtain correct ideas on the subject of the first peopling and the most ancient relations of our native country, it will not be sufficient to direct attention exclusively to objects exhumed from the earth. It is at the same time indispensably necessary to examine and compare with care the places in which antiquities are usually found; otherwise many most important collateral points either can not be explained at all, or [can be explained only] in a very unsatisfactory manner. Thus we should scarcely have been able to refer . . . the antiquities to three successive periods, if experience had not taught us that objects which belong to different periods are usually found by themselves. . . . It will not be the places where antiquities may be casually met with, but rather our ancient stone structures and barrows, which, with reference to the subject just mentioned, ought to be the subject of a more particular description; for as to the graves themselves we know that, generally speaking, they contain both the bones of the dead, and many of their weapons, implements, and trinkets, which were buried with them. Here we may therefore, in general, expect to find those objects together which were originally used at the same period. . . .

The barrows of Denmark, Norway, and Sweden, like the antiquities of these countries, were at an earlier time all considered as belonging to one class, so that monuments of the most different kind were mixed together, as if they belonged to one period. For this reason we will just point out very briefly the chief classes of the acknowledged Danish monuments. . . .

The Danish grave hills are, like the early antiquities, generally divisible into three classes, namely, those of the stone, those of the bronze, and those of the iron period, which last includes the inscribed monumental stones, or Runic stones, as they are termed.

Worsaae was great not only in that he knew how to study the ancient monuments of Denmark, and how to wrest prehistory from the intractable materials of archaeology, but in that he was the first real comparative archaeologist. He was succeeded by many others, of which the names of the Swede Oscar Montelius and the Australian Vere Gordon Childe are the most distinguished. He was very conscious of the stupidity of studying the past of any nation in isolation, and in the passages quoted below, from his *The Primeval Antiquities of Denmark,* we see this—his belief in the comparative method, and his passionate awareness of the necessity of getting the public interested in archaeology.

In order that the Danish memorials may appear in their true light and connection, it will be of importance to enquire in what regions of other countries similar monuments of antiquity have been observed. Without such a general examination it would scarcely be possible to derive satisfactory historical conclusions from the enquiry. . . .

This division of the ancient times in Denmark into three periods is solely and entirely founded on the accordant testimony of antiquities and barrows, for the ancient traditions do not mention that there ever was a time here, when, for want of iron, weapons and edged tools were made of bronze. On this account, many maintain that no importance, or credibility, can be attached to this division into three eras, since the objects supposed to belong to such three periods may have proceeded from the same period, but from different classes of persons. Thus, they assume that the bronze objects, which are distinguished by their beauty of workmanship, may have been used by the rich; while the iron objects belonged to those less wealthy, and those of stone to the poor. This supposition is scarcely founded on probability, much less on a perfect acquaintance with the remains of antiquity.

It is quite true that tools and weapons of stone and bronze, and perhaps also of stone, bronze, and iron have, as has already been remarked, been in use at the same time, *in periods of transition,* when bronze or iron was scarce in the country, and consequently very expensive; yet it is nevertheless no less true that there were three distinct periods, in which the use of stone, bronze, and iron severally prevailed, in a most characteristic manner.

For if it be granted that bronze objects belonged only to the rich, how is it to be imagined that there were no, or rather exceedingly few, rich people in the northern parts of Sweden, and in the whole of Norway, where, it is well known, that, comparatively speaking, bronze objects belong to the rarest finds? Moreover, it is scarcely probable that the rich would have used the inferior metal, bronze, for tools and weapons, while those less wealthy possessed the superior, iron. . . .

Experience has shown us that modes of interment and all circumstances appertaining to them are most prized and preserved by nations in an inferior degree of civilization, and are only abandoned by them when they have been subdued by foreigners more powerful than themselves, or when they have ceased to be an independent people. In the stone period, and in that of bronze, the funeral ceremonies and barrows were completely different; and we are therefore justified in concluding that the race who inhabited Denmark in the bronze period was different from that, which during that of stone, laid the foundation for peopling the country. This is clearly shown by the antiquities, since there exists no gradual transition from the simple implements and weapons of stone, to the beautifully wrought tools and arms of bronze. On the other hand, it is not decided that the people of the iron period must have been a third race, which had immigrated at a later date than that which inhabited the country during the bronze period; for though the antiquities and barrows of these two periods are by no means of the same kind, yet the difference is neither so striking nor so prominent, as to enable us to found on it the supposition of two totally different races of mankind. A greater development of civilization, and in particular a more lively intercourse with other nations, might easily, during a more advanced period of paganism, have called forth a remarkable alteration both in the prevailing taste, and in the mode of interment. The most that we can say, at present, is that Denmark, during the iron period, may possibly, by small immigrations from the neighboring countries, have received new constituent parts of its population.

As an appendix to his book, Worsaae published a short essay entitled "On the Examination of Barrows and the Preservation of Antiquities," and the following extract comes from this essay. It is remarkable in its modern outlook, particularly when it is remembered that it was first published in Denmark in 1843; and is broadly contemporary with the barrow digging of the British Archaeological Association's first meeting at Canterbury in 1843, and appeared only twenty years after Belzoni's death.

In general, it is not to be desired that the ancient barrows belonging to the times of paganism should be either opened or removed. It is true they occur, in certain parts of the country, in such numbers as to offer serious impediments to agriculture; while they contain besides large masses of stone, which in many cases might be used with advantage. Still they deserve to be protected and preserved, in as great a number as possible. They are national memorials, which may be said to cover the ashes of our forefathers; and by this means constitute a national possession, which has been handed down for centuries, from race to race. Would we then unconcernedly destroy those venerable remains of ancient times, without any regard to our posterity? Would we disturb the peace of the dead, for the sake of some trifling gain?

Innumerable barrows have been destroyed by persons who believed that they should find great treasures in them. Experience, however, shows that objects of value are so rare that scarcely one in a hundred contains an article of any worth . . . there is no inducement to open barrows. The only case which can render it desirable is when the object is to gain information respecting the ancient history of our forefathers. But even investigations of this kind cannot always be regarded as desirable, they ought never to be undertaken from unseasonable [sic, but surely "unreasonable"?—G.D.] or superficial curiosity: they should be carried on with care and by persons of intelligence, who will know how to apply the objects discovered to the positive advantage of science. . . .

If a barrow must, of necessity, be removed, a complete description of its external form, its height, and circumference should first be made. This description should explain whether it is surrounded, or enclosed, with large stones; whether chambers of stone are found in the middle of it; whether it has borne any peculiar name; whether any traditions are associated with it; and finally whether there are similar memorials in the same district and what is their number. If the description were accompanied with drawings of the appearance of the barrow, it would naturally be an advantage. As it is of importance to know what is the internal condition of the barrow, and what may be the relation between the tomb itself and the objects deposited within it, the tomb must now be examined with all possible precaution. If the barrow is one of the usual conical kind, it will be best to cut through it from southeast to northwest, with a trench of about eight feet broad, which, in more complete investigations may again be intersected by a similar trench from southwest to northeast. It will often be sufficient so to excavate the barrow from the top, as to form a large, round cavity as far as the bottom of the mound, which is always on a level with the surrounding field, for it is in the middle of this base that the most important tombs are usually situated. In this proceeding it is, however, advisable to form a trench from the cavity in the middle to the southeast side of the barrow, since tombs are often found here, and it might otherwise be extremely difficult to bring up the earth from the central cavity, when such cavity had obtained a depth of several feet.

As soon as the trench is begun, and the first covering of grass and heath is removed, we must examine whether vessels of clay with burnt bones and ashes are not to be met with under such stones. These vessels, from their great antiquity, are so extremely fragile that it is only with the greatest care they can be brought from the barrow in an uninjured state. When the surrounding stones are carefully removed, the best and safest mode of extracting the urns is by introducing a board beneath them, then placing them in the open air, and after a few hours the clay becomes firm again. . . . Skeletons, and in particular sculls, must be preserved; and even the bones of those animals which have been interred with the deceased may have a value for science. . . .

It is generally considered of importance, in such excavations, that the cavities should not be made too narrow, in fact they ought to be very wide at the top, because it is always necessary to make them narrower in descending, with the view to prevent their falling in. . . .

Next to the barrows, the peat bogs are the most important deposits of antiquities. The objects discovered in them have this advantage over those exhumed from the earth, that they are in a much better state of preservation. In bogs we may, for instance, expect to find stone axes with the ancient handles of wood, while even bodies clothed in their garments have several times been met with in cutting through bogs. Hence it is doubly important to observe the greatest care in digging in the peat, as soon as anything remarkable is traced. The best mode is to dig cautiously round the spot, and to endeavour to extract all the objects it contains without injuring them. The mass of peat which surrounds them is not then to be removed immediately; for the earthy portions easily separate, when they have been somewhat dried in the air. At the same time, it is not expedient to dry all specimens in the sun, or in a strong heat, for articles which are not of stone, or of metal, are shrunk by this means. . . .

A very important rule is that all antiquities, even those which appear the most trivial and the most common, ought to be preserved. Trifles often afford important information, when seen in connection with a large collection. That they are of common occurrence forms no objection; for historic results can be deduced only from the comparison of numerous contemporary specimens . . . antiquities have a value with reference to the spot in which they are found. The law of Denmark provides that all gold, silver, and other valuables, which are found in the earth, shall be forwarded to the royal collections, and that the full value of the metal shall be paid to the finder. This arrangement, of course, does not apply to objects of wood, stone, or clay; yet it is to be wished that they should be sent to the national collection, where alone, in fact, they can prove of utility. . . .

Parties who do not themselves possess any knowledge of antiquities would do well, if they discover anything remarkable, to apply to the clergyman, schoolmaster, or other intelligent person on the spot, who may be able to determine what may be deserving of attention. In this respect it would of great utility if all over the country, in every large parish, for instance, or at least in every district, several intelligent men would form an association for protecting the most remarkable antiquities from destruction, and for co-operating with the lower classes in examining barrows and preserving antiquities. [See plates 16 and 17.]

Five years before the publication of Worsaae's *Danmarks Oldtid,* Sven Nilsson (1787–1883), who had then been Professor of Zoology at Lund for twenty-six years, issued the first number of his *Skandinaviska Nordens Urinvånare;* the fourth and last number came out in 1843. A third edition, revised by the author and edited with an introduction by Sir John Lubbock, was published in London in 1868 with the short title of *The Primitive Inhabitants of Scandinavia,* and with a very long subtitle which goes as follows: *An essay on Comparative Ethnography . . . containing a description of the implements, dwelling, tombs, and mode of living of the savages in the North of Europe during the Stone Age.* The following extract comes from that edition.

In the present volume I have endeavoured, by a new method, to gain a knowledge of the first inhabitants of the Scandinavian Peninsula, and thus to contribute in some measure to the history of the gradual development of mankind. I feel more and more convinced that, as in nature we are unable rightly to conceive the importance of individual objects without possessing a distinct view of nature, considered as a whole, so are we also unable properly to understand the signification of the antiquities of any individual country without at the same time clearly realizing the idea that they are the fragments of a progressive series of civili-

95

zation, and that the human race has always been, and still is, steadily advancing in civilization. . . .

The earliest tribes, of which we find traces in every country, show by what they have left behind, as far as we have been able to discover hitherto, that they have belonged to a race of beings standing on the very lowest point of civilization: mountain grottoes, subterranean caves, or stone caverns, their dwellings; rough-hewn stone flakes, their hunting and fishing implements; no domesticated animals except the dog; no cattle, no agriculture, no written language. Between this, the lowest state in which we can imagine human beings, and the most cultivated state of society which they are able to attain, there are many intermediate degrees or stages of development.

Every nation has had, or has, four stages to pass through, before attaining its highest social development. It shows itself either as savage, as nomad, as agriculturist, or as possessing a written language and coined money, and labor distributed among the various members of society.

1. The *savage* has few other than material wants, and these he endeavors to satisfy only for the moment. To appease hunger for the day; when requisite, to protect his body against heat or cold; to prepare his lair for the night; to follow the instinct of propagation, and instinctively to guard and tend his offspring —this constitutes all his care, all his enjoyment. He thinks and acts only for the day which *is,* not for the day which is *coming.* In this state man is necessarily a hunter and fisherman, especially in zones where fruits and berries are scarce, or totally wanting during the greater part of the year. The savage has, therefore, no other alternative; he is compelled to fish and to hunt, or he must perish. . . .

Even amongst the savages, also, we find traces of religion. Experience gradually awakens reflection: hunger is a troublesome guest, but is sure to call, when for a day or two the savage has not succeeded in killing any game. The prudent thought then suggests itself to him of saving a portion of the abundance of the day, and still more, that of carrying away the young calf or fawn, whose mother he has perhaps killed in the chase; and collecting several more of them, and forming at last a herd, he becomes

2. A *herdsman* (nomad), subsisting chiefly on the produce of his herds; the flesh of domestic animals his food, milk his beverage, skins his clothes. The chase and fishing, formerly his *chief,* now become his *occasional* occupations. There are various kinds of nomads: some of them have fixed habitations during all seasons, grazing their herds in the fields and in the neighboring forests; others have fixed habitations only in the winter, migrating in summer with their tents from place to place; others, again, have no fixed habitations, roving about continually with their herds, living in movable huts or sheds on wheels, *drawn* by cattle, or in tents stretched on poles, and *carried* on the back of their cattle during their wanderings. . . .

At last he tires of his wandering life (or, rather, he is obliged to give it up, since the locality has become too small for the increasing population with its flocks); he builds sheds for his cattle, and lays up stores of fodder in barns; he burns a tract of forest land, and sows corn in the ashes. His first *field* is a place where the trees are *felled,* a clearing in the forest, and his first *plough* a hoe. Thus the nomad gradually becomes

3. An *agriculturist,* and takes a more stable social position. The movable tent gives place to a permanently fixed dwelling; the tilled cornfields yield a richer harvest the more they are cultivated; the forests surrounding his home give him fuel and building materials; the fields provide him with grass and winter fodder for his cattle, and even the waters yield him their tribute. . . .

A man's cornfield and pasture ground, his forest, his mine, his lakes and rivers, supply *most* of his wants; not indeed all, but, on the other hand, some in *superfluity*. These superfluous things, then, can be exchanged by barter, and his other needs thereby be supplied; but his personal presence on his property is constantly required; the original trade by barter thus becomes inconvenient, perhaps impossible; some article which finds a demand everywhere, and which within a small compass contains a large value, is made the means of exchanging all kinds of commodities—in other words, it becomes money. At first it derives its value from its weight, but this arrangement has its attendant inconveniences; these are obviated when a piece of this article, of a fixed weight and standard, with its value stamped thereon, becomes *coined money*. With this and with the written language the agriculturist enters upon

4. The fourth stage of civilization, in a still better organized state of society, where labour is divided amongst its various members. Different professions (sometimes *ranks* so called) arise. . . . Thus the *nation* is enabled, through the organization of society, to fulfill more and more completely its allotted mission—to attain the highest degree of culture and the highest state of civilization.

5   *Archaeology Comes of Age*

In the previous three chapters we have seen how archaeology grew into a conscious and scientific discipline from the antiquarianism and dilettantism of the sixteenth, seventeenth, and eighteenth centuries. The dilettanti and the more serious travelers brought back accounts of surface antiquities abroad, and often enough, as we have seen, brought back not only accounts, but some of the actual antiquities.

In the seventeenth century Archbishop Ussher worked out an exact chronology of the world and of man based on the calculations provided in Genesis. His calculations produced the date of 4004 B.C. for the origin of the world and of man, and this chronology was widely accepted: 4004 was printed in the margin of the Authorized Version of the Bible. Half a century before Ussher, Shakespeare made Rosalind say "The poor world is almost six thousand years old" (*As You Like It,* IV, 1).

The new geology made this short chronology of the world impossible to believe in. The new doctrine was based on the principle of uniformitarianism, which held that only processes proceeding and observed at present could be accepted as explanations of the formation of the earth's surface in the past. This fluviatilist geology, as set out by Sir Charles Lyell in his *Principles of Geology* (1830–33), totally rejected the older catastrophist geology, or diluvialist geology as it was often called, since it interpreted the evidence of the rocks as proof of a universal deluge. The new fluviatilist geology not only made the earth and man much older than six thousand years: it also made people look again and anew at the earlier discoveries of men like Frere and Tournal and Father MacEnery, while new discoveries made by Boucher de Perthes in the Somme and William Pengelly in Devonshire paved the way for the famous pronouncements made in London in 1859 at the Royal Society and the Society of Antiquaries of London.

The Three-Age system organized by the Scandinavian archaeologists as a theoretical basis for examining the past of man, and as a practical way of ordering a museum, and as a fact proved by excavation in the Danish tumuli and peat bogs, suggested the way in which the long prehistory of man could be divided. And of course in 1859 there was published Charles Darwin's *Origin of Species;* the theory of evolution had in fact been set out in two separate statements by Wallace and Darwin in the *Proceedings of the Linnean Society* for 1858.

Darwin at first expressed no opinion on the effect of his theory on the question of man's ancestry, nor did he in the *Origin of Species* comment on the oft-repeated anatomical likeness between man and the apes except to say, "Light will be thrown on the origin of man and his history." This is how the sentence appeared in the first edition; Loren Eiseley has reminded us that in later editions the sentence was altered to begin "Much light will be . . ." [1] The extension of Darwinism to man was due largely to T. H. Huxley, who published in 1863 his *Man's Place in Nature:* Darwin's own *Descent of Man* came out in 1871. It is sometimes argued that it was the *Origin of Species* which was really responsible for the development of archaeology. We quote from Grahame Clark's *Archaeology and Society* (third edition, 1957).

It was possible under the old dispensation for archaeology to develop from antiquarianism, and even for the outlines of secondary prehistory to take shape in parts of Europe—after all, Thomsen's Three Ages could fit into the span of Archbishop Ussher's chronology with several thousand years to spare—but

---

[1] Loren Eiseley, *Darwin's Century*, p. 255.

quite definitely there was no room for Paleolithic man. It
needed a revolution in men's conception of the nature and antiquity of man as an organism before the bare notion of primary
prehistory could take birth.

Such a revolution was wrought by the publication in 1859 of
Charles Darwin's *Origin of Species.* The idea of transformism
had been current during the previous century, but it was not until Darwin formulated his coherent and to many scientists convincing theory of natural selection that the evolution of species
became acceptable as a hypothesis. The relevance of this to the
status of man was as manifest as it was challenging to old beliefs. In Huxley's words acceptance of Darwin's views made it
essential to "extend by long epochs the most liberal estimate
that has yet been made of the Antiquity of Man." . . . The
vast extension in the range of human history implicit in the idea
that man evolved from some antecedent animal species at a remote period of time emphasized the need to gather fossils illustrating his cultural as well as his biological development.

Others have thought that the birth of modern archaeology and
anthropology was not the result of the *Origin of Species.* This was
Andrew Lang's view when he said that anthropology probably
took its rise not so much in Darwin's famous theory of evolution
as in the long-ignored or ridiculed discoveries of the relics of
Paleolithic man by M. Boucher de Perthes.[2]

The origins of any subject are complex and can rarely be attributed to one cause; the new geology, the Three-Age system, the
discovery of the antiquities of Egypt and the Mediterranean, the
doctrine of evolution—all these brought the discipline of archaeology into existence in the sixties of the nineteenth century. Certainly
the doctrine of evolution, if accepted, produced a new climate of
thought in which archaeology and anthropology could grow and
flourish. As the present writer has said elsewhere:[3]

This new way of scientific thinking, with its emphasis on uniformitarianism and evolution, enabled the discoveries of Pen-

[2] *Anthropological Essays Presented to E. B. Tylor,* ed. Balfour and Marrett, 1907.
[3] Glyn Daniel, *A Hundred Years of Archaeology,* London, 1950, pp. 66–67.

gelly and Boucher de Perthes to be accepted readily, whereas only a generation before, when the immutability of species and catastrophist diluvialism were the orders of thought the discoveries of Schmerling and MacEnery had passed unnoticed or been rejected with scorn. The doctrine of evolution not only made people more ready to believe in the antiquity of man; it made the roughly chipped artifacts from Devon and the Somme not only credible, but essential. If man had gradually evolved from a prehuman ancestor with no culture to the cultured animal of Egypt and Greece, then there *must* be evidence of his primitive culture in the most recent geological levels. Evolutionary beliefs not only made Boucher de Perthes's hand axes easy to believe in, they made it necessary that more evidences of early human culture should be found, and that traces should also be found of other stages of culture leading from these simple tools to the complex equipment and buildings of the known early historic civilizations.

Many writers have emphasized the part played by English scholars in the birth of archaeology in the mid-nineteenth century. Thus Sir Arthur Keith wrote that "in the brief period . . . 1849–60, a small company of Englishmen . . . gave man a new history of himself and his civilization." [4] Certainly there was a brilliant company of scientists in England at that time interested in different ways in the past of man: Charles Lyell, Charles Darwin, Joseph Prestwich, John Evans, Thomas Huxley, George Busk, John Lubbock, Hugh Falconer, Francis Galton, E. B. Tylor—this short list is a galaxy of talent and genius, standing, as Sir Michael Sadleir said of one of them, "in the brilliant sunshine that flooded England between two spells of stormy weather." [5] But there were comparable men in other countries, and we may see the birth and early stages of the development of archaeology in the writings of three men from the separate countries—Morlot in Switzerland, Lubbock in England, and Montelius in Sweden.

A. Morlot, Professor of Geology at the Academy of Lausanne,

[4] In *Life-work of Lord Avebury,* ed. A. Grant Duff, 1924, p. 67.
[5] *Ibid,* p. 223.

was much interested in the development of the Danish Three-Age system; indeed he once said that the growth of prehistoric archaeology was really due to the diffusion of the ideas of Thomsen, Worsaae, and Nilsson through Europe. This system was adopted in Switzerland, and when, during the very dry winter of 1853–54, the low lake-levels of Lake Zurich revealed the remains of wooden piles, as well as stone axes, pottery, and charred wood, the Swiss soon found that they had their own proof of the Three-Age system in the lake dwellings from the Stone Age, Bronze Age, and Iron Age. Dr. Ferdinand Keller of Zurich examined these various finds from the Swiss lake dwellings. His memoirs, with additions, were translated into English and published in 1866 under the title of *The Lake Dwellings of Switzerland and Other Parts of Europe.* Morlot, in his *Leçon d'ouverture d'un cours sur la haute antiquité fait à l'Académie de Lausanne,* published in 1860, summarized these lake-dwelling discoveries. In the same year he published his *Études géologico-archéologiques en Danemark et en Suisse* (Volume 46 of the *Bulletin de la Société vaudoise des sciences naturelles*). This was translated into English as *General Views on Archaeology* and published by the Smithsonian Institution in 1861. The following extract is from this translation.

A century has scarcely elapsed since the time when it would have been thought impossible to reconstruct the history of our globe prior to the appearance of mankind; but though contemporary historians were wanting during this immense pre-human era, this era has not failed to leave us a well-arranged series of most significant vestiges. The animal and vegetable tribes which have successively appeared and disappeared have left their fossil remains in the successively deposited strata. Thus has been composed, gradually and slowly, a history of creation written, as it were, by the Creator himself. It is a great book, the leaves of which are the stratified rocks, following each other in the strictest chronological order, the chapters being the mountain chains. . . .

The development of Archaeology has been very similar to that of Geology. Not long ago we should have smiled at the idea of reconstructing the bygone days of our race previous to the

ιg of history properly so called. The void was partly
ɔ by representing that ante-historical antiquity as having
ly of short duration, and partly by exaggerating the value
e age of those vague and confused notions which con-
stituted tradition. . . .

The infancy of mankind, at least in Europe, has passed without having any reminiscences; and history fails here entirely, for
what is history but the memory of mankind. But before the beginning of history there were life and industry, of which various
monuments still exist; while others lie buried in the soil, much as
we find the organic remains of former creations entombed in the
strata composing the crust of the globe. The antiquities enact
here a similar part to that of the fossils; and if Cuvier calls the
geologist an antiquarian of a new order, we can reverse that
remarkable saying, and consider the antiquarian as a geologist,
apply his method to reconstruct the first ages of mankind previous to all recollection, and to work out what may be termed
pre-historical history. This is Archaeology pure and proper. But
Archaeology cannot be considered as coming to a full stop with
the first beginning of history, for the further we go back in our
historical researches, the more incomplete they become, leaving
gaps which the study of material remains helps to fill up. Archaeology, therefore, pursues its course in a parallel line with
that of history, and henceforth the two sciences mutually en-
lighten each other. But with the progress of history the part
taken by Archaeology goes on decreasing, until the invention of
printing almost brings to a close the researches of the antiquarian. . . .

To understand the past ages of our species, we must first
begin by examining its present state, following man wherever he
has crossed the waters and set his foot upon dry land. The
different nations which at present inhabit our earth must be
studied with respect to their industry, their habits, and their
general mode of life. We thus make ourselves acquainted with
the different degrees of civilization, ranging from the highest
summit of modern development to the most abject state, hardly
surpassing that of the brute. By that means Ethnology supplies

us with what may be called a contemporaneous scale of development, the stages of which are more or less fixed and invariable; whilst Archaeology traces a scale of successive development, with one movable stage passing generally along the whole line.

Ethnography is, consequently, to Archaeology what physical geography is to geology, namely: a thread of induction in the labyrinth of the past, and a starting point into those comparative researches of which the end is the knowledge of mankind and its development through successive generations.

In following out the principles above laid down, the Scandinavian *savants* have succeeded in unravelling the leading features in the progress of pre-historical European civilization, and in distinguishing three principal eras which they have called the Stone Age, the Bronze Age, and the Iron Age. This great conquest in the realm of science is due chiefly to the labors of Mr. Thomsen, director of the Ethnological and Archaeological Museums at Copenhagen, and to those of Mr. Nilsson, professor at the flourishing University of Lund, in Sweden. These illustrious veterans of the school of northern antiquarians have ascertained that Europe, at present so civilized, was at first inhabited by tribes to whom the use of metal was totally unknown, and whose industry and domestic habits must have borne a considerable analogy to what we now see practised among certain savages. . . .

The question arises whether, previous to the discovery of bronze, man, owing to the great rarity of tin, may not have begun by using copper in a pure state. If so, there would have been a Copper Age between the Stone and Bronze Ages. In America this has really been the case. When they were discovered by the Spaniards, both the two centers of civilization, Mexico and Peru, had bronze composed of copper and tin, which was used for manufacturing arms and cutting instruments, in the absence of iron and steel, which were unknown in the New World; but the admirable researches of Messrs. Squier and Davis on the antiquities of the Mississippi valley have brought to light an ancient civilization of a remarkable nature, and distinguished by the use of raw virgin copper, worked in a cold state by hammering without the aid of fire . . . the "mound builders," as the Americans call the race of the Copper Age, seem to have preceded and prepared the Mexican civilization destroyed by the Spaniards. . . .

The preceding pages present a sketch, certainly very rough and imperfect, of the developments of civilization. They establish, however, in a very striking manner, the fact of a progress, slow, but uninterrupted and immense, when the starting point is considered. . . . And yet there are persons who deny all general progress, seeing everywhere nothing but decay and ruin, like that worthy specimen of a northern pessimist who exclaimed, "See how man has degenerated; he has even lost his likeness to the monkey!" . . .

We do not here entertain any idea of writing a treatise on the archaeology of Switzerland; our intention is merely to bring out the rather remarkable features of resemblance and correspondence that Switzerland presents with the North. In Switzerland, the three ages of stone, bronze, and iron, are quite as well represented as in Scandinavia, but the most important discoveries in this order of things are of tolerably recent date. . . .

The general chronology of the three great phases in the development of civilization in Europe, called the age of stone, the age of bronze, and the age of iron, is purely relative, like the chronology of the geological formations. It is not known when the age of stone or that of bronze, or even that of iron, commenced, nor how long a time each of them lasted. We merely know that what belongs to the age of bronze succeeded the order of things of the age of stone, and preceded that event, so important to the destinies of mankind, the introduction of the manufacture of iron. This is itself a great deal, for it is but a short time since nothing at all was known of what had occurred previous to the present age of iron. But we are so accustomed to precise dates in what has hitherto been understood as *history,* without troubling ourselves whether the figure indicated was true or purely imaginary, that we cannot become accustomed at once to the system of simply relative data of archaeology—to a history without dates. . . .

If nothing is known respecting the absolute date of the age of stone and the age of bronze, it is at least evident from the large accumulation of their remains that they have each lasted a very long while. . . . The Danish *savants* estimate that the age of stone goes back at least 4,000 years, perhaps very much further. . . . But such estimates cannot end in positive results. To arrive at dates in archaeology it will be necessary to call in the aid of geology, just as no absolute chronological data in geology can be obtained without the assistance of archaeology, starting from a sufficiently thorough knowledge of what has happened since the appearance of man on the earth. The two sciences are thus called upon reciprocally to complete each other.

In this last extract Morlot referred to Squier and Davis, *Ancient Monuments of the Mississippi Valley*, published in Washington in 1848, and described by him as "one of the most splendid archaeological works ever published." Morlot's own work is a remarkable and indeed splendid piece of archaeology. He is well aware of the historical background of his subject, its limitations, possibilities, and future. His remarks on chronology are sound and sage: he is looking forward to geochronological techniques. All this was written in 1860. It bears the stamp of mid-Victorian faith in progress, and this he shared, together with many other things such as his sense of the importance of ethnology to archaeology, with our English representative of these first archaeologists, John Lubbock.

Morlot was a professional scholar. John Lubbock (1834–1913), later Sir John Lubbock, and later Lord Avebury, was not a professional scholar; he did not even go to a university. He was a banker and politician responsible for getting passed into law thirty bills, including the Ancient Monuments Act of 1882 and the Bank Holidays Act of 1871 (indeed for a short while bank holidays were called St. Lubbock's days). These professional activities he combined with an intense interest and great competence in natural history and archaeology. He had an amazing capacity for work; Charles Darwin once wrote to him: "How on earth you find time to do all you do is a mystery to me." He was particularly fascinated by archaeology and the development of prehistory into civilization, and his first book, *Prehistoric Times as illustrated by an-*

cient remains and the manners and customs of modern savages,
published in 1865, was, as the title shows, an archaeological and
ethnographical treatise. In it we find for the first time the words
Paleolithic and *Neolithic.* This is how *Prehistoric Times* begins:

> The first appearance of man in Europe dates from a period
> so remote that neither history, nor tradition, can throw any light
> on his origin or mode of life. Under these circumstances, some
> have supposed that the past is hidden from the present by a veil,
> which time will probably thicken, but never can remove. Thus
> our prehistoric antiquities have been valued as monuments of
> ancient skill and perseverance, not regarded as pages of ancient
> history; recognized as interesting vignettes, not as historical
> pictures. Some writers have assured us that, in the words of
> Palgrave, "We must give it up, that speechless past; whether
> fact or chronology, doctrine or mythology; whether in Europe,
> Asia, Africa, or America; at Thebes or Palenque, on Lycian
> shore or Salisbury Plain: lost is lost; gone is gone for ever."
> Others have taken a more hopeful view, but in attempting to re-
> construct the story of the past, they have too often allowed
> imagination to usurp the place of research, and have written in
> the spirit of the novelist, rather than in that of the philosopher.
> Of late years, however, a new branch of knowledge has
> arisen; a new Science has, so to say, been born among us, which
> deals with times and events far more ancient than any which
> have yet fallen within the province of the archaeologist. The
> geologist reckons not by days or by years; the whole six thou-
> sand years, which were until lately looked on as the sum of the
> world's existence, are to him but one unit of measurement in the
> long succession of past ages. Our knowledge of geology is, of
> course, very incomplete; on some questions we shall no doubt
> see reason to change our opinion, but, on the whole, the conclu-
> sions to which it points are as definite as those of zoology, chem-
> istry, or any of the kindred sciences. Nor does there appear to
> be any reason why those methods of examination which have
> proved so successful in geology, should not also be used to
> throw light on the history of man in prehistoric times. Archae-
> ology forms, in fact, the link between geology and history. It is

true that in the case of other animals we can, from their bones and teeth, form a definite idea of their habits and mode of life, while in the present state of our knowledge the skeleton of a savage could not always be distinguished from that of a philosopher. But on the other hand, while other animals leave only teeth and bones behind them, the men of past ages are to be studied principally by their works: houses for the living, tombs for the dead, fortifications for defence, temples for worship, implements for use, and ornaments for decoration.

From the careful study of the remains which have come down to us, it would appear that Prehistoric Archaeology may be divided into four great epochs.

I. That of the Drift; when man shared the possession of Europe with the Mammoth, the Cave Bear, the Woolly-haired Rhinoceros, and other extinct animals. This I have proposed to call the "Palaeolithic" Period.

II. The later or Polished Stone Age; a period characterized by beautiful weapons and instruments made of flint and other kinds of stone; in which, however, we find no trace of the knowledge of any metal, excepting gold, which seems to have been sometimes used for ornaments. For this period I have suggested the term "Neolithic."

III. The Bronze Age, in which bronze was used for arms and cutting instruments of all kinds.

IV. The Iron Age, in which that metal had superseded bronze for arms, axes, knives, etc.; bronze, however, still being in common use for ornaments, and frequently also for the *handles* of swords and other arms, though never for the blades.

Stone weapons, however, of many kinds were still in use during the Age of Bronze, and lingered on even into that of Iron, so that the mere presence of a few stone implements is not in itself sufficient evidence that any given "find" belongs to the Stone Age. In order to prevent misapprehension, it may also be well to state at once that, for the present, I only apply this classification to Europe, though in all probability it might be extended also to the neighboring regions of Asia and Africa. The civilization of the south of Europe, moreover, preceded that of northern Europe. As regards other civilized countries, China and Japan, for instance, we, as yet, know but little of their prehistoric archaeology, though recent researches have gone far to prove that the use of iron was there also preceded by bronze, and bronze by stone. Some nations, indeed, such as the Fuegians, Andamaners, etc., are even now, or were very lately, in an Age of Stone.

In the last chapter of *Prehistoric Times* Lubbock explained his principles, and set out his views about the origins of man and civilization and the value of studying archaeology and the past, and reaffirmed his belief in progress and the future of man.

I have already expressed my belief that the simple arts and implements have been independently invented by various tribes, at different times, and in different parts of the world. . . .

It is probable that man originated in a warm climate, and so long as he was confined to the tropics he may have found a succession of fruits, and have lived as the monkeys do now. Indeed, according to Bates, this is still the case with some of the Brazilian Indians. "The monkeys," he says, "lead in fact a life similar to that of the Parárauate Indians." . . .

It is too often supposed that the world was peopled by a series of "migrations." But migrations, properly so called, are compatible only with a comparatively high state of organization. . . .

The most sanguine hopes for the future are justified by the whole experience of the past. It is surely unreasonable to suppose that a process which has been going on for so many thousand years should have now suddenly ceased; and he must be blind indeed who imagines that our civilization is unsusceptible of improvement, or that we ourselves are in the highest state attainable by man.

Lubbock wrote many books on subjects ranging from *British Wild Flowers considered in relation to Insects, Ants, Bees, and Wasps,* to *The Pleasures of Life* and *The Hundred Best Books,* but in addition to *Prehistoric Times,* he wrote only one other archaeological and anthropological treatise. This was *The Origin of Civilization and the Primitive Condition of Man: Mental and*

Social Condition of Savages, first published in 1870, and actually his second book. Incidentally both these books were widely read; both went into seven editions, the seventh edition of *Prehistoric Times,* which came out in 1913, having been revised by him a few months before his death. In the passage quoted from *Prehistoric Times* Lubbock showed himself to be strongly in favor of independent invention and indeed of a natural cultural evolution in man. In *The Origin of Civilization* he repeats this viewpoint clearly:

> So that, as I shall attempt to show, races in a similar state of mental development, however distinct their origin may be, and however distant the regions they inhabit, have very similar religious concepts.

Lubbock was not much engaged in excavation but was on one occasion startled into digging by James Fergusson's assertion that the Roman road from Bath to Marlborough "passes under Silbury Hill or makes a sudden bent to get round it in a manner that no Roman road, in Britain at least, was ever known to do. . . . From a careful examination of all the circumstances of the case, the conclusion seems inevitable that Silbury Hill stands *on* the Roman road." Lubbock writes:

> Startled by this argument, and yet satisfied that there must be some error. . . . I caused excavations to be made. . . . The ditches running along the Roman road could still be followed and it is clear that the road swerved shortly before arriving at and in order to avoid the tumulus. I quite agree therefore, with old Stukeley, that the Roman road curved abruptly southward to avoid Silbury Hill, and that "this shows Silbury Hill was ancienter than the Roman road." . . . As regards Stonehenge we have, I think, satisfactory reasons for attributing it to the Bronze Age.

One final quotation from Lubbock, who so much epitomizes the birth of archaeology in northwestern Europe and the sense of discovery and purpose that informed scientists in the third quarter of the nineteenth century. We have already heard John Evans on his visit to the Somme gravels in 1859. It was Lubbock's lifelong regret that a pressing engagement prevented him from accompanying Prestwich and Evans to the Somme on that visit, but he went the next year with Prestwich. Of his visit Lubbock wrote:

> I am sure no geologist could return from such a visit without an overpowering sense of the change which has taken place and the enormous time which must have elapsed since the first appearance of Man in Western Europe. . . .
>
> While we have been straining our eyes to the East, and eagerly watching excavations in Egypt and Assyria, suddenly a new light has arisen in the midst of us, and the oldest relics of man yet discovered have occurred, not among the ruins of Nineveh or Heliopolis, not on the sandy plains of the Nile or the Euphrates, but in the pleasant valleys of England and France, along the banks of the Seine and Somme, the Thames and the Waveney.

Following in the wake of the great northern pioneers of archaeology, Thomsen, Worsaae, and Nilsson, came the Swede Oscar Montelius (1843–1921). Montelius traveled extensively in Europe and in the Mediterranean. He realized the possibilities of cross-dating and was prepared to give exact dates to the subdivisions of the Bronze Age. He distinguished five or six subdivisions of the Bronze Age and four in the Neolithic. The following extracts from his *The Civilization of Sweden in Heathen Times* (London, 1888) make interesting reading, written as they were midway between Thomsen and the systematists of the 1920's, like Sir Cyril Fox and Gordon Childe.

> The history of the earliest inhabitants of the North was till about fifty years ago shrouded in obscurity. It was not till then that antiquarians began generally to recognize that the antiquities which are dug up from time to time, and the barrows and stone monuments which still abound throughout the country, do not all belong to that part of heathen times which immediately preceded the introduction of Christianity, and of which the Icelandic sagas relate. When Ansgar first came to Sweden in the

ninth century, the use of iron was universal in the country, and had been so for a long time. A careful investigation of the antiquities has shown, however, that before that period, now usually known as the Iron Age, there was another, when iron was altogether unknown, in which weapons and tools were made of bronze, a mixture of copper and tin. This period, called the Bronze Age, had, as well as the Iron Age, continued for many centuries. But before the beginning of the Bronze Age, Sweden had for a very long time been inhabited by people who lived in entire ignorance of the use of the metals, and were therefore compelled to make their instruments and weapons of such materials as stone, horn, bone, and wood. This last period is known therefore as the Stone Age.

This division of heathen times in the North into three great periods was already made and published as long ago as the last century, but it was not till 1830–40 that it had any special importance in antiquarian researches. The honor of developing a scientific system based upon this triple division—a work so important for gaining an insight into the earliest condition of the whole human race—belongs to the *savants* of the North. The first place among them is occupied by Councillor Christian Jürgensen Thomsen (died 1865), to whose labors we are mainly indebted for the celebrated Museum of Northern Antiquities in Copenhagen. Next to him we must place as the founders of the prehistoric archaeology of the North, Professor Sven Nilsson of Lund (died 1883), and Chamberlain J. J. A. Worsaae (died 1885). Thomsen's system was soon taken up by the Royal Antiquary Bror Emil Hildebrand (died 1884), who did the greatest service by his development of the National Historical Museum at Stockholm. The Three-Age system was also quickly adopted in almost every other country. The attack long made against it in Germany may now be regarded as ceased and the correctness of this division has been generally recognized, even in that country. . . . We can now form a very clear idea of the circumstances under which the first settlers in our land lived, and we can follow, step by step, the slow but sure development whereby the inhabitants of Sweden, once a horde of savages, have reached their present condition.

It is true that we meet with no line of kings, no heroic names dating from these earliest times. But is not the knowledge of the people's life, and of the progress of their culture, of more worth than the names of saga heroes? And ought we not to give more credence to the contemporary, irrefutable witnesses to which alone archaeology now listens, than to the poetical stories which for centuries were preserved only in the memory of skalds? . . .

How far the beginning of each period coincides with the appearance of a new race which subdued the earlier settlers in the country, is a further question which we must for the present distinguish from that which concerns only the order in which the several heathen periods followed each other. . . .

With respect to the important question *how* the Bronze Age began in the North, different opinions have been expressed. Some have supposed that it was due to the immigration of a Celtic race, others to a Teutonic immigration. Professor Nilsson has endeavored to show that the North is indebted to Phoenician colonists for the earliest knowledge of metals, while Herr Wiberg, in Gefle, regarded the Bronze Age to have begun in the North through the influence of the Etruscans. Also Professor Lindenschmidt of Mainz, who does not believe in the existence of a Bronze Age in the sense understood by the Northern antiquarians, considers that most of the bronze works in question were Etruscan.

It seems to us that there are strong grounds for the opinion that the beginning of the Bronze Age in Scandinavia was not connected with any great immigration of a new race, but that the people of the North learnt the art of working bronze by intercourse with other nations. The resemblance of the graves during the last part of the Stone Age and the early part of the Bronze Age, as well as other circumstances, points to such a conclusion. From Asia the "Bronze Culture," if we may so express the higher civilization dependent on the knowledge of bronze, had gradually spead itself over the continent of Europe in a northerly and northwesterly direction, until at last it reached the coasts of the Baltic . . . the end of the Stone Age, and therefore the beginning of the Bronze Age, in the North, must be regarded as having taken place 3,500 years ago. The latest investigations have shown that the Bronze Age proper came to an end in these regions in the beginning of the fifth century B.C. It lasted therefore about a thousand years.

As the Bronze Age comprises so long a period, attempts have naturally been made to distinguish the antiquities belonging to its earlier and later parts. Such attempts might have been supposed almost useless, when we consider that among the thousand of finds of the Bronze Age in the North as yet known, there is not a single coin, or any other object, with an inscription, either native or foreign. Nevertheless by a careful and thorough examination of the many antiquities and graves of the Bronze Age now known, it has fortunately proved possible to distinguish in it six consecutive periods.

Just as archaeology was born in the two decades between 1850 and 1870, so was its collateral science of anthropology. Indeed anthropology, defined as the study of man, at least in theory, and the study of primitive man in practice, might be said to include some aspects of archaeology. This is certainly how it was understood by some of the pioneers of anthropology like E. B. Tylor, and how it is still understood in many universities, particularly in America, where prehistoric archaeology is a part of anthropology. But all archaeology is not a part of anthropology, and the archaeology of the ancient civilizations of the Near East or of the Dark and Middle Ages in Europe and the Industrial Revolution cannot be claimed to be anthropology. Where anthropology and archaeology meet is in prehistory, and the development of prehistoric archaeology in the middle of the nineteenth century was much helped by the development of anthropology. Indeed there was for fifty years or more a cross-fertilization between prehistoric archaeology and anthropology; the development of the idea of culture in prehistory as we shall see later (chapter 8) was a direct effect of anthropology.

Here we consider one English and one American anthropologist—namely E. B. Tylor and L. H. Morgan. Edward Burnett Tylor (1832–1917) became interested in anthropology as the result of a casual contact in the spring of 1856 in an omnibus at Havana with Henry Christy, an English banker and businessman, whose role in the early study of Paleolithic man and the discovery of Paleolithic art will be discussed in the next chapter.

Tylor's first book was *Anahuac or Mexico and the Mexicans,*

Ancient and Modern (1861), and this was followed by *Researches into the Early History of Mankind and the Development of Civilization* (1865), *Primitive Culture* (1871), and *Anthropology* (1881). Tylor was made Reader in Anthropology at Oxford University in 1884, and Professor in 1896. In his inaugural address to the University he declared that "to trace the development of civilization and the laws by which it is governed nothing is so valuable as the possession of material objects," and he was always very well aware of the importance of archaeology, although he himself was an anthropologist, practicing what his contemporaries referred to, sometimes kindly and sometimes rudely, as "Mr. Tylor's science." Here are some extracts from his *Researches,* published in the same year as Lubbock's *Prehistoric Times.*

In studying the phenomena of knowledge and art, religion and mythology, law and custom, and the rest of the complex whole which we call Civilization, it is not enough to have in view the more advanced races, and to know their history so far as direct records have preserved it for us. The explanation of the state of things in which we live has often to be sought in the condition of rude and early tribes; and without a knowledge of this to guide us, we may miss the meaning even of familiar thoughts and practices. . . .

It is indeed hardly too much to say that Civilization, being a process of long and complex growth, can only be thoroughly understood when studied through its entire range; that the past is continually needed to explain the present, and the whole to explain the part. . . .

As, however, the earlier civilization lies very much out of the beaten track of history, the place of direct records has to be supplied in great measure by indirect evidence, such as Antiquities, Language, and Mythology. This makes it generally difficult to get a sound historical basis to work on, but there happens to be a quantity of material easily obtainable, which bears on the development of some of the more common and useful arts . . .

In the remote times and places where direct history is at fault, the study of Civilization, Culture-History as it is conveniently called in Germany, becomes itself an important aid to the historian, as a means of reconstructing the lost records of early or barbarous times. But its use as contributing to the early history of mankind depends mainly on the answering of the following question. . . .

When similar arts, customs, beliefs, or legends are found in several distant regions, among peoples not known to be of the same stock, how is this similarity to be accounted for? Sometimes it may be ascribed to the like working of men's minds under like conditions, and sometimes it is proof of blood relationship or of intercourse, direct or indirect, between the races among whom it is found. In the one case it has no historical value whatever, while in the other it has this value in a high degree, and the ever-recurring problem is how to distinguish between the two. . . .

Direct record is the mainstay of History, and where this fails us in remote places and times, it becomes much more difficult to make out where civilization has gone forward, and where it has fallen back. As to progress in the first place; when any important movement has been made in modern times, there have usually been well-informed contemporary writers only too glad to come before the public with something to say that the world cared to hear. But in going down to the lower levels of traditional history, this state of things changes. It is not only that real information becomes more and more scarce, but that the same curiosity that we feel about the origin and growth of civilization, unfortunately combined with a disposition to take any semblance of an answer rather than live in face of mere blank conscious ignorance, has favoured the growth of the crowd of mythic inventors and civilizers who have their place in the legends of so many distant ages and countries. . . .

The early Culture-History of Mankind is capable of being treated as an inductive science, by collecting and grouping facts. It is true that very little has as yet been done in this way, as regards the lower races at least; but the evidence has only to a very slight extent been got into a state to give definite results, and the whole argument is extremely uncertain and difficult: a fact which sufficiently accounts for writers on the origin of civilization being able to tell us all about it, with that beautiful ease and confidence which belong to the speculative philosopher, whose course is but little obstructed by facts. . . .

In the arguments given here in illustration of the general method, only one side of history has been kept in view, and the facts have been treated generally as evidence of movement only in a forward direction, or (to define more closely what is here treated as Progress) the appearance and growth of new arts and new knowledge, whether of a profitable or hurtful nature, developed at home or imported from abroad. Yet we know by what has taken place within the range of history, that Decline as well as Progress in art and knowledge really goes on in the world. Is there not then evidence forthcoming to prove that degradation as well as development has happened to the lower races beyond the range of direct history? The known facts bearing on this subject are scanty and obscure, but by examining some direct evidence of decline, it may perhaps be possible to form an opinion as to what indirect evidence there may probably be, and how it is to be treated; though actually to find this and use it, is a very different matter. . . .

The Chinese do not make now the magnificent cloisonné enamels and the high-class porcelain of their ancestors; we do not build churches, or even cast church bells, as our forefathers did. In Egypt the extraordinary development of masonry, goldsmiths' work, weaving, and other arts which rose to such a pitch of excellence there thousands of years ago have died out under the influence of foreign civilizations which contented themselves with a lower level of excellence in these things, and there seems to be hardly a characteristic native art of any importance practiced there, unless it be the artificial hatching of eggs, and even this is found in China. As Sir Thomas Browne writes in his "Fragment on Mummies," "Egypt is now become the land of obliviousness and doteth. Her ancient civility is gone, and her glory hath vanished as a phantasma. Her youthful days are over, and her face hath become wrinkled and tetrick. She poreth not upon the heavens, astronomy is dead unto her, and knowledge maketh other cycles" . . .

The want of evidence leaves us as yet much in the dark as to the share which decline in civilization may have had in bringing the lower races into the state in which we find them. But perhaps this difficulty rather affects the whole of particular tribes, than the history of Culture as a whole. To judge from experience, it would seem that the world, when it has once got a firm grasp of new knowledge or a new art, is very loth to lose it altogether, especially when it relates to matters important to man in general, for the conduct of his daily life, and the satisfaction of his daily wants, things that come home to men's "business and bosoms." An inspection of the geographical distribution of art and knowledge among mankind seems to give some grounds for the belief that the history of the lower races, as of the higher, is not the history of a course of degeneration, or even of equal oscillations to and fro, but of a movement which, in spite of frequent stops and relapses, has on the whole been forward; that there has been from age to age a growth in Man's power over Nature, which no degrading influences have been able permanently to check. . . .

The present series of Essays affords no sufficient foundation for a definite theory of the Rise and Progress of Human Civilization in early times. Nor, indeed, will any such foundation be ready for building upon, until a great deal of preparatory work has been done. . . . The facts collected seem to favour the view that the wide differences in the civilization and mental state of the various races of mankind are rather differences of development than of origin, rather of degree than of kind. . . . I do not think I have ever met with a single fact which seems to me to justify the theory, of which Dr. von Martius is perhaps the leading advocate, that the ordinary condition of the savage is the result of degeneration from a far higher state. . . .

The question then arises, how any particular piece of skill or knowledge has come into any particular place where it is found. Three ways are open, independent invention, inheritance from ancestors in a distant region, transmission from one race to another; but between these three ways the choice is commonly a difficult one. Sometimes, indeed, the first is evidently to be preferred. Thus, though the floating gardens of Mexico and Cashmere are very similar devices, it seems more likely that the Mexican *chinampa* was invented on the spot than that the idea of it was imported from a distant region. Though the wattled cloth of the Swiss lake dwellings is so similar in principle to that of New Zealand, it is much easier to suppose it the result of separate invention than of historical connexion. Though both the Egyptians and Chinese came upon the expedient of making the picture of an object stand for the sound which was the name of that object, there is no reason to doubt their having done so independently.

Tylor's *Researches*, which, as we have said, came out in the same year as Lubbock's *Prehistoric Times*, had a chapter entitled "The Stone Age: Past and Present": Lubbock's terms "Paleolithic" and "Neolithic" had not yet appeared, and Tylor was using phrases like "Unground Stone Age" and "Ground Stone Age." Six years later, in his *Primitive Culture*, Tylor was freely using the word "prehistory" and wrote proudly, "The history and prehistory of man have taken their proper places in the general scheme of knowledge." This was in 1871. Ten years later Tylor published his *Anthropology*, the first textbook of that name to appear, and here are extracts from what he says about archaeology and the antiquity and development of ancient man in that remarkable work.

The student who seeks to understand how mankind came to be as they are, and to live as they do, ought first to know clearly whether men are newcomers on the earth, or old inhabitants. Did they appear with their various races and ways of life ready-made, or were these shaped by the long, slow growth of ages? . . .

The historic ages are to be looked on as but the modern period of man's life on earth. Behind them lies the prehistoric period, when the chief work was done of forming and spreading over the world the races of mankind. Though there is no scale to measure the length of this period by, there are substantial reasons for taking it as a long stretch of time. . . .

It does not follow . . . that civilization is always on the move, or that its movement is always progress. On the contrary, history teaches that it remains stationary for long periods and often falls back. To understand such decline of culture, it must be borne in mind that the highest arts and the most elaborate arrangements of society do not always prevail, in fact that they may be too perfect to hold their ground, for people must have what fits their circumstances. . . .

It is reasonably inferred that even in countries now civilized, savage and low barbaric tribes must have once lived. Fortunately it is not left altogether to the imagination to picture the lives of these rude and ancient men, for many relics of them are found which may be seen and handled in museums. . . . When an antiquary examines the objects dug up in any place, he can generally judge in what state of civilization its inhabitants have been . . .

In judging how mankind may have once lived, it is also a great help to observe how they are actually found living. Human life may be roughly classed into three great stages, Savage, Barbaric, Civilized, which may be defined as follows. The lowest or *savage* state is that in which man subsists on wild plants and animals, neither tilling the soil nor domesticating creatures for his food. Savages may dwell in tropical forests where the abundant fruit and game may allow small clans to live in one spot and find a living all the year round, while in barer and colder regions they have to lead a wandering life in quest of the wild food which they soon exhaust in any place. In making their rude implements, the materials used by savages are what they find ready to hand, such as wood, stone, and bone, but they cannot extract metal from the ore, and therefore belong to the Stone Age. Men may be considered to have risen into the next or *barbaric* state when they take to agriculture. With the certain supply of food which can be stored till next harvest, settled village and town life is established, with immense results in the improvement of arts, knowledge, manners, and government. Pastoral tribes are to be reckoned in the barbaric stage, for although their life of shifting camp from pasture to pasture may prevent settled habitation and agriculture, they have from their herds a constant supply of milk and meat. Some barbaric nations have not come beyond using stone implements, but most have risen into the Metal Age. Lastly, *civilized* life may be taken as beginning with the art of writing, which, by recording history, law, knowledge, and religion for the service of ages to come, binds together the past and the future in an unbroken chain of intellectual and moral progress. This classification of three great stages of culture is practically convenient, and has the advantage of not describing imaginary states of society, but such as are actually known to exist. So far as the evidence goes, it seems that civilization has actually grown up in the world through these three stages, so that to look at a savage of the Brazilian forests, a barbarous New Zealander or Dahoman, and a civilized European may be the student's best guide to understanding the progress of civilization, only he must be cautioned that the comparison is but a guide, not a full explanation.

The American counterpart of E. B. Tylor was Lewis H. Morgan (1818–81), but unlike Tylor, Morgan never served on the staff of any scientific or educational institution. He was a lawyer practicing in Rochester, New York, who became very interested in the social organization and origins of the American Indians and the light that their study threw on the general problem of cultural origins. In the 1850's the problem of American origins was an open one: after several field trips Morgan thought that he had obtained at last "decisive evidence of the Asiatic origin of the American Indian race." His first book was *The League of the Iroquois* (1851); in 1877 he published his *Ancient Society or Researches in the Lines of Human Progress from Savagery through Barbarism to Civilization,* and it was here that he set out his ethnical periods in human history. The following passage summarizes his argument.

The great antiquity of mankind upon the earth has been conclusively established. It seems singular that the proofs should have been discovered as recently as within the last thirty years, and that the present generation should be the first called upon to recognize so important a fact.

Mankind are now known to have existed in Europe in the glacial period, and even back of its commencement, with every probability of their origination in a prior geological age. They have survived many races of animals with whom they were contemporaneous, and passed through a process of development, in the several branches of the human family, as remarkable in its courses as in its progress.

Since the probable length of their career is connected with geological periods, a limited measure of time is excluded. One hundred or two hundred thousand years would be an unextravagant estimate of the period from the disappearance of the glaciers in the northern hemisphere to the present time. Whatever doubt may attend any estimate of a period, the actual duration of which is unknown, the existence of mankind extends backward immeasurably, and loses itself in a vast and profound antiquity.

This knowledge changes materially the views which have prevailed respecting the relations of savages to barbarians, and of barbarians to civilized men. It can now be asserted upon convincing evidence that savagery preceded barbarism in all the tribes of mankind, as barbarism is known to have preceded civilization. The history of the human race is one in source, one in experience, and one in progress.

It is both a natural and a proper desire to learn, if possible, how all these ages upon ages of past time have been expended by mankind; how savages, advancing by slow, almost imperceptible steps, attained the higher condition of barbarians; how barbarians, by similar progressive advancement, finally attained to civilization; and why other tribes and nations have been left behind in the race of progress—some in civilization, some in barbarism, and others in savagery. . . .

As it is undeniable that portions of the human family have existed in a state of savagery, other portions in a state of barbarism, and still other portions in a state of civilization, it seems equally so that these three distinct conditions are connected with each other in a natural as well as necessary sequence of progress. Moreover that this sequence has been historically true of the entire human family, up to the status attained by each branch respectively, is rendered probable by the conditions under which all progress occurs, and by the known advancement of several branches of the family through two or more of these conditions. . . .

The theory of human degradation to explain the existence of savages and of barbarians is no longer tenable. It came in as a corollary from the Mosaic cosmogony; and was acquiesced in from a supposed necessity which no longer exists. As a theory, it is not only incapable of explaining the existence of savages, but is without support in the facts of human experience. . . .

The experience of mankind has run in nearly uniform channels: that human necessities in similar conditions have been substantially the same; and that the operations of the mental principle have been uniform in virtue of the specific identity of the brain of all the races of mankind. This, however, is but a part of the explanation of uniformity in results. The germs of the principal institutions and arts of life were developed while man was still a savage. To a very great extent the experience of the subsequent periods of barbarism and of civilization have been expended in the further development of these original conceptions. Wherever a connection can be traced on different continents between a present institution and a common germ, the derivation of the people themselves from a common original stock is implied.

The discussion of these several classes of facts will be facilitated by the establishment of a certain number of Ethnical Periods, each representing a distinct condition of society, and distinguishable by a mode of life peculiar to itself. The terms "Age of *Stone,*" "of *Bronze,*" and "of *Iron,*" introduced by Danish archaeologists, have been extremely useful for certain purposes, and will remain so for the classification of objects of ancient art; but the progress of knowledge has rendered other and different subdivisions necessary. Stone implements were not entirely laid aside with the introduction of tools of iron, nor of those of bronze. The invention of the process of smelting iron ore created an ethnical epoch, yet we could scarcely date another from the production of bronze. Moreover, since the period of stone implements overlaps those of bronze and of iron, and since that of bronze also overlaps that of iron, they are not capable of a circumscription that would leave each independent and distinct.

It is probable that the successive arts of subsistence which arose at long intervals will ultimately, from the great influence they must have exercised upon the condition of mankind, afford the most satisfactory bases for these divisions. But investigation has not been carried far enough in this direction to yield the necessary information. With our present knowledge the main result can be attained by selecting such other inventions or discoveries as will afford sufficient tests of progress to characterize the commencement of successive ethnical periods. Each of those about to be proposed will be found to cover a distinct culture, and to represent a particular mode of life. Even though accepted as provisional, these periods will be found convenient and useful.

The period of savagery, of the early part of which very little is known, may be divided, provisionally, into three sub-periods. These may be named respectively the *Older,* the *Middle,* and the *Later* period of savagery. . . . In like manner, the period of barbarism divides naturally into three sub-periods, which will be called, respectively, the *Older,* the *Middle,* and the *Later* period of barbarism. . . .

I. *Lower Status of Savagery.* This period commenced with the infancy of the human race, and may be said to have ended with the acquisition of a fish subsistence and of a knowledge of the use of fire. Mankind were then living in their original restricted habitat, and subsisting upon fruits and nuts. The commencement of articulate speech belongs to this period. . . .

II. *Middle Status of Savagery.* It commenced with the acquisition of a fish subsistence and a knowledge of the use of fire, and ended with the invention of the bow and arrow. Mankind, while in this condition, spread from their original habitat over the greater portion of the earth's surface. . . .

III. *Upper Status of Savagery.* It commenced with the invention of the bow and arrow, and ended with the invention of the art of pottery. . . .

IV. *Lower Status of Barbarism.* The invention or practice of the art of pottery, all things considered, is probably the most effective and conclusive test that can be selected to fix a boundary line, necessarily arbitrary, between savagery and barbarism. . . . All such tribes, then, as never attained to the art of pottery will be classed as savages, and those possessing this art but who never attained a phonetic alphabet and the use of writing will be classed as barbarians. . . .

v. *Middle Status of Barbarism.* It commenced with the domestication of animals in the Eastern hemisphere, and in the Western with cultivation by irrigation and with the use of adobe-brick and stone in architecture. Its termination may be fixed with the invention of the process of smelting iron ore. . . .

vi. *Upper Status of Barbarism.* It commenced with the manufacture of iron, and ended with the invention of a phonetic alphabet, and the use of writing in literary composition. Here civilization begins. . . .

vii. *Status of Civilization.* It commenced, as stated, with the use of a phonetic alphabet and the production of literary records, and divides into *Ancient* and *Modern.* As an equivalent, hieroglyphical writing upon stone may be admitted.

In the foregoing extract from *Ancient Society,* Morgan glosses over many important points. For example, he does not say where "the original restricted habitat" of mankind was. Nor does he explain the contradiction between his oft-repeated assertion that the progress of mankind from lower savagery to civilization is everywhere the same, and the difficulty he had in defining the criteria for the middle status of barbarism differently in the New World and the Old. Morgan's system was, of course, a model, and it was interesting in the eighties of the nineteenth century to have such a model, and to have one different from the Scandinavian Three-Age system, which, as Morgan said, was extremely useful "for the classification of objects of ancient art," by which I think he really meant artifacts. In devising his model he was going back to the Nilsson model,[6] but not having the evidence to apply it, regretfully used other cultural facts like pottery and fire. Morgan identified certain of his seven ethnical periods with existing primitive peoples: thus "the Australians and the greater part of the Polynesians when discovered" were in the state of middle savagery, the Athapascan tribes of the Hudson's Bay Territory were upper sav-

[6] Sven Nilsson's model of man's past is summarized in the extract given above (pp. 95–98) from his *The Primitive Inhabitants of Scandinavia.*

ages, and the Village Indians of New Mexico, Mexico, Central America, and Peru were in the middle status of barbarism. This line of comparative ethnographical parallels was one followed by Sollas in his *Ancient Hunters and Their Modern Representatives* (1911).

But the most remarkable result of the publication of Morgan's *Ancient Society* was its virtual canonization by Marxism. Karl Marx was much impressed by the book and altered some of his views on social evolution after having read it; he made copious notes, intending to write a book about Morgan and his theories. He died, and his coworker, Friedrich Engels (1820–95), completed the project in *Der Ursprung der Familie, des Privateigenthums und des Staates,* published in Zurich in 1884; the first English translation, *The Origin of the Family, Private Property and the State,* was published in Chicago in 1902. Surprisingly, the first translation printed in England did not appear until 1940. The following extract is from the English edition.

The following chapters are, in a sense, the execution of a bequest. No less a man than Karl Marx had made it one of his future tasks to present the results of Morgan's researches in the light of the conclusions of his own—within certain limits, I may say our—materialistic examination of history, and thus to make clear their full significance. For Morgan in his own way had discovered afresh in America the materialistic conception of history discovered by Marx forty years ago, and in his comparison of barbarism and civilization it had led him, in the main points, to the same conclusions as Marx. And just as the professional economists in Germany were for years as busy plagiarizing *Capital* as they were persistent in attempting to kill it by silence, so Morgan's *Ancient Society* received precisely the same treatment from the spokesmen of "prehistoric" science in England. . . .

It is Morgan's great merit that he has discovered and reconstructed in its main lines this prehistoric basis of our written history, and that in the kinship groups of the North American Indians he has found the key to the most important and hitherto insoluble riddles of earliest Greek, Roman and German history. His book is not the work of a day. For nearly forty years he wrestled with his material, until he was completely master of it. But that also makes his book one of the few epoch-making works of our time. . . .

Morgan is the first man who with expert knowledge has attempted to introduce a definite order into human prehistory: so long as no important additional material makes changes necessary, his classification will undoubtedly remain in force. . . .

The sketch which I have given here, following Morgan, of the development of mankind through savagery and barbarism to the beginnings of civilization, is already rich enough in new features; what is more, they cannot be disputed, since they are drawn directly from the process of production. Yet my sketch will seem flat and feeble compared with the picture to be unrolled at the end of our travels: only then will the transition from barbarism to civilization stand out in full light and in all its striking contrasts. For the time being, Morgan's division may be summarized thus: Savagery—the period in which man's appropriation of products in their natural state predominates; the products of human art are chiefly instruments which assist this appropriation. Barbarism—the period during which man learns to breed domestic animals and to practise agriculture, and acquires methods of increasing the supply of natural products by human agency. Civilization—the period in which man learns a more advanced application of work to the products of nature, the period of industry proper and art.

One of Lewis Morgan's key points was the evolution of the family, which cannot be worked out by prehistoric archaeology, and is a theoretical model or construct invented from a study of, and often a misapprehension of, modern primitive peoples. As Leslie A. White has said, "Morgan's whole theory of the evolution of the family, from the promiscuous horde to monogamy, has been shown by modern anthropologists to be invalid; the only adherents to the theory are die-hard Marxists who feel . . . that any criticism of Morgan is a betrayal of the Marxist faith." [7] Here we leave Morgan and his ideas as overpraised uncritically by

[7] L. A. White's preface to his edition of Morgan's *Ancient Society* (Cambridge, Mass., 1964, p. xxv).

Marx and Engels to return to them later (chapter 8) when we see the interesting attempts made by Gordon Childe and Grahame Clark to combine the Scandinavian Three-Age model and the Morgan model in one, and the elaboration and persistent use of the Morgan model in Russian and other archaeological work. But before we leave him, one comment; when Engels wrote that Morgan was "the first man who with expert knowledge has attempted to introduce a definite order into human prehistory," he was not only revealing that Morgan was introducing a model into the apparent facts of the past, but further revealing his own remarkable ignorance of prehistoric archaeology to date. A reading of Worsaae, Morlot, Lubbock, and De Mortillet might not have converted him from his view that Morgan was one of the greatest writers of all time; he might still have thought that *Ancient Society* was "one of the few epoch-making works of our time," but he would at least have realized that there were other views on prehistoric archaeology, and that between 1859 and 1877, those two decades which saw the birth of archaeology, some other epoch-making works had been written.

But let us end this chapter on a less controversial note. On November 2, 1870, J. H. Parker, Keeper of the Ashmolean Museum in Oxford, gave a lecture to the Oxford Architectural and Historical Society entitled "The Ashmolean Museum; Its History, Present State, and Prospects." It was published the same year at Oxford, and here are some extracts from it.

> What is Archaeology? It is *History in detail,* and the details are tenfold more interesting than the dry skeletons called School Histories. Details give life and interest to any subject. Archaeology is also history taught by the eye, by showing a series of tangible objects; and what we have once *seen* we can remember far better than anything of which we have only heard or read . . .
>
> Architecture has long been the most popular branch of Archaeology . . . we should never forget the weighty words of Mr. Goldwin Smith . . . "The buildings of every nation are an important part of its history, but a part that has been neglected by all historians, because the historians themselves have been entirely ignorant of the subject" . . .

When Archaeology is made part of the system of Education at Oxford, as I trust it will be, with the help of this Museum, any educated man will feel it a disgrace to be ignorant of it. The subject in itself, in its general outline, is so simple and easy, and when that outline is once understood is so easily followed up in one branch or another, and so useful for assisting to understand other branches of history, that it seems impossible that it should not be taken up in earnest.

The ladies are already taking the lead in this matter. Architecture or Archaeology is now part of the course of study in the education of young ladies, and I have frequently observed in society that to find out whether a young lady knows anything of Archaeology or not is a test whether she has been highly educated or not. The daughters of our higher nobility, who have generally had the best education that can be obtained, are almost always well acquainted with Archaeology. Some of my most favourite pupils have been young ladies of this class, our future Duchesses or Countesses. I could mention names, but for the fear of offending the modesty, or rather the shyness of the English character. . . .

I will now remind you of the words of another distinguished Oxford man—Dean Stanley: *What Comparative Anatomy is to the study of Medicine, that Archaeology is to the study of History.* As the two names I have mentioned both belong to the Liberal party, and party spirit sometimes lays hold of names, and our object might possibly be misrepresented in consequence, it may be as well to mention some names on the other side. In the early days of our Society, Dr. Newman sometimes attended our meetings, and he said that *It was a pleasure to attend the meetings of this Society, because it was the only neutral ground in Oxford.* At that time, Polemics ran very high in Oxford; but Archaeology has nothing to do with Politics or Polemics. . . .

The spirit of Archaeology is necessarily Conservative. At the same time, we see the necessity of taking Liberal views of progress, and giving up the bigotry and exclusiveness of our fathers—the Antiquaries of the old School. Archaeology must necessarily be Cosmopolitan, if it is to attain its object, as we cannot

130

really study it without the power of comparison, or comparing one country or one district with another.

There is a tremendous feeling of modernity in Parker's address, delivered nearly a hundred years ago—except for the reference to future Duchesses and Countesses who do not at the present fill archaeological lecture rooms. There is one passage however which makes it memorable in any account of the origins and growth of archaeology, and we excerpt it here: Parker is in 1870 recommending to a doubtless surprised audience, the great advantages of "this modern art of photography."

It is by comparing small remains in one place with more perfect remains of the same kind and of the same period in other places, that we learn to understand the smaller remains. To carry on this study formerly required the power of traveling far and wide but the art of photography enables us to pursue this study by our own fireside, and sometimes even better than we could do by traveling, because we can place the objects side by side, and not have to trust to memory or to drawings, which are not always to be depended on.

C. T. Newton had already made use of photography in his excavations in Greece and Turkey; but while he used photography on his excavations he had lithographs made from the photographs to illustrate his reports. Alexander Conze dug in Samothrace in 1873 and 1875; his excavation report, perhaps the first modern archaeological excavation account we have, was illustrated by photographs, and this is probably the first time photographs were used in such a way. Conze's illustrated excavation report shows that archaeology had really come of age in the quarter century following 1859.

6 Discovery and Decipherment

The previous four chapters have given us a picture of the origins of archaeology from its antiquarian and dilettante beginnings. In 1871, as we have said, Tylor wrote in his *Primitive Culture:* "The history and prehistory of man have taken their proper places in the general scheme of knowledge." Four years before, the Paris Exhibition had an archaeological section: the Great Exhibition in London in 1851 had had none. It could be said with fairness that archaeology had grown up between those two exhibitions. Gabriel de Mortillet wrote a guide to the archaeological collections in the Paris Exhibition, entitled *Promenades préhistoriques à l'Exposition Universelle,* and was already prepared to describe in it the three main historical facts that had emerged from the new science, namely the *Loi de Progrès de l'Humanité,* the *Loi de Développement Similaire,* and the *Haute Antiquité de l'Homme.*

From the early seventies on there was no longer any question of the origins of archaeology; the story from now on is a story of growth, and in this long, complicated, and exciting story of growth and development we can select only a few essential themes; the first is Discovery and Decipherment and that is our concern here.

Of the many great archaeological discoveries made by chance and by deliberately planned excavations in the last hundred years, we can single out, here, only a few examples. The discovery of Upper Paleolithic cave art in the nineteenth century is an exciting one because it combines discovery and excavation, chance and purpose, and also that element of suspicion that, unhappily, surrounds some genuine discoveries from time to time, and, happily, promotes justifiable skepticism about discoveries that are not genuine.

Upper Paleolithic art was first established by the proper recognition of *art mobilier,* small decorated objects found in the debris of rock shelters where Upper Paleolithic man had lived, fifteen to thirty thousand years ago. After the demonstration by Lartet and Christy, more especially in their posthumous *Reliquiae Aquitanicae* (1875), one could not refuse to believe that the savages of the later stages of the Old Stone Age were artists. It was when art comparable in style with the decorated objects found in Upper Paleolithic habitation sites was found on the walls of caves—not used for living in, and sometimes set deep in the hillsides—that doubts and suspicions began to grow.

Our next extract deals with the discovery of some of these early sites like Altamira, but also with the sites of La Mouthe and Pair-non-Pair, which persuaded the scientific world that skepticism had gone too far. It comes from the pen of perhaps the greatest, or one of the three greatest French archaeologists, Joseph Déchelette, who, before his sudden and untimely death at the age of fifty-two as a soldier in 1914, was engaged in completing a general guide to the prehistoric and protohistoric archaeology of Europe, particularly of France and Western Europe. Incidentally the loss to French archaeology, and to all archaeology, by his death, is shown by the fact that no one since his time has attempted the synthesis he planned on the level he achieved. The truth may well be that no one since his time could do what he planned to do and nearly achieved. Déchelette was prepared to range from the beginning of the Paleolithic to the Dark Age. No anthology of great archaeologists should be without a passage from him; the following is from his *Manuel d'archéologie préhistorique, celtique, et gallo-romaine,* first published in 1908.

Movable objects carved of stone, ivory, bone, and horn by Magdalenian artists had been known for a number of years when unexpected discoveries brought to light new revelations concerning the art of the primitive reindeer hunters. In some of the deep caves . . . there were discovered drawings, often very numerous, of animals and other designs carved or painted on walls and ceilings. The question arose at once as to whether these unusual designs were contemporary with the quaternary inhabitants of the caves. A Spaniard, Don Marcelino de Sautuola, the first to call the attention of investigators to these discoveries, did not hesitate to affirm this hypothesis, without, however, succeeding in dissipating the doubts which the novelty and strangeness of his discoveries had rightly evoked. In 1880 he published a summary description of the paintings of animals which he had recognized the year before on the ceiling of the cave of Altamira. . . . An engineer, M. Édouard Harlé, however, after studying these paintings, denied their antiquity. Later, even though Vilanova y Piera, Professor of Palaeontology in Madrid, took the same position as did his compatriot, maintaining firmly that these paintings were contemporary with the Upper Palaeolithic settlement sites, many circumstances seemed to favor the incredulity of others. How could one explain the remarkably fine state of preservation of these frescoes, supposed to be many thousands of years old, if the walls were constantly moist and in places even covered with stalagmitic formations? Besides, what could be the meaning of these animal figures occupying completely obscure points of the cave that were, moreover, difficult of access? Objections were also raised against the complete absence of any trace of smoke on the walls. This circumstance seemed to exclude the hypothesis of a prolonged habitat in these dark subterranean passages. Nonetheless, certain of the facts which M. Harlé himself had observed were irreconcilable with the supposition that these designs had been faked and also made it difficult to attribute a recent date to them. Several designs were covered by a stalagmitic layer. Furthermore the entrance to the cave had remained obstructed and unknown until 1868. It was therefore impossible to consider all these designs as recent works, without encountering serious difficulties.

Nevertheless, MM. de Sautuola and Vilanova did not succeed in dissipating the doubts, and the discoveries at Altamira fell into oblivion until, in 1895, M. Émile Rivière, the successful explorer of the caves at Mentone, in his turn, came across signs engraved upon the walls of the Grotte de la Mouthe, in the commune of Tayac in the Dordogne. Prior to M. Rivière's excavations, Palaeolithic and Neolithic deposits had completely obstructed the entrance to this cave. . . . In the rock shelter of Pair-non-Pair, in the Gironde, M. Daleau had begun excavations in 1883. In 1897, stimulated by the discoveries at La Mouthe, he published the important wall paintings from Pair-non-Pair, which he had known about for many years previous to this. There the designs had been completely covered. The last doubts were thus dissipated and, since then, the attention of archaeologists has been focused on the walls of caves. They ceased denying the authenticity and importance of the discoveries of Sautuola.

It was the discovery at La Mouthe that caused Émile Cartailhac, then Professor of Prehistory at Toulouse and doyen of French archaeology, to take with him to Altamira the young seminarist who was in due course himself to become the doyen of Paleolithic studies not only in France but the whole world—namely Henri Breuil (1877–1961). Hitherto Cartailhac had disbelieved in Altamira, but after his visit with the young Breuil, he recounted his conversion not only to the authenticity of Altamira but to the existence and authenticity of Upper Paleolithic cave art in general: this was in the famous paper "Mea culpa d'un sceptique" published in *L'Anthropologie* for 1902. This conversion included Breuil. One of the most successful and important aspects of Henri Breuil's archaeological career was the discovery and recording of Upper Paleolithic cave art. Here is an account from his own pen of the astonishing discoveries of the decorated caves of Les Trois Frères and Le Tuc d'Audoubert in 1912 and 1914.[1]

Few discoveries have more of the flavor of romantic fiction than these. I only wish the Comte H. Begouen could tell the story himself.

The Comte was a friend of the prehistorian Émile Cartailhac, and was himself of wide intellectual interests, having given very

[1] *Les Cavernes du Volp,* tr. by Jacquetta Hawkes, *The World of the Past* (1963).

many years of his life to travel and to political and historical writing. He had given up his business in Toulouse and retired to his small estate of Montesquieu-Avantés—at least for so long as the Ariège sun tempered the chill of the Pyrenean foothills. His three young sons, Max, Jacques, and Louis, came there for their holidays. . . .

The whole family was very much aware of cave prehistory, for the Mas d'Azil, with its gigantic vault, like an earthfast cathedral, and its labyrinth of dim passages, was only a few kilometres away, while at no great distance there were the deep caverns of Niaux, Bédeilhac, Portel, and Gargas, already famous for their prehistoric paintings and engravings.

At that time the river Volp offered the strongest lure to exploration. . . . A little way from Montesquieu-Avantés it had cut deep tunnels between the point where it went underground at Enlène and le Tuc d'Audoubert, where the limestone hill disgorged it. Two systems of underground galleries, one dry and the other flooded, honeycombed the slopes where the manors of Pujol and Espas stood—and near them the ruins of a medieval building.

Long ago those seasoned diggers the Abbé Cau-Durban and Félix Regnault had partially removed the Neolithic deposits from the Enlène entry; nearby Comte Begouen had found a piece of sculpture, a reindeer antler carved in full relief in the best Magdalenian IV style. In 1912 his three boys decided to use a frail craft which they had made out of packing cases and petrol cans to explore beyond the deep lake where the Volp emerged after its two kilometres underground.

On July 12, without too much difficulty, they reached some huge, half-flooded galleries with a small annex containing engravings, and made their way underground to another lake. . . . An eighteenth-century inscription soon proved to them that they were not the first to penetrate so far.

An ascending passage led the boys into a narrow upper gallery where there were a few engravings. It was there that on the morning of October 12, 1912, Max Begouen had an intuition that certain hanging folds of stalactite concealed a further corridor. He broke them off and pushed on into a vast gallery—

knowing that he was the first human being to tread there since the Reindeer Age. In the afternoon he and his brothers . . . explored the gallery, penetrating to the last chamber. There, leaning against a rock, they saw the forms of two bison, marvellously modelled in clay. The very same evening their father was taken to see their great discovery.

Four days later Émile Cartailhac and I arrived from Toulouse and Paris. We, too, made our way into the chamber and were confronted by the bisons.

Two years later, on July 21, 1914, the three Begouen brothers . . . determined to go down a shaft which a peasant working a nearby field declared to be always very draughty and to cause the snow to melt in wintertime. Comte Begouen stationed himself at the entrance to wait for their return.

Several hours dragged by and the sentinel was beginning to suffer from fatherly anxiety, when suddenly he saw his sons above ground, and capering towards him. They had dropped through a hole pierced in the roof of a narrow passage, then entered another, one end of which, so cramped and low that they had to crawl, had led them into the dry cave of Enlène. The other end, however, took them up to a maze of galleries, all quite unknown, which were decorated with many groups of splendid engravings and a few little paintings. The now famous cave of Les Trois Frères had been discovered. Since that day it has been thoroughly explored.

The last two extracts indicate the beginning of the discovery of Upper Paleolithic art. It is a process of discovery—mainly by chance—that continues to the present day. Perhaps, after Altamira, the most exciting discovery is that of Lascaux near the village of Montignac, fifteen miles from Les Eyzies. Here, by accident, on September 12, 1940, four schoolboys, retrieving their dog Robot who had fallen into a hole in a hill caused by the uprooting of a tree in the previous winter's gale, discovered themselves in the great hall of Lascaux with its magnificent painted and engraved animals. The entrance to Lascaux has still not been found but thousands of visitors have flocked to see these paintings, visiting the cave by a specially constructed entrance. Lascaux has come much into the news in the last few years since it was realized that some of the paintings were fading and others being covered by a fungus. Lascaux was closed to the public in 1964 and research continues on how best to preserve the heritage of Upper Paleolithic cave art. It would be sad if what was first found only in the 1880's and recognized as authentic only sixty years ago, should disappear from the eyes of its modern discoverers.

Our next extract of great discovery must be from the work of Heinrich Schliemann (1822–90), the German businessman and banker who, having collected together a great fortune, retired at forty-six to devote himself to the archaeology of the eastern Mediterranean. "Every profession has its hero, the man of genius whose struggles and accomplishment seem to personify the highest aspirations of his chosen field and who captures the imagination of the general public," wrote Leo Deuel in his *The Treasures of Time,* and he adds, "In archaeology that unique hero has long been Heinrich Schliemann." Schliemann believed from childhood that Troy existed and that reconnaissance and excavation would reveal the material culture of the great ones of Homer. His excavations at Hissarlik on the west coast of Asia Minor, and at Mycenae, Tiryns, and Orchomenos on the mainland of Greece entirely justified his faith and discovered for us the early Trojans and the Myceneans. The following passage is from his *Ilios, the City and Country of the Trojans* (1880).

At last I was able to realize the dream of my life, and to visit at my leisure the scene of those events which had always had such an intense interest for me, and the country of the heroes whose adventures had delighted and comforted my childhood. I started therefore, in April 1868, by way of Rome and Naples, for Corfu, Cephalonia, and Ithaca. This famous island I investigated carefully; but the only excavations I made there were in the so-called Castel of Ulysses, on the top of Mount Aëtos. I found the local character of Ithaca to agree perfectly with the indications of the *Odyssey.* . . .

I afterwards visited the Peloponnesus, and particularly examined the ruins of Mycenae, where it appeared to me that the passage in Pausanias in which the Royal Sepulchres are mentioned, and which has now become so famous, had been wrongly interpreted; and that, contrary to the general belief, those tombs were not at all understood by that writer to be in the lower town, but in the Acropolis itself. I visited Athens, and started from the Piraeus for the Dardanelles, whence I went to the village of Bounarbashi, at the southern extremity of the Plain of Troy. Bounarbashi, together with the rocky heights behind it, called the Bali Dagh, had until then, *in recent times,* been almost universally considered to be the site of the Homeric Ilium, the springs at the foot of that village having been regarded as the two springs mentioned by Homer, one of which sent forth warm, the other cold water. But, instead of only two springs, I found thirty-four, and probably there are forty. . . . The distance of Bounarbashi from the Hellespont is, in a straight line, eight miles, whilst all the indications of the *Iliad* seem to prove that the distance between Ilium and the Hellespont was but very short, hardly exceeding three miles. Nor would it have been possible for Achilles to have pursued Hector in the plain round the walls of Troy, had Troy stood on the summit of Bounarbashi. I was therefore at once convinced that the Homeric city could not possibly have been here. Nevertheless, I wished to investigate so important a matter by actual excavations, and took a number of workmen to sink pits in hundreds of different places, between the forty springs and the extremity of the heights. But at the springs, as well as in Bounarbashi and everywhere else, I found only pure virgin soil, and struck the rock at a very small depth. At the southern end of the heights alone there are some ruins belonging to a very small fortified place, which I hold with the learned archaeologist, my friend Mr. Frank Calvert, United States Vice-Consul at the Dardanelles, to be identical with the ancient city of Gergis. . . .

Bounarbashi having thus given negative results, I next carefully examined all the heights to the right and left of the Trojan Plain, but my researches bore no fruits until I came to the site of the city called by Strabo New Ilium, which is at a distance of only three miles from the Hellespont, and perfectly answers in this, as well as in all other respects, to the topographical requirements of the *Iliad*. My particular attention was attracted to the spot by the imposing position and natural fortifications of the hill called Hissarlik, which formed the northwestern corner of Novum Ilium, and seemed to me to mark the site of its Acropolis as well as of the Pergamus of Priam. . . . The elevation of this hill is 49.43 metres or 162 feet above the level of the sea.

In a hole dug here at random by two villagers, some twenty-five years ago, on the brink of the northern slope . . . there was found a small treasure of about 1,200 silver staters of Antiochus III [223–187 B.C.].

The first recent writer who asserted the identity of Hissarlik with the Homeric Troy was Maclaren. He showed by the most convincing arguments that Troy could never have been on the heights of Bounarbashi, and that, if it ever existed, Hissarlik must mark its site. . . . Such weighty authorities as George Grote, Julius Braun, and Gustav von Eckenbrecher, have also declared in favor of Hissarlik. Mr. Frank Calvert further, who began by upholding the theory which placed Troy at Bounarbashi, became, through the arguments of the above writers, and particularly, it appears, through those of Maclaren and Barker Webb, a convert to the Troy–Hissarlik theory and a valiant champion of it. He owns nearly one half of Hissarlik, and in two small ditches he had dug on his property he had brought to light before my visit some remains of the Macedonian and Roman periods, as well as part of the wall of Hellenic masonry, which, according to Plutarch (in his Life of Alexander), was built by Lysimachus. I at once decided to commence excavations here, and announced this intention in the work *Ithaque, le Péloponnèse et Troie,* which I published at the end of 1868. Having sent a copy of this work, together with a dissertation in ancient Greek, to the University of Rostock, that learned body honoured me with the diploma of Doctor of Philosophy. With unremitting zeal I have ever since endeavoured to show myself worthy of the dignity conferred on me.

In the book referred to I mentioned . . . that, according to my interpretation of the passage of Pausanias . . . in which he speaks of the sepulchres at Mycenae, the Royal Tombs must be looked for in the Acropolis itself, and not in the lower town. As this interpretation of mine was in opposition to that of all other scholars, it was at the time refused a hearing; now, however, that in 1876 I have actually found these sepulchres, with their immense treasures, on the very site indicated by me, it would seem that my critics were in the wrong and not myself.

Circumstances obliged me to remain nearly the whole of the year 1869 in the United States, and it was therefore only in April 1870 that I was able to return to Hissarlik and make a preliminary excavation, in order to test the depth to which the artificial soil extended. I made it at the northwestern corner, in a place where the hill had increased considerably in size, and where, consequently, the accumulation of debris of the Hellenic period was very great. Hence it was only after digging 16 feet below the surface that I laid bare a wall of huge stones, 6½ feet thick, which, as my later excavations have shown, belonged to a tower of the Macedonian epoch.

In order to carry on more extensive excavations I needed a firman from the Sublime Porte, which I only obtained in September 1871. . . .

At length, on the twenty-seventh of September, I made my way to the Dardanelles, together with my wife, Sophia Schliemann, who is a native of Athens and a warm admirer of Homer, and who, with glad enthusiasm, joined me in executing the great work which, nearly half a century ago, my childish simplicity had agreed upon with my father. . . . But we met with ever-recurring difficulties on the part of the Turkish authorities, and it was not until the eleventh of October that we could fairly commence our work. There being no other shelter, we were obliged to live in the neighbouring Turkish village of Chiblak, a mile and a quarter from Hissarlik. After working with an average number of eighty labourers daily up to the twenty-fourth of November, we were compelled to cease the excavations for the winter. But during that interval we had been able to make a large trench on the face of the steep northern slope, and to dig down to a depth of 33 feet below the surface of the hill.

We first found there the remains of the later Aeolic Ilium, which on an average, reached to a depth of 6½ feet. . . .

Below these Hellenic ruins, and to a depth of about 13 feet, the debris contained a few stones, and some very coarse handmade pottery. Below this stratum I came to a large number of house walls, of unwrought stones cemented with earth, and, for the first time, met with immense quantities of stone implements and saddle querns, together with more coarse handmade pottery. From about 20 feet to 30 feet below the surface, nothing was found but calcined debris, immense masses of sun-dried or slightly baked bricks and house walls of the same, numbers of saddle querns, but fewer stone implements of other kinds, and much better handmade pottery. At a depth of 30 feet and 33 feet we discovered fragments of house walls of large stones, many of them rudely hewn; we also came upon a great many very large blocks. The stones of these house walls appeared as if they had been separated from one another by a violent earthquake. My instruments for excavating were very imperfect: I had to work with only pickaxes, wooden shovels, baskets, and eight wheelbarrows.

I returned to Hissarlik with my wife at the end of March 1872, and resumed the excavations with 100 workmen. But I was soon able to increase the number of my labourers to 130, and had often even 150 men at work. I was now well prepared for the work, having been provided by my honoured friends Messrs. John Henry Schröder & Co. of London with the very best English wheelbarrows, pickaxes, and spades, and having also procured three overseers and an engineer, Mr. A. Laurent, to make the maps and plans. The last received monthly £20, the overseer £6 each, and my servant £7 4s.; whilst the daily wages of my common labourers were 1 fr. 80 c., or about 18 pence sterling. I now built on the top of Hissarlik a wooden house, with three rooms and a magazine, kitchen, etc., and covered the buildings with waterproof felt to protect them from the rain.

On the steep northern slope of Hissarlik, which rises at an angle of 45°, and at a perpendicular depth of 46½ feet below the surface, I dug out a platform 233 feet wide, and found there an immense number of poisonous snakes; among them remarkably numerous specimens of the small brown adder called *antelion* . . . which is hardly thicker than an earthworm, and gets its name from the vulgar belief that the person bitten by it only survives till sunset.

I first struck the rock at a depth of about 53 feet below the surface of the hill, and found the lowest stratum of artificial soil to consist of very compact debris of houses, as hard as stone, and house walls of small pieces of unwrought or very rudely cut limestone, put together so that the joint between two of the stones in a lower layer is always covered by a single stone in the course above it. This lowest stratum was succeeded by house walls built of large limestone blocks, generally unwrought, but often rudely cut into something resembling a quadrangular shape. Sometimes I came upon large masses of such massive blocks lying close upon one another, and having all the appearance of being the broken walls of some large building. There is no trace of a general conflagration, either in this stratum of buildings built with large stones or in the lowest layer of debris; indeed, the multitudinous shells found in these two lowest strata are uninjured, which sufficiently proves that they have not been exposed to a great heat. I found in these two lowest strata the same stone implements as before, but the pottery is different. The pottery differs also from that in the upper strata.

As the cutting of the great platform on the north side of Hissarlik advanced but slowly, I began on the first of May a second large trench from the south side; but the slope being there but slight, I was forced to give it a dip of 14°. I here brought to light, near the surface, a pretty bastion, composed of large blocks of limestone, which may date from the time of Lysimachus. The southern part of Hissarlik has been formed principally by the debris of the later or Novum Ilium, and for this reason Greek antiquities are found here at a much greater depth than on the top of the hill.

As it was my object to excavate Troy, which I expected to find in one of the lower cities, I was forced to demolish many interesting ruins in the upper strata. . . .

With the consent of Mr. Frank Calvert, I also began on the twentieth of June, with the help of seventy labourers, to excavate in his field on the north side of Hissarlik, where, close to my large platform and at a perpendicular depth of 40 feet below the plateau of the hill, I dug out of its slope another platform, about 109 feet broad, with an upper terrace and side galleries, in order to facilitate the removal of the debris. No sooner had I commenced the work than I struck against a marble triglyph with a splendid metope, representing Phoebus Apollo and the four horses of the Sun. This triglyph, as well as a number of drums of Doric columns which I found there, can leave no doubt that a temple of Apollo of the Doric order once existed on the spot, which had, however, been so completely destroyed that I did not discover even a stone of its foundations *in situ*.

When I had dug this platform for a distance of 82 feet into the hill, I found that I had commenced it at least 16½ feet too high, and I therefore abandoned it, contenting myself with cutting into its centre a trench 26 feet wide at the top and 13 feet wide at the bottom. At a distance of 131 feet from the slope of the hill, I came upon a great wall, 10 feet high and 6½ feet thick, the top of which is just 34 feet below the surface. It is built in the so-called Cyclopean manner, of large blocks joined together with small ones; it had at one time been much higher, as the quantity of stones lying beside it seemed to prove. It evidently belonged to the city built with large stones, the second in succession from the virgin soil. At a depth of 6 feet below this wall I found a retaining wall of smaller stones, rising at an angle of 45°. This latter wall must of course be much older than the former; it evidently served to support the slope of the hill, and it proves beyond any doubt that, since its erection, the hill had increased 131 feet in breadth and 34 feet in height. As my friend Professor A. H. Sayce was the first to point out, this wall is built in exactly the same style as the house walls of the first and lowest city, the joint between two of the stones in the lower layer being always covered by a third in the upper layer. Accordingly, in agreement with him, I do not hesitate to attribute this wall to the first city. The debris of the lower stratum being as hard as stone, I had very great difficulty in excavating it in the ordinary way, and I found it easier to undermine it by cutting it vertically, and with the help of windlasses and enormous iron levers, nearly 10 feet in length and 6 inches in circumference, to loosen and so break it down in fragments 16 feet high,

16 feet broad, and 10 feet thick. But I found this manner of excavating very dangerous, two workmen having been buried alive
under a mass of debris of 2,560 cubic feet, and having been
saved as by a miracle. In consequence of this accident I gave up
the idea of running the great platform 233 feet broad through
the whole length of the hill, and decided on first digging a
trench, 98 feet wide at the top and 65 feet at the bottom.

As the great extent of my excavations rendered it necessary
for me to work with no less than from 120 to 150 labourers, I
was obliged, on the first of June, on account of the harvest season, to increase the daily wages to 2 francs. But even this would
not have enabled me to collect the requisite number of men, had
not the late Mr. Max Müller, German Consul at Gallipoli, sent
me 40 workmen from that place. After the first of July, however, I easily procured a constant supply of 150 workmen.
Through the kindness of Mr. Charles Cookson, English Consul
at Constantinople, I secured 10 hand-carts, which are drawn by
two men and pushed by a third. I thus had 10 hand-carts and 88
wheelbarrows to work with, in addition to which I kept 6 horse-
carts, each of which cost 5 francs or 4 shillings a day, so that
the total cost of my excavations amounted to more than 400
francs (£16) a day. Besides screw jacks, chains, and windlasses,
my implements consisted of 24 large iron levers, 108 spades,
and 103 pickaxes, all of the best English manufacture. I had
three capital foremen, and my wife and myself were present at
the work from sunrise to sunset; but our difficulties increased continually with the daily augmenting distance to which we had to
remove the debris. Besides this, the constant strong gale from
the north, which drove a blinding dust into our eyes, was exceedingly troublesome.

On the south side of the hill, where on account of the slight
natural slope I had to make my great trench with an inclination
of 76°, I discovered, at a distance of 197 feet from its entrance,
a great mass of masonry, consisting of two distinct walls, each
about 15 feet broad, built close together, and founded on the
rock at a depth of 46½ feet below the surface. Both are 20 feet
high; the outer wall slopes on the south side at an angle of 15°,
and is vertical on the north side. The inner wall falls off at an

angle of 45° on its south side, which is opposite to the north side of the outer wall. There is thus a deep hollow between the two walls. The outer wall is built of smaller stones cemented with clay, but it does not consist of solid masonry. The inner wall is built of large unwrought blocks of limestone; it has on the north side solid masonry to a depth of only 4 feet, and leans here against a sort of rampart 65½ feet broad and 16½ feet high, partly composed of the limestone which had to be removed in order to level the rock for building the walls upon it. These two walls are perfectly flat on the top, and have never been higher; they are 140 feet long, their aggregate breadth being 40 feet on the east and 30 feet at the west end. The remnants of brick walls and masses of broken bricks, pottery, whorls, stone implements, saddle-quern stones, etc., with which they were covered, appear to indicate that they were used by the inhabitants of the third or burnt city, as the substructions of a great tower; and I shall . . . call these walls . . . "the Great Tower," though they may originally have been intended by their builders for a different purpose. . . .

Up to the beginning of May 1873, I had believed that the hill of Hissarlik, where I was excavating, marked the site of the Trojan citadel only; and it certainly is the fact that Hissarlik was the acropolis of Novum Ilium. I therefore imagined that Troy was larger than the latter town, or at least as large; but I thought it important to discover the precise limits of the Homeric city, and accordingly I sank twenty shafts as far down as the rock, on the west, southwest, south-southeast, and east of Hissarlik, directly at its foot or at some distance from it, on the plateau of the Ilium of the Greek colony. As I found in these shafts no trace of fragments either of pre-historic pottery or of pre-historic house walls, and nothing but fragments of Hellenic pottery and Hellenic house walls; and as, moreover, the hill of Hissarlik has a very steep slope toward the north, the northeast, and the northwest, facing the Hellespont, and is also very steep on the west side towards the Plain, the city could not possibly have extended in any one of these directions beyond the hill itself. It therefore appears certain that the ancient city cannot have extended on any side beyond the primeval plateau of Hissarlik, the circumference of which is indicated on the south and southwest by the Great Tower and the double gate; and on the northwest, northeast, and east, by the great boundary wall. . . .

The inhabitants of the five pre-historic sites of Hissarlik seem generally to have burnt the dead, as I found in 1872 two tripod urns with calcined human remains on the virgin soil in the first city; and in 1871, 1872, and 1873, a vast number of large funeral urns, containing human ashes, in the third and fourth cities. I found no bones however except a single tooth, and on one occasion among the ashes a human skull, which is well preserved, with the exception of the lower jaw, which is missing: as I found a brooch of bronze along with it, I suppose it may have belonged to a woman. . . .

It is true that nearly all the pottery found in the pre-historic ruins of Hissarlik is broken, and that there is hardly one large vessel out of twenty which is not in fragments; nay, in the first two cities the pottery has all been shattered by the weight and pressure of the stones with which the second city was built. But still, even if all the funeral urns with human ashes ever deposited in Hissarlik had been well preserved, yet, judging from the fragments of them—in spite of the abundance of these fragments—I can hardly think that I could have found even a thousand entire urns. It is, therefore, evident that the inhabitants of the five prehistoric cities of Hissarlik buried only a small part of their funeral urns in the city itself, and that we must look for their principal necropolis elsewhere.

Whilst these important excavations were going on, I neglected the trenches on the north side, and only worked there when I had workmen to spare. But I brought to light here the prolongation of the great wall which I agree with Prof. Sayce in attributing to the second stone city.

Wishing to investigate the fortifications on the west and northwest sides of the ancient city, in the beginning of May 1873 I also commenced making a trench, 33 feet broad and 141 feet long, on the northwest side of the hill, at the very point where I had made the first trench in April 1870. I broke first through an Hellenic circuit wall, probably that which, according to Plutarch in his Life of Alexander, was built by Lysimachus, and found it to be 13 feet high and 10 feet thick, and to consist of large hewn blocks of limestone. Afterwards I broke through an older wall, 8¾ feet high and 6 feet thick, composed of large blocks cemented with earth. This second wall is attached to the large wall which I brought to light in April 1870, and the two form two sides of a quadrangular Hellenic tower, a third wall of which I had to break through later on.

This part of the hill was evidently much lower in ancient times, as seems to be proved not only by the wall of Lysimachus, which must at one time have risen to a considerable height above the surface of the hill, whereas it is now covered by 16½ feet of rubbish, but also by the remains of the Hellenic period, which are here found to a great depth. It appears, in fact, as if the rubbish and debris of habitations had been thrown down on this side for centuries, in order to increase the height of the place.

In order to hasten the excavations on the northwest side of the hill, I cut a deep trench from the west side also, in which, unfortunately, I struck obliquely the circuit wall of Lysimachus, here 13 feet high and 10 feet thick. . . .

While following up this circuit wall, and bringing more and more of it to light, close to the ancient building and northwest of the Gate, I struck upon a large copper article of the most remarkable form, which attracted my attention all the more as I thought I saw gold behind it. On the top of it was a layer of red and calcined ruins, from 4¾ to 5¼ feet thick, as hard as stone, and above this again the above-mentioned wall of fortification (5 feet broad and 20 feet high), built of large stones and earth, which must have been erected shortly after the destruction of Troy. In order to secure the treasure from my workmen and save it for archaeology, it was necessary to lose no time; so, although it was not yet the hour for breakfast, I immediately had *païdos* called. This is a word of uncertain derivation, which has passed over into Turkish, and is here employed in place of ἀνάπαυσις or time for rest. While the men were eating and resting, I cut out the Treasure with a large knife. This required great exertion and involved great risk, since the wall of fortification, beneath which I had to dig, threatened every moment to fall down

148

upon me. But the sight of so many objects, every one of which is of inestimable value to archaeology, made me reckless, and I never thought of any danger. It would, however, have been impossible for me to have removed the treasure without the help of my dear wife, who stood at my side, ready to pack the things I cut out in her shawl, and to carry them away. . . .

As I found all these articles together, in the form of a rectangular mass, or packed into one another, it seems certain that they were placed on the city wall in a wooden chest. This supposition seems to be corroborated by the fact that close by the side of these articles I found a copper key. It is therefore possible that someone packed the treasure in the chest, and carried it off, without having had time to pull out the key; when he reached the wall, however, the hand of an enemy, or the fire, overtook him, and he was obliged to abandon the chest, which was immediately covered, to a height of 5 feet, with the ashes and stones of the adjoining house.

Perhaps the articles found a few days previously in a room of the chief's house, close to the place where the treasure was discovered, belonged to this unfortunate person. These articles consisted of a helmet and a silver vase, with a cup of electrum. . . .

That the treasure was packed together at a moment of supreme peril appears to be proved, among other things, by the contents of the largest silver vase, consisting of nearly 9,000 objects of gold. . . . The person who endeavoured to save the Treasure had, fortunately, the presence of mind to place the silver vase, with the valuable articles inside it, upright in the chest, so that nothing could fall out, and everything has been preserved uninjured. . . .

I now perceived that the trench which I had made in April 1870 had exactly struck the right point for excavating, and that, if I had only continued it, I should, in a few weeks, have uncovered the most remarkable buildings in Troy.

Another man who realized in the eastern Mediterranean one of the dreams of his life was Sir Arthur Evans (1851-1941), son of the John Evans whose account of his visit to see Boucher de Perthes at Amiens and Abbeville we have already quoted. Schliemann had been attracted to Crete, and thought that perhaps here might be found the origins of the Bronze Age civilization of Troy and Mycenae. Schliemann died before he could dig in Crete, and it was left to Sir Arthur Evans to excavate at Knossos, discover the civilization which he called Minoan, and add another chapter to the early history of man. This following extract is from an article by Evans on "The Palace of Minos," in *The Monthly Review,* for March 1901.

Less than a generation back the origin of Greek civilization, and with it the sources of all great culture that has ever been, were wrapped in an impenetrable mist. That ancient world was still girt round within its narrow confines by the circling "Stream of Ocean." Was there anything beyond? The fabled kings and heroes of the Homeric Age, with their palaces and strongholds, were they aught, after all, but more or less humanized sun myths?

One man had faith, accompanied by works, and in Dr. Schliemann the science of classical antiquity found its Columbus. Armed with the spade, he brought to light from beneath the mounds of ages a real Troy; at Tiryns and Mycenae he laid bare the palace and the tombs and treasures of Homeric Kings. A new world opened to investigation, and the discoveries of its first explorer were followed up successfully by Dr. Tsountas and others on Greek soil. The eyes of observers were opened, and the traces of this prehistoric civilization began to make their appearance far beyond the limits of Greece itself. From Cyprus and Palestine to Sicily and southern Italy, and even to the coasts of Spain, the colonial and industrial enterprise of the "Mycenaeans" has left its mark throughout the Mediterranean basin. Professor Petrie's researches in Egypt have conclusively shown that as early at least as the close of the Middle Kingdom, or, approximately speaking, the beginning of the Second Millennium B.C., imported Aegean vases were finding their way into the Nile Valley. By the great days of the Eighteenth Dynasty, in the sixteenth and succeeding centuries B.C., this intercourse was of such a kind that Mycenaean art, now in its full maturity of bloom, was reacting on that of the contemporary Pharaohs and infusing a living European element into the old conventional style of the land of the Pyramids and the Sphinx.

But the picture was still very incomplete. Nay, it might even be said that its central figure was not yet filled in. In all these excavations and researches the very land to which ancient tradition unanimously pointed as the cradle of Greek civilization had been left out of count. To adapt the words applied by Gelon to slighted Sicily and Syracuse, "The spring was wanting from the year" of that earlier Hellas. Yet Crete, the central island—a halfway house between three continents—flanked by the great Libyan promontory and linked by smaller island steppingstones to the Peloponnese and the mainland of Anatolia, was called upon by Nature to play a leading part in the development of the early Aegean culture.

Here, in his royal city of Knossos, ruled Minos, or whatever historic personage is covered by that name, and founded the first sea empire of Greece, extending his dominion far and wide over the Aegean isles and coastlands. Athens paid to him its human tribute of youths and maidens. His colonial plantations extended east and west along the Mediterranean basin till Gaza worshipped the Cretan Zeus and a Minoan city rose in western Sicily. But it is as the first lawgiver of Greece that he achieved his greatest renown, and the Code of Minos became the source of all later legislation. As the wise ruler and inspired lawgiver there is something altogether biblical in his legendary character. He is the Cretan Moses, who every nine years repaired to the Cave of Zeus, whether on the Cretan Ida or on Dicta, and received from the God of the Mountain the laws for his people. Like Abraham, he is described as the "friend of God." Nay, in some accounts, the mythical being of Minos has a tendency to blend with that of his native Zeus.

This Cretan Zeus, the God of the Mountain, whose animal figure was the bull and whose symbol was the double axe, had indeed himself a human side which distinguishes him from his more ethereal namesake of classical Greece. In the great Cave of Mount Dicta, whose inmost shrine, adorned with natural pillars of gleaming stalactite, leads deep down to the waters of an unnavigated pool, Zeus himself was said to have been born and

151

fed with honey and goat's milk by the nymph Amaltheia. On the conical height immediately above the site of Minos' City—now known as Mount Juktas—and still surrounded by a Cyclopean enclosure, was pointed out his tomb. Classical Greece scoffed at this primitive legend, and for this particular reason, first gave currency to the proverb that "the Cretans are always liars." . . .

If Minos was the first lawgiver, his craftsman Daedalus was the first traditional founder of what may be called a "school of art." Many were the fabled works wrought by them for King Minos, some gruesome, like the brass man Talos. In Knossos, the royal city, he built the dancing ground, or "Choros," of Ariadne, and the famous Labyrinth. In its inmost maze dwelt the Minotaur, or "Bull of Minos," fed daily with human victims, till such time as Theseus, guided by Ariadne's ball of thread, penetrated to its lair, and, after slaying the monster, rescued the captive youths and maidens. Such, at least, was the Athenian tale. A more prosaic tradition saw in the Labyrinth a building of many passages, the idea of which Daedalus had taken from the great Egyptian mortuary temple on the shores of Lake Moeris, to which the Greeks gave the same name; and recent philological research has derived the name itself from the *labrys,* or double ax, the emblem of the Cretan and Carian Zeus. . . .

When one calls to mind these converging lines of ancient tradition it becomes impossible not to feel that, without Crete, "the spring is taken away" indeed from the Mycenaean world. Great as were the results obtained by exploration on the sites of this ancient culture on the Greek mainland and elsewhere, there was still a sense of incompleteness. In nothing was this more striking than in the absence of any written document. A few signs had, indeed, been found on a vase handle, but these were set aside as mere ignorant copies of Hittite or Egyptian hieroglyphs. In the volume of his monumental work which deals with Mycenaean art, M. Perrot was reduced to the conclusion that "as at present advised, we can continue to affirm that, for the whole of this period, neither in Peloponnese nor in Central Greece, no more upon the buildings nor upon the thousand-and-one objects of domestic use and luxury that have come forth from the tombs, has anything been discovered that resembles any form of writing."

But was this indeed, the last word of scientific exploration? Was it possible that a people so advanced in other respects— standing in such intimate relations with Egypt and the Syrian lands where some form of writing had been an almost immemorial possession—should have been absolutely wanting in this most essential element of civilization? I could not believe it. Once more one's thoughts turned to the land of Minos, and the question irresistibly suggested itself—was that early heritage of fixed laws compatible with a complete ignorance of the art of writing? An abiding tradition of the Cretans themselves, preserved by Diodorus, shows that they were better informed. The Phoenicians, they said, had not invented letters, they had simply changed their forms—in other words, they had only improved on an existing system.

It is now seven years since a piece of evidence came into my hands which went far to show that long before the days of the introduction of the Phoenician alphabet, as adopted by the later Greeks, the Cretans were, in fact, possessed of a system of writing. While hunting out ancient engraved stones at Athens I came upon some three- and four-sided seals showing on each of their faces groups of hieroglyphic and linear signs distinct from the Egyptian and Hittite, but evidently representing some form of script. On inquiry I learnt that these seals had been found in Crete. A clue was in my hands, and like Theseus, I resolved to follow it, if possible to the inmost recesses of the Labyrinth. That the source and centre of the great Mycenaean civilization remained to be unearthed on Cretan soil I had never doubted, but the prospect now opened of finally discovering its written records.

From 1894 onwards I undertook a series of campaigns of exploration chiefly in central and eastern Crete. In all directions fresh evidence continually came to light. Cyclopean ruins of cities and strongholds, beehive tombs, vases, votive bronzes, exquisitely engraved gems, amply demonstrating that in fact the great days of that "island story" lay far behind the historic period. From the Mycenaean sites of Crete I obtained a whole series of inscribed seals, such as I had first noticed at Athens, showing the existence of an entire system of hieroglyphic or quasi-pictorial writing, with here and there signs of the co-existence of more linear forms. From the great Cave of Mount Dicta—the birthplace of Zeus—the votive deposits of which have now been thoroughly explored by Mr. Hogarth, I procured a stone Libation Table inscribed with a dedication of several characters in the early Cretan script. But for more exhaustive excavation my eyes were fixed on some ruined walls, the great gypsum blocks of which were engraved with curious symbolic characters, that crowned the southern slope of a hill known as Kephala, overlooking the ancient site of Knossos, the City of Minos. They were evidently part of a large prehistoric building. Might one not uncover here the palace of King Minos, perhaps even the mysterious Labyrinth itself?

These blocks had already arrested the attention of Schliemann and others, but the difficulties raised by the native proprietors had defeated all efforts at scientific exploration. In 1895 I succeeded in acquiring a quarter of the site from one of the joint owners. But the obstruction continued, and I was beset by difficulties of a more serious kind. The circumstances of the time were not favourable. The insurrection had broken out, half the villages in Crete were in ashes, and in the neighbouring town of Candia the most fanatical part of the Mahomedan population were collected together from the whole of the island. The Faithful Herakles, who was at that time my "guide, philosopher and muleteer," was seized by the Turks and thrown into a loathsome dungeon, from which he was with difficulty rescued. Soon afterwards the inevitable massacre took place, of which the nominal British "occupants" of Candia were in part themselves the victims. Then at last the sleeping lion was aroused. Under the guns of Admiral Noel the Turkish commander evacuated the Government buildings at ten minutes' notice and shipped off the Sultan's troops. Crete once more was free.

At the beginning of this year I was at last able to secure the remaining part of the site of Kephala, and with the consent of Prince George's Government at once set about the work of excavation. I received some pecuniary help from the recently started Cretan Exploration Fund, and was fortunate in securing the services of Mr. Duncan Mackenzie, who had done good work for the British School in Melos, to assist me in directing the works. From about eighty to one hundred and fifty men were employed in the excavation which continued till the heat and fevers of June put an end to it for this season.

The result has been to uncover a large part of a vast prehistoric building—a palace with its numerous dependencies, but a palace on a far larger scale than those of Tiryns and Mycenae. About two acres of this has been unearthed, for by an extraordinary piece of good fortune the remains of walls began to appear only a foot or so, often only a few inches, below the surface. This dwelling of prehistoric kings had been overwhelmed by a great catastrophe. Everywhere on the hilltop were traces of a mighty conflagration; burnt beams and charred wooden columns lay within the rooms and corridors. There was here no gradual decay. The civilization represented on this spot had been cut short in the fulness of its bloom. Nothing later than remains of the good Mycenaean period was found over the whole site. Nothing even so late as the last period illustrated by the remains of Mycenae itself. From the day of destruction to this the site has been left entirely desolate. For three thousand years or more not a tree seems to have been planted here; over a part of the area not even a ploughshare had passed. At the time of the great overthrow, no doubt, the place had been methodically plundered for metal objects, and the fallen debris in the rooms and passages turned over and ransacked for precious booty. Here and there a local bey or peasant had grubbed for stone slabs to supply his yard or threshing floor. But the party walls of clay and plaster still stood intact, with the fresco painting on them, still in many cases perfectly preserved at a few inches' depth from the surface, a clear proof of how severely the site had been let alone for these long centuries.

Who were the destroyers? Perhaps the Dorian invaders who seem to have overrun the island about the eleventh or twelfth century before our era. More probably, still earlier invading swarms from the mainland of Greece. The Palace itself had a long antecedent history and there are frequent traces of remodelling. Its early elements may go back to a thousand years before its final overthrow, since, in the great Eastern Court, was found the lower part of an Egyptian seated figure of diorite, with a triple inscription, showing that it dates back to the close of the Twelfth or the beginning of the Thirteenth Dynasty of Egypt; in other words approximately to 2000 B.C. But below the foundation of the later building, and covering the whole hill, are the remains of a primitive settlement of still greater antiquity, belonging to the insular Stone Age. In parts this "Neolithic" deposit was over twenty-four feet thick, everywhere full of stone axes, knives of volcanic glass, dark polished and incised pottery, and primitive images such as those found by Schliemann in the lowest strata of Troy.

The outer walls of the Palace were supported on huge gypsum blocks, but there was no sign of an elaborate system of fortification such as at Tiryns and Mycenae. The reason of this is not far to seek. Why is Paris strongly fortified, while London is practically an open town? The city of Minos, it must be remembered, was the centre of a great sea power, and it was in "wooden walls" that its rulers must have put their trust. The mighty blocks of the Palace show, indeed, that it was not for want of engineering power that the acropolis of Knossos remained unfortified. But in truth Mycenaean might was here at home. At Tiryns and Mycenae itself it felt itself threatened by warlike Continental neighbors. It was not till the mainland foes were masters of the sea that they could have forced an entry into the House of Minos. Then, indeed, it was an easy task. In the Cave of Zeus on Mount Ida was found a large brooch (or *fibula*) belonging to the race of northern invaders, on one side of which a war galley is significantly engraved.

The Palace was entered on the southwest side by a portico and double doorway opening from a spacious paved court. Flanking the portico were remains of a great fresco of a bull, and on the walls of the corridor leading from it were still preserved the lower part of a procession of painted life-size figures, in the centre of which was a female personage, probably a queen, in magnificent apparel. This corridor seems to have led round to a great southern porch or *Prophylaeum* with double

156

columns, the walls of which were originally decorated with figures in the same style. Along nearly the whole length of the building ran a spacious paved corridor, lined by a long row of fine stone doorways, giving access to a succession of magazines. On the floor of these magazines huge store jars were still standing, large enough to have contained the "forty thieves." One of these jars, contained in a small separate chamber, was nearly five feet in height.

Here occurred one of the most curious discoveries of the whole excavation. Under the closely compacted pavement of one of these magazines, upon which the huge jars stood, there were built in, between solid piles of masonry, double tiers of stone cists lined with lead. Only a few were opened and they proved to be empty, but there can be little doubt that they were constructed for the deposit of treasure. Whoever destroyed and plundered the Palace had failed to discover these receptacles, so that when more come to be explored there is some real hope of finding buried hoards.

On the east side of the Palace opened a still larger paved court, approached by broad steps from another principal entrance to the north. From this court access was given by an anteroom to what was certainly the most interesting chamber of the whole building, almost as perfectly preserved—though some twelve centuries older—as anything found beneath the volcanic ash of Pompeii or the lava of Herculaneum. Already a few inches below the surface freshly preserved fresco began to appear. Walls were shortly uncovered decorated with flowering plants and running water, while on each side of the doorway of a small inner room stood guardian griffins with peacocks' plumes in the same flowery landscape. Round the walls ran low stone benches, and between these on the north side, separated by a small interval and raised on a stone base, rose a gypsum throne with a high back, and originally coloured with decorative designs. Its lower part was adorned with a curiously carved arch, with crocketed mouldings, showing an extraordinary anticipation of some most characteristic features of Gothic architecture. Opposite the throne was a finely wrought tank of gypsum slabs—a feature borrowed perhaps from an Egyptian palace—

approached by a descending flight of steps, and originally surmounted by cyprus wood columns supporting a kind of *implu-
vium*. Here truly was the council chamber of a Mycenaean King
or Sovereign Lady. It may be said today that the youngest of
European rulers has in his dominions the oldest throne in Europe.

The frescoes discovered on the Palace site constitute a new
epoch in the history of painting. Little, indeed, of the kind even
of classical Greek antiquity has been hitherto known earlier at
least than the Pompeian series. The first find of this kind marks
a red-letter day in the story of the excavation. In carefully uncovering the earth and debris in a passage at the back of the
southern Propylaeum there came to light two large fragments of
what proved to be the upper part of a youth bearing a gold-
mounted silver cup. The robe is decorated with a beautiful
quatrefoil pattern; a silver ornament appears in front of the
ear, and silver rings on the arms and neck. What is specially
interesting among the ornaments is an agate gem on the left
wrist, thus illustrating the manner of wearing the beautifully
engraved signets of which many clay impressions were found in
the Palace.

The colours were almost as brilliant as when laid down over
three thousand years before. For the first time the true portraiture of a man of this mysterious Mycenaean race rises before us. The flesh tint, following perhaps an Egyptian prece-
dent, is of a deep reddish-brown. The limbs are finely moulded,
though the waist, as usual in Mycenaean fashions, is tightly
drawn in by a silver-mounted girdle, giving great relief to the
hips. The profile of the face is pure and almost classically
Greek. This, with the dark curly hair and high brachycephalic
head, recalls an indigenous type well represented still in the
glens of Ida and the White Mountains—a type which brings
with it many reminiscences from the Albanian highlands and the
neighbouring regions of Montenegro and Herzegovina. The lips
are somewhat full, but the physiognomy has certainly no Semitic
cast. The profile rendering of the eye shows an advance in human portraiture foreign to Egyptian art, and only achieved by
the artists of classical Greece in the early fine-art period of the
fifth century B.C.—after some eight centuries, that is, of barbaric decadence and slow revival.

There was something very impressive in this vision of brilliant youth and of male beauty, recalled after so long an interval to our upper air from what had been till yesterday a forgotten world. Even our untutored Cretan workmen felt the spell and fascination. They, indeed, regarded the discovery of such a painting in the bosom of the earth as nothing less than miraculous, and saw in it the "icon" of a saint!   .   .   .

To the north of the Palace, in some rooms that seem to have belonged to the women's quarter, frescoes were found in an entirely novel miniature style. Here were ladies with white complexions—due, we may fancy, to the seclusion of harem life—*décolletées,* but with fashionable puffed sleeves and flounced gowns, and their hair as elaborately curled and *frisé* as if they were fresh from a *coiffeur's* hands. *"Mais,"* exclaimed a French savant who honoured me with a visit, *"ce sont des Parisiennes!"*

They were seated in groups, engaged in animated conversation, in the courts and gardens and on the balconies of a palatial building, while in the walled spaces beyond were large crowds of men and boys, some of them hurling javelins. In some cases both sexes were intermingled. These alternating scenes of Peace and War recall the subjects of Achilles' shield and we have here at the same time a contemporary illustration of that populousness of the Cretan cities in the Homeric age which struck the imagination of the bard. Certain fragments of fresco belong to the still earlier period of Aegean art, which precedes the Mycenaean, well illustrated in another field by the elegant painted vases found by Mr. Hogarth in some private houses on this site. A good idea of the refinement already reached in these earlier days of the Palace is given by the subject of one fresco fragment in this "pre-Mycenaean" style—a boy namely, in a field of white crocuses, some of which he has gathered and is placing in an ornamental vase.

Very valuable architectural details were supplied by the walls and buildings of some of the miniature frescoes above described. In one place rose the façade of a small temple, with triple cells containing sacred pillars, and representing in a more advanced form the arrangement of the small golden shrines, with doves perched upon them, found by Schliemann in the shaft graves at Mycenae. This temple fresco has a peculiar interest, as showing the character of a good deal of the upper structure of the Palace itself, which has now perished. It must largely have consisted of clay and rubble walls, artfully concealed under brilliantly painted plaster, and contained and supported by a woodwork framing. The base of the small temple rests on the huge gypsum blocks which form so conspicuous a feature in the existing remains, and below the central opening is inserted a frieze, recalling the alabaster reliefs of the palace hall of Tiryns, with triglyphs, the prototypes of the Doric, and the half-rosettes of the "metopes" inlaid with blue enamel, the Kyanos of Homer.

A transition from painting to sculpture was supplied by a great relief of a bull in hard plaster, coloured with the natural tints, large parts of which, including the head, were found near the northern gate. It is unquestionably the finest plastic work of the time that has come down to us, stronger and truer to life than any classical sculpture of the kind.

Somewhat more conventional, but still showing great naturalistic power, is the marble head of a lioness, made for the spout of a fountain. It too had been originally tinted, and the eyes and nostrils inlaid with brightly coloured enamels. A part of a stone frieze with finely undercut rosettes recalled similar fragments from Tiryns and Mycenae, but far surpasses them in execution.

Vases of marble and other stones abounded, some exquisitely carved. Among these was one cut out of alabaster in the shape of a great Triton shell, every coil and fold of which was accurately reproduced. A porphyry lamp, supported on a quatrefoil pillar, with a beautiful lotus capital, well illustrates the influence of an Egyptian model. But the model was here surpassed.

Among the more curious arts practised in prehistoric Knossos was that of miniature painting on the back of plaques of crystal. A galloping bull thus delineated on an azure background is a little masterpiece in its way. A small relief on a banded agate, representing a dagger in an ornamental sheath resting on an artistically folded belt, to a certain extent anticipates by many centuries the art of cameo carving. A series of clay seals was also discovered, exhibiting impressions of intaglios in the fine bold Mycenaean style; one of these, with two bulls, larger than any known signet gem of the kind, may well have been a royal seal. The subjects of some of these intaglios show the development of a surprisingly picturesque style of art. We see fish naturalistically grouped in a rocky pool, a hart beside a water brook in a mountain glen, and a grotto, above which some small monkeylike creatures are seen climbing the over-hanging crags.

But manifold as were the objects of interest found within the palace walls of Knossos, the crowning discovery—or, rather, series of discoveries—remains to be told. On the last day of March, not far below the surface of the ground, a little to the right of the southern portico, there turned up a clay tablet of elongated shape, bearing on it incised characters in a linear script, accompanied by numeral signs. My hopes now ran high of finding entire deposits of clay archives, and they were speedily realized. Not far from the scene of the first discovery there came to light a clay receptacle containing a hoard of tablets. In other chambers occurred similar deposits, which had originally been stored in coffers of wood, clay, or gypsum. The tablets themselves are of various forms, some flat, elongated bars, from about 2 to 7½ inches in length, with wedgelike ends; others, larger and squarer, ranging in size to small octavo. In one particular magazine tablets of a different kind were found—perforated bars, crescent and scallop-like "labels," with writing in the same hieroglyphic style as that on the seals found in eastern Crete. But the great mass, amounting to over a thousand inscriptions, belonged to another and more advanced system with linear characters. It was, in short, a highly developed form of script, with regular divisions between the words, and for elegance hardly surpassed by any later form of writing.

A clue to the meaning of these clay records is in many cases supplied by the addition of pictorial illustrations representing the objects concerned. Thus we find human figures, perhaps slaves; chariots and horses; arms or implements and armor, such as axes and cuirasses; houses or barns; ears of barley or other cereal; swine; various kinds of trees; and a long-stamened flower, evidently the saffron crocus, used for dyes. On some tablets appear ingots, probably of bronze, followed by a balance (the Greek τάλαντον), and figures which probably indicate their

161

value in Mycenaean gold talents. The numerals attached to many of these objects show that we have to do with accounts referring to the royal stores and arsenals.

Some tablets relate to ceramic vessels of various forms, many of them containing marks indicative of their contents. Others, still more interesting, show vases of metallic forms, and obviously relate to the royal treasures. It is a highly significant fact that the most characteristic of these—such as a beaker like the famous gold cups found in the Vapheio tomb near Sparta, a high-spouted ewer, and an object, perhaps representing a certain weight of metal, in the form of an ox's head, recur—together with the ingots with incurving sides among the gold offerings in the hands of the tributary Aegean princes—on Egyptian monuments of Thothmes III's time. These tributary chieftains, described as Kefts and People of the Isles of the Sea, who have been already recognized as the representatives of the Mycenaean culture, recall in their dress and other particulars the Cretan youths, such as the cupbearer above described, who take part in the processional scenes on the palace frescoes. The appearance in the records of the royal treasury at Knossos of vessels of the same form as those offered by them to Pharaoh is itself a valuable indication that some of these clay archives go back approximately to the same period—in other words, to the beginning of the fifteenth century B.C.

Other documents, in which neither ciphers nor pictorial illustrations are to be found, may appeal even more deeply to the imagination. The analogy of the more or less contemporary tablets, written in cuneiform script, found in the palace of Tell-el-Amarna, might lead us to expect among them the letters from distant governors or diplomatic correspondence. It is probable that some are contracts of public acts, which may give some actual formulas of Minoan legislation. There is, indeed, an atmosphere of legal nicety, worthy of the House of Minos, in the way in which these clay records were secured. The knots of string which, according to the ancient fashion, stood in the place of locks for the coffers containing the tablets, were rendered inviolable by the attachment of clay seals, impressed with the finely engraved signets, the types of which represent a great variety of subjects, such as ships, chariots, religious scenes, lions, bulls, and other animals. But—as if this precaution was not in itself considered sufficient—while the clay was still wet the face of the seal was countermarked by a controlling official, and the back countersigned and endorsed by an inscription in the same Mycenaean script as that inscribed on the tablets themselves.

Much study and comparison will be necessary for the elucidation of these materials, which it may be hoped will be largely supplemented by the continued exploration of the Palace. If, as may well be the case, the language in which they were written was some primitive form of Greek we need not despair of the final decipherment of these Knossian archives, and the bounds of history may eventually be so enlarged as to take in the "heroic age" of Greece. In any case the weighty question, which years before I had set myself to solve on Cretan soil, has found, so far at least, an answer. That great early civilization was not dumb, and the written records of the Hellenic world are carried back some seven centuries beyond the date of the first known historic writings. But what, perhaps, is even more remarkable than this is that, when we examine in detail the linear script of these Mycenaean documents, it is impossible not to recognize that we have here a system of writing, syllabic and perhaps partly alphabetic, which stands on a distinctly higher level of development than the hieroglyphs of Egypt or the cuneiform script of contemporary Syria and Babylonia. It is not till some five centuries later that we find the first dated examples of Phoenician writing.

The signs already mentioned as engraved on the great gypsum blocks of the Palace must be regarded as distinct from the script proper. These blocks go back to the earliest period of the building, and the symbols on them, which are of very limited selection but of constant recurrence, seem to have had a religious significance. The most constantly recurring of these, indeed, is the *labrys,* or double axe, already referred to—the special symbol of the Cretan Zeus—votive deposits of which, in bronze, have been found in the cave sanctuaries of the God on Mount Ida and Mount Dicta. The double axe is engraved on the principal blocks, such as the corner stones and door jambs throughout the building, and recurs as a sign of dedication on every side of every block of a sacred pillar that forms the centre of what seems to have been the inmost shrine of an aniconic cult connected with this indigenous divinity.

The "House of Minos" thus turns out to be also the House of the Double Axe—the *labrys* and its Lord—in other words, it is the true *Labyrinthos*. The divine inspirer of Minos was not less the Lord of the Bull, and it is certainly no accidental coincidence that huge figures of bulls in painting and plaster occupied conspicuous positions within it. Nay, more, on a small steatite relief, a couchant bull is seen above the doorway of a building probably intended to represent the Palace, and this would connect it in the most direct way with the sacred animal of the Cretan Zeus.

There can be little remaining doubt that this vast edifice, which in a broad historic sense we are justified in calling the "Palace of Minos," is one and the same as the traditional "Labyrinth." A great part of the ground plan itself, with its long corridors and repeated succession of blind galleries, its tortuous passages and spacious underground conduit, its bewildering system of small chambers, does in fact present many of the characteristics of a maze.

Let us place ourselves for a moment in the position of the first Dorian colonists of Knossos after the great overthrow, when features now laboriously uncovered by the spade were still perceptible amid the mass of ruins. The name was still preserved, though the exact meaning, as supplied by the native Cretan dialect, had been probably lost. Hard by the western gate in her royal robes, today but partially visible, stood Queen Ariadne herself—and might not the comely youth in front of her be the hero Theseus, about to receive the coil of thread for his errand of liberation down the mazy galleries beyond? Within, fresh and beautiful on the walls of the inmost chambers, were the captive boys and maidens locked up here by the tyrant of old. At more than one turn rose a mighty bull, in some cases, no doubt, according to the favourite Mycenaean motive, grappled with by a half-naked man. The type of Minotaur itself as a man-bull was not wanting on the soil of prehistoric Knossos, and more than one gem found on this site represents a monster with the lower body of a man and forepart of a bull.

One may feel assured that the effect of these artistic creations on the rude Greek settler of those days was not less than that of the disinterred fresco on the Cretan workman of today. Everything around—the dark passages, the lifelike figures surviving from an older world—would conspire to produce a sense of the supernatural. It was haunted ground, and then, as now, "phantasms" were about. The later stories of the grisly king and his man-eating bull sprang, as it were, from the soil, and the whole site called forth a superstitious awe. It was left severely alone by the newcomers. Another Knossos grew up on the lower slopes of the hill to the north, and the old Palace site became a "desolation and hissing." Gradually earth's mantle covered the ruined heaps, and by the time of the Romans the Labyrinth had become nothing more than a tradition and a name.

There can be no doubt that two of the greatest and most exciting discoveries in archaeology were made in the twenties of this present century, namely, the discovery of the tomb of Tut-ankh-Amen in Egypt by Lord Carnarvon and Howard Carter in 1922, and the discovery of the royal graves at Ur by Leonard Woolley four years later. No anthology illustrating the growth of archaeology could be without these stories, well known though they are.

The fifth Earl of Carnarvon (1866–1923) excavated at Thebes from 1906 onward, publishing in 1912 his *Five Years Explorations at Thebes*. Howard Carter (1873–1939) first dug under Newberry and Petrie, and from 1907 worked with Lord Carnarvon. After the First World War the winters of 1919 to 1922 were spent in the Valley of the Kings and in November 1922, in what was to be their last season, the tomb of Tut-ankh-Amen was discovered. Carnarvon did not live to see the full excavation of the tomb. The following account of the opening of the tomb comes from the book by Howard Carter and A. C. Mace, *The Tomb of Tut-ankh-Amen*, published in 1923.

This was to be our final season in the Valley. Six full seasons we had excavated there, and season after season had drawn a blank; we had worked for months at a stretch and found nothing, and only an excavator knows how desperately depressing that can be; we had almost made up our minds that we were beaten, and were preparing to leave the Valley and try our luck elsewhere; and then—hardly had we set hoe to ground in our last despairing effort than we made a discovery that far exceeded our wildest dreams. Surely, never before in the whole history of excavation has a full digging season been compressed within the space of five days.

Let me try and tell the story of it all. It will not be easy, for the dramatic suddenness of the initial discovery left me in a dazed condition, and the months that have followed have been so crowded with incident that I have hardly had time to think. Setting it down on paper will perhaps give me a chance to realize what has happened and all that it means.

I arrived in Luxor on October 28, and by November 1 I had enrolled my workmen and was ready to begin. Our former excavations had stopped short at the northeast corner of the tomb of Rameses VI, and from this point I started trenching southwards. It will be remembered that in this area there were a number of roughly constructed workmen's huts, used probably by the labourers in the tomb of Rameses. . . . By the evening of November 3 we had laid bare a sufficient number of these huts for experimental purposes, so, after we had planned and noted them, they were removed, and we were ready to clear away the three feet of soil that lay beneath them.

Hardly had I arrived on the work next morning (November 4) than the unusual silence, due to the stoppage of the work, made me realize that something out of the ordinary had happened, and I was greeted by the announcement that a step cut in the rock had been discovered underneath the very first hut to be attacked. This seemed too good to be true, but a short amount of extra clearing revealed the fact that we were actually in the entrance of a steep cut in the rock, some thirteen feet below the entrance to the tomb of Rameses VI, and a similar depth from the present bed level of the Valley. The manner of cutting was that of the sunken stairway entrance so common in the Valley, and I almost dared to hope that we had found our tomb at last. Work continued feverishly throughout the whole of that day and the morning of the next, but it was not until the afternoon of November 5 that we succeeded in clearing away the masses of rubbish that overlay the cut, and were able to demarcate the upper edges of the stairway on all its four sides.

It was clear by now beyond any question that we actually had before us the entrance to a tomb, but doubts, born of previous disappointments, persisted in creeping in. There was always the horrible possibility, suggested by our experience in the Thothmes III valley, that the tomb was an unfinished one, never completed and never used: if it had been finished there was the depressing probability that it had been completely plundered in ancient times. On the other hand, there was just the chance of an untouched or only partially plundered tomb, and it was with ill-suppressed excitement that I watched the descending steps of the staircase, as one by one they came to light. The cutting was excavated in the side of a small hillock, and, as the work progressed, its western edge receded under the slope of the rock until it was, first partially, and then completely, roofed in, and became a passage, 10 feet high by 6 feet wide. Work progressed more rapidly now; step succeeded step, and at the level of the twelfth, towards sunset, there was disclosed the upper part of a doorway, blocked, plastered, and sealed.

A sealed doorway—it was actually true, then! Our years of patient labour were to be rewarded after all, and I think my first feeling was one of congratulation that my faith in the Valley had not been unjustified. With excitement growing to fever heat I searched the seal impressions on the door for evidence of the identity of the owner, but could find no name: the only decipherable ones were those of the well-known royal necropolis seal, the jackal and nine captives. Two facts, however, were clear: first, the employment of this royal seal was certain evidence that the tomb had been constructed for a person of a very high standing; and second, that the sealed door was entirely screened from above by workmen's huts of the Twentieth Dynasty was sufficiently clear proof that at least from that date it had never been entered. With that for the moment I had to be content.

While examining the seals I noticed, at the top of the door-way, where some of the plaster had fallen away, a heavy wooden lintel. Under this, to assure myself of the method by which the doorway had been blocked, I made a small peephole, just large enough to insert an electric torch, and discovered that the passage beyond the door was filled completely from floor to ceiling with stones and rubble—additional proof this of the care with which the tomb had been protected.

It was a thrilling moment for an excavator. Alone, save for my native workmen, I found myself, after years of compara-tively unproductive labour, on the threshold of what might prove to be a magnificent discovery. Anything, literally anything, might lie beyond that passage, and it needed all my self-control to keep from breaking down the doorway, and investigating then and there.

One thing puzzled me, and that was the smallness of the opening in comparison with the ordinary Valley tombs. The de-sign was certainly of the Eighteenth Dynasty. Could it be the tomb of a noble buried here by royal consent? Was it a royal cache, a hiding place to which a mummy and its equipment had been removed for safety? Or was it actually the tomb of the king for whom I had spent so many years in search?

Once more I examined the seal impressions for a clue, but on the part of the door so far laid bare only those of the royal necropolis seal already mentioned were clear enough to read. Had I but known that a few inches lower down there was a per-fectly clear and distinct impression of the seal of Tut-ankh-Amen, the king I most desired to find, I would have cleared on, had a much better night's rest in consequence, and saved myself nearly three weeks of uncertainty. It was late, however, and darkness was already upon us. With some reluctance I reclosed the small hole that I had made, filled in our excavation for pro-tection during the night, selected the most trustworthy of my workmen—themselves almost as excited as I was—to watch all night above the tomb, and so home by moonlight, riding down the Valley.

Naturally my wish was to go straight ahead with our clearing to find out the full extent of the discovery, but Lord Carnarvon was in England, and in fairness to him I had to delay matters until he could come. Accordingly, on the morning of November 6 I sent him the following cable: "At last have made wonderful discovery in Valley; a magnificent tomb with seals intact; recovered same for your arrival; congratulations."

My next task was to secure the doorway against interference until such time as it could finally be reopened. This we did by filling our excavation up again to surface level, and rolling on top of it the large flint boulders of which the workmen's huts had been composed. By the evening of the same day, exactly forty-eight hours after we had discovered the first step of the staircase, this was accomplished. The tomb had vanished. So far as the appearance of the ground was concerned there never had been any tomb, and I found it hard to persuade myself at times that the whole episode had not been a dream.

I was soon to be reassured on this point. News travels fast in Egypt, and within two days of the discovery congratulations, inquiries, and offers of help descended upon me in a steady stream from all directions. . . . On the 8th I had received two messages from Lord Carnarvon in answer to my cable, the first of which read "Possibly come soon," and the second, received a little later, "Propose arrive Alexandria 20th."

. . . On the night of the 18th I went to Cairo for three days, to meet Lord Carnarvon and made a number of necessary purchases, returning to Luxor on the 21st. On the 23rd Lord Carnarvon arrived in Luxor with his daughter Lady Evelyn Herbert, his devoted companion in all his Egyptian work, and everything was in hand for the beginning of the second chapter of the discovery of the tomb. . . .

By the afternoon of the 24th the whole staircase was clear, sixteen steps in all, and we were able to make a proper examination of the sealed doorway. On the lower part the seal impressions were much clearer, and we were able without any difficulty to make out on several of them the name of Tut-ankh-Amen. This added enormously to the interest of the discovery. If we had found, as seemed almost certain, the tomb of that shadowy monarch, whose tenure of the throne coincided with one of the most interesting periods in the whole of Egyptian history, we should indeed have reason to congratulate ourselves.

With heightened interest, if that were possible, we renewed our investigation of the doorway. Here for the first time a disquieting element made its appearance. Now that the whole door was exposed to light it was possible to discern a fact that had hitherto escaped notice—that there had been two successive openings and reclosings of a part of its surface: furthermore, that the sealing originally discovered, the jackal and nine captives, had been applied to the reclosed portions, whereas the sealings of Tut-ankh-Amen covered the untouched part of the doorway, and were therefore those with which the tomb had been originally secured. The tomb then was not absolutely intact, as we had hoped. Plunderers had entered it, and entered it more than once—from the evidence of the huts above, plunderers of a date not later than the reign of Rameses VI—but that they had not rifled it completely was evident from the fact that it had been resealed.

Then came another puzzle. In the lower strata of rubbish that filled the staircase we found masses of broken potsherds and boxes, the latter bearing the names of Akh-en-Aten, Smenkh-ka-Re and Tut-ankh-Amen, and, what was much more upsetting, a scarab of Thothmes III and a fragment with the name of Amenhotep III. Why this mixture of names? The balance of evidence so far would seem to indicate a cache rather than a tomb. . . .

So matters stood on the evening of the 24th. On the following day the sealed doorway was to be removed . . . Mr. Engelbach, Chief Inspector of the Antiquities Department, paid us a visit during the afternoon, and witnessed part of the final clearing of rubbish from the doorway.

On the morning of the 25th the seal impressions on the doorway were carefully noted and photographed, and then we removed the actual blocking of the door, consisting of rough stones carefully built from floor to lintel, and heavily plastered on their outer faces to take the seal impressions.

This disclosed the beginning of a descending passage (not a staircase), the same width as the entrance stairway, and nearly seven feet high. As I had already discovered from my hole in the doorway, it was filled completely with stone and rubble, probably the chip from its own excavation. This filling, like the doorway, showed distinct signs of more than one opening and reclosing of the tomb, the untouched part consisting of clean white chip, mingled with dust, whereas the disturbed part was composed mainly of dark flint. It was clear that an irregular tunnel had been cut through the original filling at the upper corner on the left side, a tunnel corresponding in position with that of the hole in the doorway.

As we cleared the passage we found, mixed with the rubble of the lower levels, broken potsherds, jar sealings, alabaster jars, whole and broken, vases of painted pottery, numerous fragments of smaller articles, and water skins, these last having obviously been used to bring up the water needed for the plastering of the doorways. These were clear evidence of plundering, and we eyed them askance. By night we had cleared a considerable distance down the passage, but as yet saw no sign of second doorway or of chamber.

The day following (November 26) was the day of days, the most wonderful that I have ever lived through, and certainly one whose like I can never hope to see again. Throughout the morning the work of clearing continued, slowly perforce, on account of the delicate objects that were mixed with the filling. Then, in the middle of the afternoon, thirty feet down from the outer door, we came upon a second sealed doorway, almost an exact replica of the first. The seal impressions in this case were less distinct, but still recognizable as those of Tut-ankh-Amen and of the royal necropolis. Here again the signs of opening and reclosing were clearly marked upon the plaster. We were firmly convinced by this time that it was a cache that we were about to open, and not a tomb. . . . We were soon to know. There lay the sealed doorway, and behind it was the answer to the question.

Slowly, desperately slowly it seemed to us as we watched, the remains of passage debris that encumbered the lower part of the doorway were removed, until at last we had the whole door clear before us. The decisive moment had arrived. With trembling hands I made a tiny breach in the upper left-hand corner. Darkness and blank space, as far as an iron testing-rod could reach, showed that whatever lay beyond was empty, and not filled like the passage we had just cleared. Candle tests were applied as a precaution against possible foul gases, and then, widening the hole a little, I inserted the candle and peered in. . . . At first I could see nothing, the hot air escaping from the chamber causing the candle flame to flicker, but presently, as my eyes grew accustomed to the light, details of the room within emerged slowly from the mist, strange animals, statues, and gold—everywhere the glint of gold. For the moment—an eternity it must have seemed to the others standing by—I was struck dumb with amazement, and when Lord Carnarvon, unable to stand the suspense any longer, inquired anxiously, "Can you see anything?" it was all I could do to get out the words,. "Yes, wonderful things." Then widening the hole a little further, so that we both could see, we inserted an electric torch.

I suppose most excavators would confess to a feeling of awe—embarrassment almost—when they break into a chamber closed and sealed by pious hands so many centuries ago. For the moment, time as a factor in human life has lost its meaning. Three thousand, four thousand years maybe, have passed and gone since human feet last trod the floor on which you stand, and yet, as you note the signs of recent life around you—the half-filled bowl of mortar for the door, the blackened lamp, the finger mark upon the freshly painted surface, the farewell garland dropped upon the threshold—you feel it might have been but yesterday. The very air you breathe, unchanged throughout the centuries, you share with those who laid the mummy to its rest. Time is annihilated by little intimate details such as these, and you feel an intruder.

That is perhaps the first and dominant sensation, but others follow thick and fast: the exhilaration of discovery, the fever of suspense, the almost overmastering impulse, born of curiosity, to break down seals and lift the lids of boxes, the thought— pure joy to the investigator—that you are about to add a page to history, or solve some problem of research, the strained expectancy—why not confess it?—of the treasure seeker. Did these thoughts actually pass through our minds at the time, or have I imagined them since? I cannot tell. . . .

Surely never before in the whole history of excavation had such an amazing sight been seen as the light of our torch revealed to us. . . .

Gradually the scene grew clearer, and we could pick out individual objects. First, right opposite to us—we had been conscious of them all the while, but refused to believe in them—were three great gilt couches, their sides carved in the form of monstrous animals curiously attenuated in body, as they had to be to serve their purpose, but with heads of startling realism. Uncanny beasts enough to look upon at any time; seen as we saw them, their brilliant gilded surfaces picked out of the darkness by our electric torch, as though by limelight, their heads throwing grotesque distorted shadows on the wall behind them, they were almost terrifying. Next, on the right, two statues caught and held our attention: two life-sized figures of a king in black, facing each other like sentinels, gold kilted, gold sandalled, armed with mace and staff, the protective sacred cobra upon their foreheads.

These were the dominant objects that caught the eye at first. Between them, around them, piled on top of them, there were countless others—exquisitely painted and inlaid caskets; alabaster vases, some beautifully carved in open-work designs; strange black shrines, from the open door of one a great gilt snake peeping out; bouquets of flowers or leaves; beds; chairs beautifully carved; a golden inlaid throne; a heap of curious white oviform boxes; staves of all shapes and designs; beneath our eyes, on the very threshold of the chamber, a beautiful lotiform cup of translucent alabaster; on the left a confused pile of overturned chariots, glistening with gold and inlay; and peeping from behind them another portrait of a king. . . .

By the middle of February our work in the antechamber was finished. With the exception of the two sentinel statues, left for a special reason, all its contents had been removed to the laboratory, every inch of its floor had been swept and sifted for the last bead or fallen piece of inlay, and it now stood bare and empty. We were ready at last to penetrate the mystery of the sealed door.

Friday, the 17th, was the day appointed, and at two o'clock those who were to be privileged to witness the ceremony met by appointment above the tomb. . . . In the antechamber everything was prepared and ready. . . .

My first care was to locate the wooden lintel above the door: then very carefully I chipped away the plaster and picked out the small stones which formed the uppermost layer of the filling. The temptation to stop and peer inside at every moment was irresistible, and when, after about ten minutes' work, I had made a hole large enough to enable me to do so, I inserted an electric torch. An astonishing sight its light revealed, for there, within a yard of the doorway, stretching as far as one could see and blocking the entrance to the chamber, stood what to all appearance was a solid wall of gold. For the moment there was no clue as to its meaning, so as quickly as I dared I set to work to widen the hole. This had now become an operation of considerable difficulty, for the stones of the masonry were not accurately squared blocks built regularly upon one another, but rough slabs of varying size, some so heavy that it took all one's strength to lift them: many of them, too, as the weight above was removed, were left so precariously balanced that the least false movement would have sent them sliding inwards to crash upon the contents of the chamber below. We were also endeavouring to preserve the seal impressions upon the thick mortar of the outer face, and this added considerably to the difficulty of handling the stones. . . .

With the removal of a very few stones the mystery of the golden wall was solved. We were at the entrance of the actual burial chamber of the king, and that which barred our way was the side of an immense gilt shrine built to cover and protect the sarcophagus. It was visible now from the antechamber by the light of the standard lamps, and as stone after stone was removed, and its gilded surface came gradually into view, we could, as though by electric current, feel the tingle of excitement which thrilled the spectators behind the barrier. . . . We who were doing the work were probably less excited, for our whole energies were taken up with the task in hand—that of removing the blocking without an accident. The fall of a single stone might have done irreparable damage to the delicate surface of the shrine, so, directly the hole was large enough, we made an additional protection for it by inserting a mattress on the inner side of the door blocking, suspending it from the wooden lintel of the doorway. Two hours of hard work it took us to clear away the blocking, or at least as much of it as was necessary for the moment; and at one point, when near the bottom, we had to delay operations for a space while we collected the scattered beads from a necklace brought by the plunderers from the chamber within and dropped upon the threshold. This last was a terrible trial to our patience, for it was a slow business, and we were all of us excited to see what might be within; but finally it was done, the last stones were removed, and the way to the innermost chamber lay open before us.

In clearing away the blocking of the doorway we had discovered that the level of the inner chamber was about four feet lower than that of the antechamber, and this, combined with the fact that there was but a narrow space between door and shrine, made an entrance by no means easy to effect. Fortunately, there were no smaller antiquities at this end of the chamber, so I lowered myself down, and then, taking one of the portable lights, I edged cautiously to the corner of the shrine and looked beyond it. At the corner two beautiful alabaster vases blocked the way, but I could see that if these were removed we should have a clear path to the other end of the chamber; so, carefully marking the spot on which they stood, I picked them up—with the exception of the king's wishing cup they were of finer quality and more graceful shape than any we had yet found—and passed them back to the antechamber. Lord Carnarvon and M. Lacau now joined me, and, picking our way along the narrow passage between shrine and wall, paying out the wire of our light behind us, we investigated further.

It was, beyond any question, the sepulchral chamber in which we stood, for there, towering above us, was one of the great gilt shrines beneath which kings were laid. So enormous was this

structure (17 feet by 11 feet, and 9 feet high, we found afterwards) that it filled within a little the entire area of the chamber,
a space of some two feet only separating it from the walls on all
four sides, while its roof, with cornice top and torus moulding,
reached almost to the ceiling. From top to bottom it was overlaid with gold, and upon its sides there were inlaid panels of
brilliant blue faïence, in which were represented, repeated over
and over, the magic symbols which would ensure its strength
and safety. Around the shrine, resting upon the ground, there
were a number of funerary emblems, and, at the north end, the
seven magic oars the king would need to ferry himself across
the waters of the underworld. The walls of the chamber, unlike
those of the antechamber, were decorated with brightly painted
scenes and inscriptions, brilliant in their colours, but evidently
somewhat hastily executed.

The last details we must have noticed subsequently, for at the
time our one thought was of the shrine and of its safety. Had
the thieves penetrated within it and disturbed the royal burial?
Here, on the eastern end, were the great folding doors, closed
and bolted, but not sealed, that would answer the question for
us. Eagerly we drew the bolts, swung back the doors, and there
within was a second shrine with similar bolted doors, and upon
the bolts a seal, intact. This seal we determined not to break,
for our doubts were resolved, and we could not penetrate further without risk of serious damage to the monument. I think at
the moment we did not even want to break the seal, for a feeling
of intrusion had descended heavily upon us with the opening of
the doors, heightened, probably, by the almost painful impres-
siveness of a linen pall, decorated with golden rosettes, which
drooped above the inner shrine. We felt that we were in the
presence of the dead king and must do him reverence, and in
imagination could see the doors of the successive shrines open
one after the other till the innermost disclosed the king himself.
Carefully, and as silently as possible, we reclosed the great
swing doors, and passed on to the farther end of the chamber.

Here a surprise awaited us, for a low door, eastwards from
the sepulchral chamber, gave entrance to yet another chamber,
smaller than the outer ones and not so lofty. This doorway, un-

like the others, had not been closed and sealed. We were able, from where we stood, to get a clear view of the whole of the contents, and a single glance sufficed to tell us that here, within this little chamber, lay the greatest treasures of the tomb. Facing the doorway, on the farther side, stood the most beautiful monument that I have ever seen—so lovely that it made one gasp with wonder and admiration. The central portion of it consisted of a large shrine-shaped chest, completely overlaid with gold, and surmounted by a cornice of sacred cobras. Surrounding this, free-standing, were statues of the four tutelary goddesses of the dead—gracious figures with outstretched protective arms, so natural and lifelike in their pose, so pitiful and compassionate the expression upon their faces, that one felt it almost sacrilege to look at them. One guarded the shrine on each of its four sides, but whereas the figures at front and back kept their gaze firmly fixed upon their charge, an additional note of touching realism was imparted by the other two, for their heads were turned sideways, looking over their shoulders towards the entrance, as though to watch against surprise. There is a simple grandeur about this monument that made an irresistible appeal to the imagination, and I am not ashamed to confess that it brought a lump to my throat. It is undoubtedly the Canopic chest and contains the jars which play such an important part in the ritual of mummification.

There were a number of other wonderful things in the chamber, but we found it hard to take them in at the time, so inevitably were one's eyes drawn back again and again to the lovely little goddess figures. Immediately in front of the entrance lay the figure of the jackal god Anubis, upon his shrine, swathed in linen cloth, and resting upon a portable sled, and behind this the head of a bull upon a stand—emblems, these, of the underworld. In the south side of the chamber lay an endless number of black shrines and chests, all closed and sealed save one, whose open doors revealed statues of Tut-ankh-Amen standing upon black leopards. On the farther wall were more shrine-shaped boxes and miniature coffins of gilded wood, these last undoubtedly containing funerary statuettes of the king. In the centre of the room, left of the Anubis and the bull, there was a row of magnificent caskets of ivory and wood, decorated and inlaid with gold and blue faïence, one, whose lid we raised, containing a gorgeous ostrich-feather fan with ivory handle, fresh and strong to all appearance as when it left the maker's hand. There were also, distributed in different quarters of the chamber, a number of model boats with sails and rigging all complete, and, at the north side, yet another chariot.

Such, from a hurried survey, were the contents of this innermost chamber. We looked anxiously for evidence of plundering, but on the surface there was none. Unquestionably the thieves must have entered, but they cannot have done more than open two or three of the caskets. Most of the boxes, as has been said, have still their seals intact, and the whole contents of the chamber, in fortunate contrast to those of the antechamber and the annex, still remain in position exactly as they were placed at the time of burial.

How much time we occupied in this first survey of the wonders of the tomb I cannot say, but it must have seemed endless to those anxiously waiting in the antechamber. Not more than three at a time could be admitted with safety so . . . it was curious as we stood in the antechamber, to watch their faces as, one by one, they emerged from the door. Each had a dazed, bewildered look in his eyes, and each in turn, as he came out, threw up his hands before him, an unconscious gesture of impotence to describe in words the wonders that he had seen. They were indeed indescribable, and the emotions they had aroused in our minds were of too intimate a nature to communicate, even though we had the words at our command. It was an experience which, I am sure, none of us who were present is ever likely to forget, for in imagination—and not wholly in imagination either—we had been present at the funeral ceremonies of a king long dead and almost forgotten. At a quarter past two we had filed down into the tomb, and when, three hours later, hot, dusty, and disheveled, we came out once more into the light of day, the very Valley seemed to have changed for us and taken on a more personal aspect. We had been given the Freedom.

Our next extract is from Sir Leonard Woolley's *Ur of the Chaldees,* published in 1929, in which he gives an account of the discovery of the Royal Tombs in 1926. The work here, more than anything else, put the Sumerians on the map of the ancient civilizations of the world—as perhaps the most ancient civilization of all. Leonard Woolley (1880–1960) was a Classical undergraduate at Oxford, and tells amusingly in his *Spadework* (1953) the story of how he became an archaeologist at the direction of the Warden of New College, the famous Dr. Spooner (see pp. 233–236). He began work in Roman Britain and then transferred to the Near and Middle East. After the First World War he started important excavations in southern Mesopotamia and at Ur made one of the really great archaeological discoveries of all time.

Ur lies about half way between Baghdad and the head of the Persian Gulf, some ten miles west of the present course of the Euphrates. A mile and a half to the east of the ruins runs the single line of railway which joins Basra to the capital of Iraq, and between the rail and the river there is sparse cultivation, and little villages of mud huts or reed-mat shelters are dotted here and there; but westward of the line is desert, blank and unredeemed. Out of this waste rise the mounds which were Ur, called by the Arabs after the highest of them all, the ziggurat hill, "Tel al Muqayyar," the Mound of Pitch.

Standing on the summit of this mound, one can distinguish along the eastern skyline the dark-tasselled fringe of the palm-gardens on the river's bank, but to north and west and south as far as the eye can see stretches a waste of unprofitable sand. To the southwest the flat line of the horizon is broken by a grey, upstanding pinnacle, the ruins of the staged tower of the sacred city of Eridu, which the Sumerians believed to be the oldest city upon earth, and to the northwest a shadow thrown by the low sun may tell the whereabouts of the low mound of al 'Ubaid; but otherwise nothing relieves the monotony of the vast plain over which the shimmering heat waves dance and the mirage spreads its mockery of placid waters. It seems incredible that such a wilderness should ever have been habitable for man, and yet the weathered hillocks at one's feet cover the temples and houses of a very great city. . . .

The greater part of three seasons' work has been devoted to the clearing of the great cemetery which lay outside the walls of the old town and occupied the rubbish heaps piled up between them and the water channel, and the treasures which have been unearthed from the graves during that time have revolutionized our ideas of the early civilization of the world.

The cemetery (there are really two cemeteries, one above the other, but I am speaking now only of the lower and older) consists of burials of two sorts, the graves of commoners and the tombs of kings. Because the latter have yielded the richest works of art one is inclined to think of them alone, but the graves of the common folk, as well as being a hundredfold as many in number, have also produced very fine objects, and have afforded precious evidence for the dating of the cemetery.

The tombs of the kings appear to be on the whole earlier in date than the graves of their subjects, and this not so much because they lie at a deeper level, for that might be explained as a natural precaution, the larger and richer graves being dug deeper as a protection against robbers, but because of their relative positions. It is a common sight to see in a Moslem graveyard the tomb of some local saint surrounded by its little domed chapel and the other graves crowded round this as close as may be, as if the occupants sought the protection of the holy man. So it is with the royal tombs of Ur. The older private graves are clustered round them . . . later it seems as if the visible monuments of the dead kings vanished and their memory faded, leaving only a vague tradition of this being holy ground, and we find the newer graves invading the shafts of the royal tombs and dug right down into them.

The private graves are found at very varying levels, partly perhaps because there was no regular standard of depth, partly because the ground surface of the cemetery was far from uniform; but, generally speaking, the higher graves are the later, and this is due to the rise in the ground level, which went on steadily throughout the time that the graveyard was in use. The result of this rise, obliterating the position of the older graves, was that a new grave might be placed directly above an old, but, being started from a higher level, would not go quite so far down, and we may find as many as half a dozen graves superimposed one above the other. When this is so, the position in

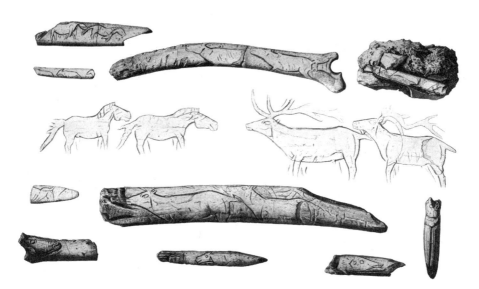

23. Reindeer, from Edouard Lartet and Henry Christy, *Reliquiae Aquitanicae*. The authors of this book were responsible for the discovery and appreciation of Upper Palaeolithic mobiliary art, which consisted of small decorated objects found in the debris of rock shelters.

24. Drawing from Les Trois Frères, France, a fine example of an Upper Palaeolithic painted cave, discovered purely by chance in 1914.

25. Photograph of the excursion to the cave of La Mouthe, August 1902.

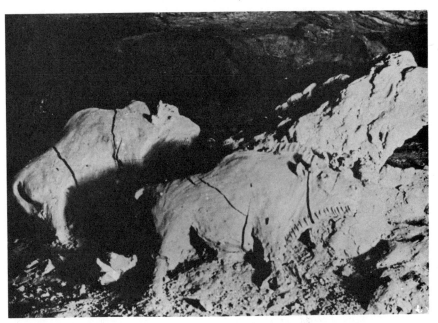

26. Three clay bison, 25,000 years old.

27. An example of the magnificent painted and engraved animals found in the great hall of Lascaux. This perfectly preserved horse was painted 20,000 to 25,000 years ago.

28. Sophia Schliemann wearing an elaborate headdress, a
necklace, and two sets of earrings—one pair at her throat.
This was only a small part of the treasures found at Troy
in 1873.

29. Heinrich Schliemann and crew digging at Troy in 1890. Note the special tracks for trundle cars to haul away debris.

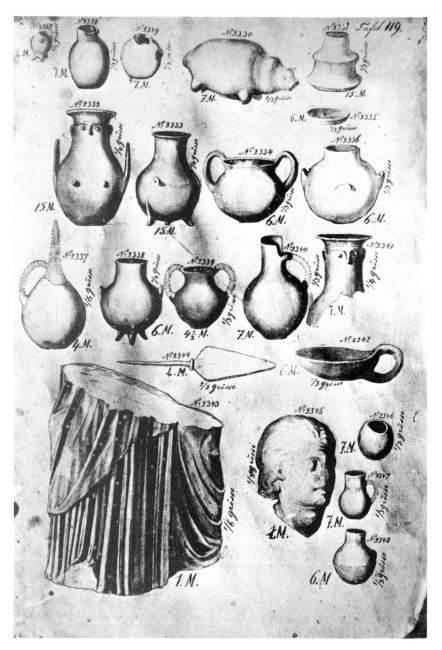

30. Notebook page from Heinrich Schliemann's *Tro-
janische Alterhümer.*

31. Clay potsherds of
Mycenae, assembled by
Schliemann, show pro-
cession of armed warriors
in battle gear.

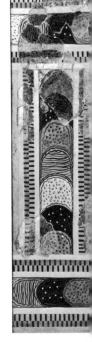

32. Bull games fresco from a small court in the eastern part of the ancient city of Knossos. Sir Arthur Evans excavated at Knossos and discovered the civilization he called Minoan.

33. The discovery of the tomb of Tut-ankh-Amen in
Egypt by Lord Carnarvon and Howard Carter in 1922
was one of the most exciting finds of this century. This
photograph shows Mr. Carter looking into the second
shrine.

34. In the tomb of Tut-ankh-Amen, Valley of the Kings, Thebes, Carter and Carnarvon wrap up one of the two statues of the king in the antechamber for removal from the tomb.

255/A.

35. Upper portion of innermost gold coffin showing floral
wreath around the king's neck.

THE ROSETTA STONE

36. The Rosetta Stone, that famous slab of black basalt, was discovered in July 1799 by a French officer named Bouchard. The parallel inscriptions in hieroglyphics, demotic characters, and Greek paved the way toward the decipherment of hieroglyphics.

Tableau des Signes Phonétiques Égyptiens, pour la lecture des noms propres Grecs et Romains.

Lettres Grecques.	Signes Démotiques.	Signes Hiéroglyphiques.
A		
B		
Γ		
Δ		
E		
Z		
Θ		
H		
I		
K		
Λ		
M		
N		
Ξ		
O		
Π		
P		
Σ		
Σ		
T		
Υ		
Φ		
X		
Ψ		
Ω		
TO		

37. Page from Jean François Champollion's famous letter to M. Dacier, in which he deciphered the Rosetta Stone.

38. The work of Sir Henry Creswicke Rawlinson brought decipherment of Mesopotamian writing to a successful conclusion. The giant Behistun inscription was carved in 516 B.C. on the orders of Darius the First. This view of the sculptures of Behistun, from Rawlinson's article which appeared in *Archaeologia,* XXXIV (1852), was taken from the foot of the rock.

39. Illustration from the *Gentleman's Magazine* for 1852 entitled "Collecting Roman remains on the Essex coast."

40. This sketch accompanies an article written by Thomas Wright which originally appeared in the *Gentleman's Magazine* for 1852. A trench of about six feet wide had been cut through the center of the barrow from east to west, and the rough drawing shows the work being done on the east side of the excavation.

41. In 1851, A. Mariette excavated the Serapeum at
Memphis, the great temple of Osiris-Apis, with its cemetery of sacred Apis bulls. The Serapeum, which was built
without any regular plan, closely resembles the other
Egyptian temples. What makes it unique is the existence
of vast subterranean vaults known as the Tomb of Apis.

42. Photograph of Sir W. Flinders Petrie (1853–1942) with pottery finds from Palestine.

43. Sir Mortimer Wheeler inspecting the prehistoric city of Mohenjo-daro in the Indus Valley.

44. Harold Barker working with a radiocarbon apparatus. The real revolution in the process of dating in archaeology took place when Professor Willard F. Libby discovered the existence of carbon 14 as well as carbon 12 in organic matters, and realized that this radioactive isotope, decaying at a fixed rate, could be used to date material in archaeological contexts.

the ground necessarily corresponds to the order in time, and from these superimposed graves we get most valuable evidence for chronology.

Judging from the character of their contents, pottery, etc., the later graves seem to come just before the beginning of the First Dynasty of Ur, which we date to about 3100 B.C., and a few are actually contemporary with that dynasty; for the cemetery age as a whole I think that we must allow a period of at least 200 years. The first of the royal tombs, then, may be dated soon after 3500 B.C., and soon after 3200 B.C. the graveyard was falling out of use. . . .

The first of the royal tombs proved a disappointment. At the very end of the season 1926–27 two important discoveries were made. At the bottom of an earth shaft, amongst masses of copper weapons, there was found the famous gold dagger of Ur, a wonderful weapon whose blade was of gold, its hilt of lapis lazuli decorated with gold studs, and its sheath of gold beautifully worked with an openwork pattern derived from plaited grass; with it was another object scarcely less remarkable, a cone-shaped reticule of gold ornamented with a spiral pattern and containing a set of little toilet instruments, tweezers, lancet, and pencil, also of gold. Nothing like these things had ever before come from the soil of Mesopotamia; they revealed an art hitherto unsuspected and they gave promise of future discoveries outstripping all our hopes.

The other discovery was less sensational. Digging down in another part of the cemetery we found what at first appeared to be walls of *terre pisée,* i.e. of earth not moulded into bricks but used as concrete is used for building. As the sun dried the soil and brought out the colours of its stratification, it became evident that these were no built walls but the clean-cut sides of a pit sunk in the rubbish; the looser filling of the pit had fallen away as we worked and had left the original face exactly as the first diggers had made it. As the excavation continued we came on slabs and blocks of rough limestone which seemed to form a paving over the pit's base. This was an astonishing thing, because there is no stone in the Euphrates delta, not so much as a pebble in its alluvium, and to obtain blocks of limestone such as these it is necessary to go some thirty miles away into the higher desert. The cost of transport would be considerable, and the result is that stone is scarcely ever found in buildings at Ur: a stone pavement underground would therefore be an unheard-of extravagance. As the season was just at its end we could do no more than clear the surface of the "pavement" and leave its fuller examination for the next autumn.

Thinking the matter over during the summer, we came to the conclusion that the stones might be not the floor of a building but its roof, and that we might have discovered a royal grave. It was with high hopes that we resumed work in the following autumn and very soon we could assure ourselves that our forecast was correct: we had found a stone-built underground structure which had indeed been the tomb of a king, but a rubbish-filled tunnel led from near the surface to the broken roof, robbers had been there before us, and except for a few scattered fragments of a gold diadem and some decayed copper pots there was nothing left for us to find.

But in spite of that disappointment the discovery was most important. We had laid bare the ruins of a two-chambered structure built of stone throughout, with one long and narrow chamber vaulted with stone and a square room which had certainly once been covered with a stone dome, though the collapse of the roof made it difficult to establish the exact method of construction. A doorway, blocked with rubble masonry, afforded entrance to the tomb and was approached by a slanting ramp cut down from the ground surface in the hard soil. Nothing of the sort had ever been found before, and the light thrown on the architectural knowledge of this remote period might well atone for the loss of the tomb's contents; moreover, there was no reason to suppose that this was an isolated tomb, and we could hope for others to which the plunderers had not made their way.

During that season (1927–28) and in the course of last winter more royal tombs came to light, and it is curious to find that never more than two of them are alike. Two large tombs, both plundered, consist of a four-roomed building occupying the whole area of the excavated shaft at the bottom of which they lie;

walls and roofs alike are of limestone rubble, and in each case there are two long outer chambers which are vaulted and two smaller central chambers crowned with domes; a ramp leads to the arched door in the outer wall, and arched doors give communication between the rooms. Two graves, those of Queen Shub-ad and her supposed husband, consist of a pit open to the sky and approached by a sloped ramp, at one end of which is a single-chamber tomb with limestone walls and a roof constructed of burnt brick, vaulted and with apsidal ends; the chamber was destined to receive the royal body, the open pit was for offerings and subsidiary burials, and was simply filled in with earth. In another case the pit was found, but the tomb chamber did not lie inside it, but seems to have been close by and on a different level. A small grave found last winter consists of a single stone-built domed chamber with a little front court at the bottom of the shaft and, higher up in the shaft, mud-brick buildings for the subsidiary burials and offerings, the whole being covered with earth; another has the same general arrangement, but instead of the domed stone chamber there was a vaulted chamber of mud brick. . . .

In 1927–28, soon after our disappointment with the plundered stone tomb, we found, in another part of the field, five bodies lying side by side in a shallow sloping trench; except for the copper daggers at their waists and one or two small clay cups, they had none of the normal furniture of a grave, and the mere fact of there being a number thus together was unusual. Then, below them, a layer of matting was found, and tracing this along we came to another group of bodies, those of ten women carefully arranged in two rows; they wore headdresses of gold, lapis lazuli, and carnelian, and elaborate bead necklaces, but they too possessed no regular tomb furnishings. At the end of the row lay the remains of a wonderful harp, the wood of it decayed but its decoration intact, making its reconstruction only a matter of care; the upright wooden beam was capped with gold, and in it were fastened the gold-headed nails which secured the strings; the sounding box was edged with a mosaic in red stone, lapis lazuli, and white shell, and from the front of it projected a splendid head of a bull wrought in gold with eyes and beard of lapis lazuli; across the ruins of the harp lay the bones of the gold-crowned harpist.

By this time we had found the earth sides of the pit in which the women's bodies lay and could see that the bodies of the five men were on the ramp which led down to it. Following the pit along, we came upon more bones, which at first puzzled us by being other than human, but the meaning of them soon became clear. A little way inside the entrance to the pit stood a wooden sledge chariot decorated with red, white, and blue mosaic along the edges of the framework and with golden heads of lions having manes of lapis lazuli and shell on its side panels; along the top rail were smaller gold heads of lions and bulls, silver lionesses' heads adorned the front, and the position of the vanished swinglebar was shown by a band of blue and white inlay and two smaller heads of lionesses in silver. In front of the chariot lay the crushed skeletons of two asses with the bodies of the grooms by their heads, and on the top of the bones was the double ring, once attached to the pole, through which the reins had passed; it was of silver, and standing on it was a gold "mascot" in the form of a donkey most beautifully and realistically modeled.

Close to the chariot were an inlaid gaming board and a collection of tools and weapons, including a set of chisels and a saw made of gold, big bowls of grey soapstone, copper vessels, a long tube of gold and lapis which was a drinking tube for sucking up liquor from the bowls, more human bodies, and then the wreckage of a large wooden chest adorned with a figured mosaic in lapis lazuli and shell which was found empty but had perhaps contained such perishable things as clothes. Behind this box were more offerings, masses of vessels in copper, silver, stone (including exquisite examples in volcanic glass, lapis lazuli, alabaster, and marble), and gold; one set of silver vessels seemed to be in the nature of a communion service, for there was a shallow tray or platter, a jug with tall neck and long spout such as we know from carved stone reliefs to have been used in religious rites, and tall slender silver tumblers nested one inside another; a similar tumbler in gold, fluted and chased, with a fluted feeding bowl, a chalice, and plain oval bowl of gold lay piled together, and two magnificent lions' heads in silver, perhaps the ornaments of a throne, were amongst the treasures in the crowded pit. The perplexing thing was that with all this wealth of objects we had found no body so far distinguished from the rest as to be that of the person to whom all were dedicated; logically our discovery, however great, was incomplete.

The objects were removed and we started to clear away the remains of the wooden box, a chest some 6 feet long and 3 feet across, when under it we found burnt bricks. They were fallen, but at one end some were still in place and formed the ring vault of a stone chamber. The first and natural supposition was that here we had the tomb to which all the offerings belonged, but further search proved that the chamber was plundered, the roof had not fallen from decay but had been broken through, and the wooden box had been placed over the hole as if deliberately to hide it. Then, digging round the outside of the chamber, we found just such another pit as that 6 feet above. At the foot of the ramp lay six soldiers, orderly in two ranks, with copper spears by their sides and copper helmets crushed flat on the broken skulls; just inside, having evidently been backed down the slope, were two wooden four-wheeled waggons each drawn by three oxen—one of the latter so well preserved that we were able to lift the skeleton entire; the waggons were plain, but the reins were decorated with long beads of lapis and silver and passed through silver rings surmounted with mascots in the form of bulls; the grooms lay at the oxen's heads and the drivers in the bodies of the cars; of the cars themselves only the impression of the decayed wood remained in the soil, but so clear was this that a photograph showed the grain of the solid wooden wheel and the grey-white circle which had been the leather tyre.

Against the end wall of the stone chamber lay the bodies of nine women wearing the gala headdress of lapis and carnelian beads from which hung golden pendants in the forms of beech leaves, great lunate earrings of gold, silver "combs" like the palm of a hand with three fingers tipped with flowers whose petals are inlaid with lapis, gold, and shell, and necklaces of lapis and gold; their heads were leaned against the masonry, their bodies extended onto the floor of the pit, and the whole space between them and the waggons was crowded with other dead, women and men, while the passage which led along the side of the chamber to its arched door was lined with soldiers carrying daggers, and with women. Of the soldiers in the central space one had a bundle of four spears with heads of gold, two had sets of four silver spears, and by another there was a re-markable relief in copper with a design of two lions trampling on the bodies of two fallen men which may have been the deco-ration of a shield.

On the top of the bodies of the "court ladies" against the chamber walls had been placed a wooden harp, of which there survived only the copper head of a bull and the shell plaques which had adorned the sounding box; by the side wall of the pit, also set on the top of the bodies, was a second harp with a won-derful bull's head in gold, its eyes, beard, and horn tips of lapis, and a set of engraved shell plaques not less wonderful; there are four of them with grotesque scenes of animals playing the parts of men, and while the most striking feature about them is that sense of humour which is so rare in ancient art, the grace and balance of the design and the fineness of the drawing make of these plaques one of the most instructive documents that we possess for the appreciation of the art of early Sumer.

Inside the tomb the robbers had left enough to show that it had contained bodies of several minor people as well as that of the chief person, whose name, if we can trust the inscription on a cylinder seal, was A-bar-gi; overlooked against the wall we found two model boats, one of copper now hopelessly decayed, the other of silver wonderfully well preserved; some 2 feet long, it has a high stern and prow, five seats, and amidships an arched support for the awning which would protect the passenger, and the leaf-bladed oars are still set in the thwarts; it is a testimony to the conservatism of the East that a boat of identical type is in use today on the marshes of the Lower Euphrates, some fifty miles from Ur.

The king's tomb chamber lay at the far end of his open pit; continuing our search behind it we found a second stone cham-ber built up against it either at the same time or, more probably, at a later period. This chamber, roofed like the king's with a vault of ring arches in burnt brick, was the tomb of the queen to whom belonged the upper pit with its ass chariot and other offerings: her name, Shub-ad, was given us by a fine cylinder seal of lapis lazuli which was found in the filling of the shaft a little above the roof of the chamber and had probably been thrown into the pit at the moment when the earth was being put back into it. The vault of the chamber had fallen in, but luckily this was due to the weight of earth above, not to the violence of tomb robbers; the tomb itself was intact.

At one end, on the remains of a wooden bier, lay the body of the queen, a gold cup near her hand; the upper part of the body was entirely hidden by a mass of beads of gold, silver, lapis lazuli, carnelian, agate, and chalcedony, long strings of which, hanging from a collar, had formed a cloak reaching to the waist and bordered below with a broad band of tubular beads of lapis, carnelian, and gold: against the right arm were three long gold pins with lapis heads and three amulets in the form of fish, two of gold and one of lapis, and a fourth in the form of two seated gazelles, also of gold.

The headdress whose remains covered the crushed skull was a more elaborate edition of that worn by the court ladies: its basis was a broad gold ribbon festooned in loops round the hair—and the measurement of the curves showed that this was not the natural hair but a wig padded out to an almost grotesque size; over this came three wreaths, the lowest, hanging down over the forehead, of plain gold ring pendants, the second of beech leaves, the third of long willow leaves in sets of three with gold flowers whose petals were of blue and white inlay; all these were strung on triple chains of lapis and carnelian beads. Fixed into the back of the hair was a golden "Spanish comb" with five points ending in lapis-centred gold flowers. Heavy spiral rings of gold wire were twisted into the side curls of the wig, huge lunate earrings of gold hung down to the shoulders, and apparently from the hair also hung on each side a string of large square stone beads with, at the end of each, a lapis amulet, one shaped as a seated bull and the other as a calf. Complicated as the headdress was, its different parts lay in such good order that it was possible to reconstruct the whole and exhibit the likeness of the queen with all her original finery in place.

For the purposes of exhibition a plaster cast was made from

187

a well-preserved female skull of the period (the queen's own skull was too fragmentary to be used), and over this my wife modelled the features in wax, making this as thin as possible so as not to obliterate the bone structure; the face was passed by Sir Arthur Keith, who has made a special study of the Ur and al 'Ubaid skulls, as reproducing faithfully the character of the early Sumerians. On this head was put a wig of the correct dimensions dressed in the fashion illustrated by terra-cotta figures which, though later in date, probably represented an old tradition. The gold hair ribbon had been lifted from the tomb without disturbing the arrangement of the strands, these having been first fixed in position by strips of glued paper threaded in and out between them and by wires twisted round the gold; when the wig had been fitted on the head, the hair ribbon was balanced on the top and the wires and paper bands were cut, and the ribbon fell naturally into place and required no further arranging. The wreaths were restrung and tied on in the order noted at the time of excavation. Though the face is not an actual portrait of the queen, it gives at least the type to which she must have conformed, and the whole reconstructed head presents us with the most accurate picture we are likely ever to possess of what she looked like in her lifetime.

By the side of the body lay a second headdress of a novel sort. Onto a diadem made apparently of a strip of soft white leather had been sewn thousands of minute lapis lazuli beads, and against this background of solid blue were set a row of exquisitely fashioned gold animals—stags, gazelles, bulls, and goats—with between them clusters of pomegranates, three fruits hanging together shielded by their leaves, and branches of some other tree with golden stems and fruit or pods of gold and carnelian, while gold rosettes were sewn on at intervals, and from the lower border of the diadem hung palmettes of twisted gold wire.

The bodies of two women attendants were crouched against the bier, one at its head and one at its foot, and all about the chamber lay strewn offerings of all sorts, another gold bowl, vessels of silver and copper, stone bowls and clay jars for food, the head of a cow in silver, two silver tables for offerings, silver lamps, and a number of large cockleshells containing green paint; such shells are nearly always found in women's graves, and the paint in them, presumably used as a cosmetic, may be white, black, or red, but the normal colour is green. Queen Shubad's shells were abnormally big, and with them were found two pairs of imitation shells, one in silver and one in gold, each with its green paint.

The discovery was now complete and our earlier difficulty was explained: King A-bar-gi's grave and Queen Shub-ad's were exactly alike, but whereas the former was all on one plane, the queen's tomb chamber had been sunk below the ground level of her grave pit. Probably they were husband and wife: the king had died first and been buried, and it had been the queen's wish to lie as close to him as might be; for this end the gravediggers had reopened the king's shaft, going down in it until the top of the chamber vault appeared; then they had stopped work in the main shaft but had dug down at the back of the chamber pit in which the queen's stone tomb could be built. But the treasures known to lie in the king's grave were too great a temptation for the workmen; the outer pit where the bodies of the court ladies lay was protected by 6 feet of earth which they could not disturb without being detected, but the richer plunder in the royal chamber itself was separated from them only by the bricks of the vault; they broke through the arch, carried off their spoil, and placed the great clothes chest of the queen over the hole to hide their sacrilege.

Nothing else would account for the plundered vault lying immediately below the untouched grave of the queen; and the connecting of Shub-ad's stone chamber with the upper "death pit," as we came to call these open shafts in which the subsidiary bodies lay, made an exact parallel to the king's grave and, in a lesser degree, to the other royal tombs. Clearly, when a royal person died, he or she was accompanied to the grave by all the members of the court: the king had at least three people with him in his chamber and sixty-two in the death pit; the queen was content with some twenty-five in all. Here we had a single stone chamber and an open death pit; where there was a larger stone building with two or four rooms, then one of these was for the royal body and the rest for the followers sacrificed in precisely the same way; the ritual was identical, only the accommodation for the victims differed in different cases.

On the subject of human sacrifice more light was thrown by the discovery of a great death pit excavated last winter. At about 26 feet below the surface we came upon a mass of mud brick not truly laid but rammed together and forming, as we guessed, not a floor but the stopping, as it were, of a shaft. Immediately below this we were able to distinguish the clean-cut earth sides of a pit, sloping inward and smoothly plastered with mud; following these down, we found the largest death pit that the cemetery has yet produced. The pit was roughly rectangular and measured 37 feet by 24 at the bottom, and was approached as usual by a sloped ramp. In it lay the bodies of six men-servants and sixty-eight women; the men lay along the side by the door, the bodies of the women were disposed in regular rows across the floor, every one lying on her side with legs slightly bent and hands brought up near the face, so close together that the heads of those in one row rested on the legs of those in the row above. Here was to be observed even more clearly what had been fairly obvious in the graves of Shub-ad and her husband, the neatness with which the bodies were laid out, the entire absence of any signs of violence or terror.

We have often been asked how the victims in the royal graves met their death, and it is impossible to give a decisive answer. The bones are too crushed and too decayed to show any cause of death, supposing that violence had been used, but the general condition of the bodies does supply a strong argument. Very many of these women wear headdresses which are delicate in themselves and would easily be disarranged, yet such are always found in good order, undisturbed except by the pressure of the earth; this would be impossible if the wearers had been knocked on the head, improbable if they had fallen to the ground after being stabbed, and it is equally unlikely that they could have been killed outside the grave and carried down the ramp and laid in their places with all their ornaments intact; certainly the animals must have been alive when they dragged the chariots down the ramps, and if so, the grooms who led them and the drivers in the cars must have been alive also: it is safe to assume that those who were to be sacrificed went down alive into the pit.

That they were dead, or at least unconscious, when the earth was flung in and trampled down on top of them is an equally safe assumption, for in any other case there must have been some struggle which would have left its traces in the attitude of the bodies, but these are always decently composed; indeed, they are in such good order and alignment that we are driven to suppose that after they were lying unconscious someone entered the pit and gave the final touches to their arrangement—and the circumstance that in A-bar-gi's grave, the harps were placed on the top of the bodies proves that someone did enter the grave at the end. It is most probable that the victims walked to their places, took some kind of drug—opium or hashish would serve—and lay down in order; after the drug had worked, whether it produced sleep or death, the last touches were given to their bodies and the pit was filled in. There does not seem to have been anything brutal in the manner of their deaths.

None the less, the sight of the remains of the victims is gruesome enough with the gold leaves and the colored beads lying thick on the crushed and broken skulls, but in excavating a great death pit such as that of last winter we do not see it as a whole, but have to clear it a little at a time. The soil was removed until the bodies were almost exposed, covered only by the few inches of broken brick which had been the first of the filling thrown over the dead; here and there a pick driven too deep might bring to view a piece of gold ribbon or a golden beech leaf, showing that everywhere there were bodies richly adorned, but these would be quickly covered up again and left until more methodical work should reveal them in due course. Starting in one corner of the pit, we marked out squares such as might contain from five to six bodies, and all these were cleared, noted, and the objects belonging to them collected and removed before the next square was taken in hand.

It was slow work, and especially so in those cases where we decided to remove the entire skull with all its ornaments in position on it. The wreaths and chains and necklaces restrung and arranged in a glass case may look very well, but it is more interesting to see them as they were actually found, and therefore a few heads on which the original order of the beads and gold-work was best preserved were laboriously cleaned with small knives and brushes, the dirt being removed without disturbing any of the ornaments—a difficult matter as they are loose in the soil—and then boiling paraffin wax was poured over them, solidifying them in one mass. The lump of wax, earth, bone, and gold was then strengthened by waxed cloth pressed carefully over it, so that it could be lifted from the ground by undercutting. Mounted in plaster, with the superfluous wax cleaned off, these heads form an exhibit which is not only of interest in itself but proves the accuracy of the restorations which we have made of others.

Of the sixty-eight women in the pit, twenty-eight wore hair ribbons of gold. At first sight it looked as if the others had nothing of the kind, but closer examination showed that many, if not all, had originally worn exactly similar ribbons of silver. Unfortunately silver is a metal which ill resists the action of the acids in the soil, and where it was but a thin strip and, being worn on the head, was directly affected by the corruption of the flesh, it generally disappears altogether, and at most there may be detected on the bone of the skull slight traces of a purplish colour, which is silver chloride in a minutely powdered state: we could be certain that the ribbons were worn, but we could not produce material evidence of them.

But in one case we had better luck. The great gold earrings were in place, but not a sign of discolouration betrayed the existence of any silver headdress, and this negative evidence was duly noted; then, as the body was cleared, there was found against it, about on the level of the waist, a flat disk a little more than 3 inches across of a grey substance which was certainly silver; it might have been a small circular box. Only when I was cleaning it in the house that evening, hoping to find something which would enable me to catalogue it more in detail, did its real nature come to light: it was the silver hair ribbon, but it had never been worn—carried apparently in the woman's pocket, it was just as she had taken it from her room, done up in a

tight coil with the ends brought over to prevent its coming un-
done; and since it formed thus a comparatively solid mass of
metal and had been protected by the cloth of her dress, it was
very well preserved and even the delicate edges of the ribbon
were sharply distinct. Why the owner had not put it on one
could not say; perhaps she was late for the ceremony and had
not time to dress properly, but her haste has in any case
afforded us the only example of a silver hair ribbon which we
are likely ever to find.

Another thing that perishes utterly in the earth is cloth, but
occasionally on lifting a stone bowl which has lain inverted over
a bit of stuff and has protected it from the soil, one sees traces
which, although only of fine dust, keep the texture of the material, or a copper vessel may by its corrosion preserve some fragment which was in contact with it. By such evidence we were
able to prove that the women in the death pit wore garments of
bright red woollen stuff; and as many of them had at the wrists
one or two cuffs made of beads which had been sewn onto cloth,
it was tolerably certain that these were sleeved coats rather than
cloaks. It must have been a very gaily dressed crowd that assembled in the open mat-lined pit for the royal obsequies, a blaze of
colour with the crimson coats, the silver, and the gold; clearly
these people were not wretched slaves killed as oxen might be
killed, but persons held in honour, wearing their robes of office,
and coming, one hopes, voluntarily to a rite which would in
their belief be but a passing from one world to another, from
the service of a god on earth to that of the same god in another
sphere.

This much I think we can safely assume. Human sacrifice was
confined exclusively to the funerals of royal persons, and in the
graves of commoners, however rich, there is no sign of anything
of the sort, not even such substitutes, clay figurines, etc., as are
so common in Egyptian tombs and appear there to be a reminis-
cence of an ancient and more bloody rite. In much later times
Sumerian kings were deified in their lifetime and honoured as
gods after their death: the prehistoric kings of Ur were in their
obsequies so distinguished from their subjects because they too
were looked upon as superhuman, earthly deities; and when the

chroniclers wrote in the annals of Sumer that "after the Flood kingship again descended from the gods," they meant no less than this. If the king, then, was a god, he did not die as men die, but was translated; and it might therefore be not a hardship but a privilege for those of his court to accompany their master and continue in his service.

The excavator deciphers the past by his careful surgery of the ground. Sometimes he meets inscriptions like the Linear B tablets of Greece and Crete, which could give him an answer to his work but which for a long time no one is able to read. The story of the decipherment of scripts that at first could not be read is an exciting part of the history of the growth of archaeology. We include here two stories of decipherment, the first that of Egyptian hieroglyphics and the second that of Mesopotamian cuneiform. The Rosetta Stone, that famous slab of black basalt which now stands at the south end of the Egyptian Sculpture Gallery in the British Museum, was found in July 1799, near the mouth of the arm of the Nile that flows through the western delta to the sea not far from the town of Rashid (or Rosetta in its Europeanized form). The finder, a French officer named Bouchard, noticed that it bore inscriptions in three different scripts and percipiently and rightly supposed that here were three versions of the same text. The last of the inscriptions was in Greek, which could of course be read, and it was immediately realized that this stone might be of the greatest importance for the decipherment of the hieroglyphics in which the first inscription was written. It had been intended that the stone and many another Egyptian antiquity should be sent to Paris and placed in the Louvre, but the fortunes of war decided otherwise. The following account by Major General Sir Tomkyns H. Turner (1766–1843) describes how the Rosetta Stone came to the British Museum. It is a letter sent by him to the secretary of the Society of Antiquaries of London, and published in *Archaeologia*, XVI, 1812, p. 212.

Argyle Street, May 30, 1810

Sir,

The Rosetta Stone having excited much attention in the learned world, and in this Society in particular, I request to offer them, through you, some account of the manner it came into the possession of the British army, and by what means it was brought to this country, presuming it may not be unacceptable to them.

By the sixteenth article of the capitulation of Alexandria, the siege of which city terminated the labours of the British army in Egypt, all the curiosities, natural and artificial, collected by the French Institute and others, were to be delivered up to the captors. This was refused on the part of the French General to be fulfilled, by saying they were all private property. Many letters passed; at length on consideration that the care in preserving the insects and animals had made the property in some degree private, it was relinquished by Lord Hutchinson; but the artificial, which consisted of antiquities and Arabian manuscripts, among the former of which was the Rosetta Stone, was insisted upon by the noble General with his usual zeal for science. Upon which I had several conferences with the French General Menou, who at length gave way, saying that the Rosetta Stone was his private property, but, as he was forced, he must comply as well as the other proprietors. I accordingly received from the under secretary of the Institute, Le Père, the secretary Fourier being ill, a paper, containing a list of the antiquities, with the names of the claimants of each piece of sculpture: the stone is there described of black granite, with three inscriptions, belonging to General Menou. From the French sçavans I learnt that the Rosetta Stone was found among the ruins of Fort Saint-Julien, when repaired by the French and put in a state of defence: it stands near the mouth of the Nile, on the Rosetta branch, where are, in all probability, the pieces broken off. I was also informed that there was a stone similar at Menouf, obliterated, or nearly so, by the earthen jugs being placed on it, as it stood near the water; and that there was a fragment of one, used and placed in the walls of the French fortifications of Alexandria. The Stone was carefully brought to General Menou's house in Alexandria, covered with soft cotton cloth, and a double matting, where I first saw it. The General had selected this precious relick of antiquity for himself. When it was understood by the French army that we were to possess the antiquities, the covering of the stone was torn off, and it was thrown upon its face, and the excellent wooden cases of the rest were broken off; for they had taken infinite pains, in the first instance, to secure and preserve from any injury all the antiquities. I made several remonstrances, but the chief difficulty I had was on account of this stone, and the great sarcophagus, which at one time was positively refused to be given up by the Capitan Pasha, who had obtained it by having possession of the ship it had been put on board of by the French. I procured, however, a sentry on the beach from M. Le Roy, prefect maritime, who, as well as the General, behaved with great civility; the reverse I experienced from some others.

When I mentioned the manner the stone had been treated to Lord Hutchinson, he gave me a detachment of artillerymen and an artillery engine, called, from its powers, a devil cart, with which that evening I went to General Menou's house, and carried off the stone, without any injury, but with some difficulty, from the narrow streets, to my house, amid the sarcasms of numbers of French officers and men; being ably assisted by an intelligent sergeant of artillery, who commanded the party, all of whom enjoyed great satisfaction in their employment: they were the first British soldiers who entered Alexandria. During the time the stone remained at my house, some gentlemen attached to the corps of sçavans requested to have a cast, which I readily granted, provided the Stone should receive no injury; which cast they took to Paris, leaving the Stone well cleared from the printing ink, which it had been covered with to take off several copies to send to France when it was first discovered.

Having seen the other remains of ancient Egyptian sculpture sent on board the Admiral, Sir Richard Bickerton's, ship, the *Madras,* who kindly gave every possible assistance, I embarked with the Rosetta Stone, determining to share its fate, on board the Egyptienne frigate, taken in the harbour of Alexandria, and arrived at Portsmouth in February 1802. When the ship came round to Deptford, [the stone] was put in a boat and landed at the customhouse; and Lord Buckinghamshire, the then Secretary of State, acceded to my request, and permitted it to remain some time at the apartments of the Society of Antiquaries, previous to its deposit in the British Museum, where I trust it will long remain, a most valuable relick of antiquity, the feeble but only yet discovered link of the Egyptian to the known languages, a proud trophy of the arms of Britain (I could almost say *spolia opima*), not plundered from defenceless inhabitants, but honourably acquired by the fortune of war.

I have the honour to be, Sir,

Your most obedient, and most humble servant,

H. Turner, Major General

The Greek text of the Rosetta Stone was translated by the Reverend Stephen Weston and read by him to the Society of Antiquaries in London in April 1802. The Englishman Thomas Young, author of *The Undulatory Theory of Light*, was the first person to recognize that Egyptian writing consisted mainly of phonetic signs. In 1822 the list of Egyptian characters that had been drawn up by Young was corrected and greatly enlarged by the young French scholar Jean François Champollion (1790–1832), who is generally and rightly regarded as the man who deciphered the ancient Egyptian hieroglyphic writing. The first clear account of his decipherment is given in his famous letter to M. Dacier, which we print here translated by V. M. Conrad.

Letter to M. Dacier concerning the alphabet of the phonetic hieroglyphs

Sir,

It is to your generous patronage that I owe the indulgent attention which the *Académie Royale des Inscriptions et Belles-Lettres* has been pleased to accord to my work on the Egyptian scripts, in allowing me to submit to it my two reports on the *hieratic,* or priestly, script and the *demotic,* or popular one; after this flattering trial, I may at last venture to hope that I have successfully shown that these two types of writing are neither of them composed of alphabetic letters, as had been so widely supposed, but consist of *ideograms,* like the hieroglyphs themselves, that is, expressing the *concepts* rather than the *sounds* of a language; and to believe that after ten years of dedicated study I have reached that point where I can put together an almost complete survey of the general structure of these two forms of writing, the origin, nature, form, and number of their signs, the rules for their combination by means of those symbols which fulfil purely logical and grammatical functions, thus laying the first foundations for what might be termed the *grammar* and *dictionary* of these two scripts, which are found on the majority of monuments, and the interpretation of which will throw so much light on the general history of Egypt. With regard to the *demotic* script in particular, there is enough of the precious Rosetta inscription to identify the whole; scholastic criticism is indebted first to the talents of your illustrious colleague, M. Silvestre de Sacy, and successively to the late M. Akerblad and Dr. Young, for the first accurate ideas drawn from this monument, and it is from this same inscription that I have deduced the series of demotic symbols which, taking on syllabic-alphabetic values, were used in *ideographic* texts to express the proper names of persons from outside Egypt. It is by this means also that the name of the Ptolemies was discovered, both in this same inscription and in a papyrus manuscript recently brought from Egypt.

Accordingly, it only remains, in completing my study of the three types of Egyptian writing, for me to produce my account of the pure *hieroglyphs*. I dare to hope that my latest efforts will also have a favourable reception from your famous society, whose good will has been so valuable in encouragement to me.

However, in the present condition of Egyptian studies, when relics abound on every side, collected by kings as much as by connoisseurs, and when, too, with regard to these relics, the world's scholars eagerly devote themselves to laborious researches and strive for an intimate understanding of those written memorials which must serve to explain the rest, I do not think I should delay in offering to these scholars, under your honoured auspices, a short but vital list of new discoveries, which belong properly to my account on the *hieroglyphic* script, and which will undoubtedly spare them the pains I took in establishing them, and perhaps also some grave misconceptions about the various periods of the history of Egyptian culture and government in general: for we are dealing with the series of *hiero-*

glyphs which, making an exception to the general nature of the signs of this script, were given the property of expressing word *sounds,* and served for the inscription on Egyptian national monuments of the *titles, names* and *surnames of the Greek or Roman rulers* who successively governed the country. Many truths concerning the history of this famous country must spring from this new result of my researches to which I was led quite naturally.

The interpretation of the *demotic* text on the Rosetta inscription, by means of the accompanying Greek text, had made me realize that the Egyptians used a certain number of *demotic* characters, which assumed the property of expressing sounds, to introduce into their ideographic writings *proper names* and *words foreign to the Egyptian language.* We see at once the indispensable need for such a practice in an ideographic system of writing. The Chinese, who also use an ideographic script, have an exactly similar provision, created for the same reason.

The Rosetta monument shows us the application of this auxiliary method of writing, which I have termed *phonetic,* that is, expressing the sounds, in the proper names of the kings *Alexander* and *Ptolemy,* the queens *Arsinoe* and *Berenice,* in the proper names of six other persons, *Aetes, Pyrrha, Philinus, Areia, Diogenes* and *Irene,* and in the Greek words ΣΥΝΤΑΞΙΣ and ΟΥΗΝΝ . . .

The hieroglyphic text of the Rosetta inscription, which would have lent itself so felicitously to this study, owing to its cracks, yielded only the name *Ptolemy.*

The obelisk found on the island of Philae and recently brought to London also contains the hieroglyphic name of a Ptolemy, written in the same symbols as on the Rosetta inscription and similarly enclosed in a cartouche, and this is followed by a second cartouche, which must contain the proper name of a woman, a Ptolemaic queen, since this cartouche ends with the feminine hieroglyphic signs which also follow the hieroglyphic proper names of every Egyptian goddess without exception. The obelisk was, as it were, tied to a pedestal bearing a Greek inscription which is a supplication from the priests of Isis at Philae to the king, Ptolemy, his sister Cleopatra and his wife

Cleopatra. If this obelisk and its hieroglyphic inscription resulted from the plea of the priests, who actually mention the consecration of a similar monument, the cartouche with the female name could only be that of a Cleopatra. This name, and that of Ptolemy, which have certain like letters in Greek, had to serve for a comparative study of the hieroglyphic symbols which composed the two; and if identical signs in these two names stood for *the same sounds* in both cartouches, they would have to be *entirely phonetic* in character.

A preliminary comparison had also made me realize that these same two names, written phonetically in the demotic script, contained a number of identical characters. The resemblance between the three Egyptian scripts in their general principles caused me to look for the same phenomenon and the same correspondences when the same names were given in *hieroglyphs:* this was soon confirmed by simple comparison of the hieroglyphic cartouche containing the name Ptolemy and that on the Philae obelisk which I believed, according to the Greek text, must contain the name Cleopatra.

The first sign in the name *Cleopatra,* which resembles a kind of *quadrant,* and which would represent the K, should have been absent from the name Ptolemy. It was.

The second sign, a *lion couchant,* which would give the Λ, is exactly similar to the fourth sign in the name Ptolemy, also a Λ (Πτολ).

The third sign in the name Cleopatra is a *feather* or *leaf,* standing for the short vowel E; we also see two similar leaves at the end of the name Ptolemy, which, from their position, can only have the value of the diphthong AI in ΑΙΟΣ.

The fourth character in the cartouche for the hieroglyphic Cleopatra, the representation of a kind of *flower with a bent stem,* would stand for the O in the Greek name of this queen. It is in fact the third character in the name Ptolemy (Πτο).

The fifth sign in the name Cleopatra, which appears as a *parallelogram* and must represent the Π, is equally the first sign in the hieroglyphic name Ptolemy.

The sixth sign, standing for the vowel A of ΚΛΕΟΠΑΤΡΑ, is a *hawk,* and does not occur in the name Ptolemy, nor should it.

The seventh character is an *open hand,* representing the T; but this hand does not occur in the word Ptolemy, where the second letter, the T, is expressed by a *segment of a circle,* which, none the less, is also a T; for we shall see below why these two hieroglyphs have the same sound.

The eighth sign of ΚΛΕΟΠΑΤΡΑ, which is a frontal *mouth,* and which would be the P, does not occur in the cartouche of Ptolemy, nor should it.

Finally, the ninth and last sign in the queen's name, which must be the vowel A, is in fact the *hawk* which we have already seen representing this vowel in the third syllable of the same name. This proper name ends in the two hieroglyphic symbols for the feminine gender: that of Ptolemy ends in another sign, which consists of a bent shaft, equivalent to the Greek . . . as we shall see below.

The combined signs from the two cartouches, analyzed phonetically, thus already yielded us twelve signs, corresponding to eleven consonants, vowels, or diphthongs in the Greek alphabet, A, AI, E, K, Λ, M, O, Π, P, Σ, T.

The phonetic value of these twelve signs, already very probable, becomes indisputable if, applying these values to other cartouches or small enclosed panels containing proper names and taken from Egyptian hieroglyphic monuments, we are enabled to read them effortlessly and systematically, producing the proper names of rulers foreign to the Egyptian language. . . .

You, sir, will doubtless share all my astonishment when the same alphabet of phonetic hieroglyphs, applied to a host of other cartouches carved on the same piece of work, will give you titles, names, and even surnames of Roman emperors, spoken in *Greek* and written with these same phonetic hieroglyphs.

We read here, in fact:

The imperial title Αυτοκρατωρ, occupying a whole cartouche to itself, or else followed by other *still persisting* ideographic titles, transcribed ΑΟΤΟΚΡΤΡ, ΑΟΤΚΡΤΟΡ, ΑΟΤΑΚΡΤΡ, and even ΑΥΤΟΚΑΤΛ, the Λ being used as a bastard substitute (pardon the expression) for the P.

The cartouches containing this title are almost always next to, or connected with, a second cartouche containing as we shall shortly see, the *proper names* of emperors. But occasionally we also find this word in absolutely isolated cartouches. . . .

But it remains, sir, for us to survey briefly the nature of the phonetic system governing the writing of these names, to form an accurate estimate of the character of the signs used, and to investigate the reasons for adopting the image of one or another object to represent a particular consonant or vowel more than another. . . .

I am in no doubt, sir, that if we could definitely determine the object represented or expressed by all the other phonetic hiero-glyphs comprised in our alphabet, it could be a relatively easy matter for me to show, in the Egyptian-Coptic lexicons, that the names of these same objects begin with the consonant or vowels which their image represents in the phonetic hieroglyph system.

This method, followed in the composition of the Egyptian phonetic alphabet, gives us an idea to what point we could, if we wished, continue multiplying the number of phonetic hieroglyphs without sacrificing the clarity of their expression. But everything seems to indicate that our alphabet, by and large, contains them. We are, in fact, justified in drawing this conclusion, since this alphabet is the result of a series of phonetic proper names carved on Egyptian monuments during a period of about *five centuries* in various parts of the country.

It is easy to see that the vowels of the hieroglyphic alphabet are used indiscriminately one for another. On this point we can do no more than establish the following general rules:

1. The hawk, the ibis, and three other kinds of birds are consistently used for A;

2. The leaf or feather can stand for both the short vowels A and E, sometimes even O.

3. The twin leaves or feathers can equally well represent the vowels I and H, or the dipthongs IA and AI.

All I have just said on the origin, formation, and anomalies of the *phonetic hieroglyph* alphabet applies almost entirely to the *demotic phonetic* alphabet. . . .

These two systems of phonetic writing were as intimately connected as the *hieratic ideographic* system was with the *popular ideographic,* which was no more than its descendant, and the *pure hieroglyphs,* which were its source. The demotic letters are generally, in fact, as I have said, the same as the *hieratic* signs for hieroglyphs which are themselves phonetic. You, sir, will have no difficulty in recognizing the truth of this assertion, if you trouble to consult the comparative table of hieratic signs classified beside the corresponding hieroglyph, the table which I presented before the *Académie des Belles-Lettres* more than a year ago. So there is basically no other difference between the *hieroglyphic* and *demotic* alphabets but the actual form of the signs, their values and even the reasons for those values being identical. Finally I would add that since these popular phonetic symbols were merely unchanged hieratic characters, there cannot, of necessity, have been more than *two* phonetic writing systems in Egypt:

1. the *phonetic hieroglyph* script, used on public monuments;
2. the *hieratic-demotic* script, used for Greek proper names in the middle text of the Rosetta inscription and the demotic papyrus in the royal library . . . and which we shall perhaps see one day used to transcribe the name of some Greek or Roman ruler in the rolls of papyrus written in the hieratic script.

Phonetic writing, then, was in use among every class of the Egyptian nation, and they employed it for a long time as a necessary adjunct to the three ideographic methods. When, as a result of their conversion to Christianity, the Egyptian people received the alphabetic Greek script from the apostles, and then had to write all the words of their maternal tongue with this new alphabet, adoption of which cut them off forever from the religion, history, and institutions of their ancestors, all monuments being, by this act, "silenced" for these neophytes and their descendants, yet these Egyptians still retained some trace of their ancient phonetic method; and we see in fact that in the oldest Coptic texts in the Theban dialect, most of the short vowels are completely omitted, and that often, like the hieroglyphic names of Roman emperors, they consist of no more than strings of consonants interspersed at long intervals by a few vowels, almost always long. This resemblance seemed to me worth noting. The Greek and Latin writers have left us no formal remarks on the Egyptian phonetic script; it is very difficult to deduce even the existence of this system, forcing the sense of certain passages where something of the kind would seem to be vaguely hinted at. So we must abandon the attempt to study through historical tradition the period when the phonetic scripts were introduced into the ancient Egyptian picture-writing.

But the facts speak well enough for themselves to enable us to say with fair certainty that the employment of an auxiliary script in Egypt to represent the sounds and articulations of certain words preceded Greek and Roman domination, although it seems most natural to attribute the introduction of the semi-alphabetic Egyptian script to the influence of these two European nations, which had long been using a true alphabet.

Here I base my opinion on the two following considerations, which, sir, may seem to you a solid enough weight to tip the scales.

1. If the Egyptians had invented their phonetic script in imitation of the Greek or Roman alphabet, they would naturally have established a number of phonetic signs equal to the known elements of the Greek or Latin alphabet. But there is nothing of the kind; and the incontestable proof that the Egyptian phonetic writing arose for a totally different purpose from that of expressing the sounds of proper names of Greek or Roman rulers is found in the Egyptian transcription of these very names, which are mostly corrupted to the point of being unrecognizable; firstly by the suppression or confusion of most of the vowels, secondly by the persistent use of the consonants T for Δ, K for T, Π for I; and lastly by the accidental use of Λ for P and P for Λ.

2. I am positive that the same signs in *phonetic hieroglyphs* used to represent the sounds of Greek and Roman proper names were also used in ideographic texts carved long before the Greeks reached Egypt, and that they already had, in certain contexts, the same value representing sounds or articulations as in the cartouches carved under the Greeks and Romans. The development of this valuable and decisive point is connected with my work on the pure hieroglyphs. I could not set out the proof in this letter without plunging into extraordinarily prolonged complications.

Thus, sir, I believe that *phonetic* writing existed in Egypt at a far distant time; that it was first a necessary part of the ideographic script; and that it was then used also, after Cambyses, as we have it, to transcribe (crudely, it is true) in ideographic texts the proper names of peoples, countries, cities, rulers, and individual foreigners who had to be commemorated in historic texts or monumental inscriptions.

I dare say more: it would be possible to recover, in this ancient Egyptian phonetic script, imperfect though it may be in itself, if not the source, at least the model on which the alphabets of the western Asiatic nations were framed, above all those of Egypt's immediate neighbours. If you note in fact, sir:

1. that each letter of the alphabets which we term Hebrew, Chaldean, and Syriac bears a distinguishing name, very ancient appellations, since they were almost all transmitted by the Phoenicians to the Greeks when the latter took over the alphabet;

2. that the *first consonant or vowel of these names* is also, in these alphabets, the *vowel or consonant to be read,* you will see, with me, in the creation of these alphabets, a perfect analogy with the creation of the phonetic alphabet in Egypt: and if alphabets of this type are, as everything indicates, primitively formed from signs representing ideas or objects, it is evident that we must recognize the nation who invented this method of written expression in those who particularly used an ideographic script; I mean, in sum, that Europe, which received from ancient Egypt the elements of the arts and sciences, is yet further in her debt for the inestimable benefit of alphabetic writing.

However, I have only tried here to indicate briefly the many important consequences of this discovery, and it arose naturally from my main subject, the *alphabet of the phonetic hieroglyphs,* the general structure of which, together with some applications, I proposed to expound at the same time. The latter produced results which have already met with a favourable response from the illustrious members of the *Académie,* whose scholastic studies have given Europe the first principles of solid learning, and continue to offer her the most valuable of examples. My attempts may perhaps add something to the record of definite achievements by which they have enriched the history of ancient peoples; that of the Egyptians, whose just fame still echoes round the world; and it is certainly no little achievement today that we can take with assurance the first step in the study of their written memorials, and thence gather some precise notion of their leading institutions, to which antiquity itself gave a name for wisdom which nothing has yet overthrown. As for the remarkable monuments erected by the Egyptians, we can at last read, in the cartouches which adorn them, their fixed chronology from Cambyses and the times of their foundation or their successive accretions under the various dynasties which ruled Egypt; the majority of these monuments bear simultaneously the names of pharaohs and of Greeks and Romans, the former, characterized by their small numbers of signs, perpetually resisting every attempt to apply to them successfully the *alphabet* I have just discovered. Such, sir, I hope, will be the value of this work, which I am flattered to produce under your honoured auspices; the enlightened public will not refuse me its admiration or its support, since I have obtained those of the venerable Nestor of scholarship and French literature, whose devoted studies honour and adorn them, and who, with a hand at once protective and encouraging, is ever pleased to support and guide, in the hard course which he has so gloriously covered, so many young imitators who have later wholly justified his enthusiastic patronage. Happy to rejoice in my turn, I would not, however, venture to make a reply but for my deep gratitude, and my respectful affection; permit me, I beg you, sir, to repeat publicly all my assurances of that affection.

J. F. Champollion the younger
Paris, 22 September, 1822.

The decipherment of Mesopotamian writing was in its way as important as the decipherment of the Rosetta Stone. Although work had been done before by Karsten Niebuhr and Georg Grotefend, it was the work of Sir Henry Creswicke Rawlinson (1810–95) that brought decipherment to a successful conclusion. The giant Behistun inscription, "a Mesopotamian Rosetta Stone," as it has been described, was carved in 516 B.C. on the orders of Darius the First. It was high up on a cliff on the road from Babylon to

Ecbatana, and measured 150 feet by 100 feet. This account tells in Rawlinson's own words how he obtained squeezes of the inscriptions with the assistance of "a wild Kurdish boy, who had come from a distance"—one of the minor heroes of the growth of archaeology. It comes from his "Notes on some Paper Casts of Cuneiform Inscriptions upon the sculptured Rock at Behistun exhibited to the Society of Antiquaries," published in *Archaeologia,* XXXIV (1852).

The rock, or, as it is usually called by the Arab geographers, the mountain of Behistun, is not an isolated hill, as has been sometimes imagined. It is merely the terminal point of a long, narrow range which bounds the plain of Kermanshah to the eastward. This range is rocky and abrupt throughout, but at the extremity it rises in height, and becomes a sheer precipice. The altitude I found by careful triangulation to be 3,087 feet, and the height above the plain at which occur the tablets of Darius is perhaps 500 feet, or something more.

Notwithstanding that a French antiquarian commission in Persia described it a few years back to be impossible to copy the Behistun inscriptions, I certainly do not consider it any great feat in climbing to ascend to the spot where the inscriptions occur. When I was living at Kermanshah fifteen years ago, and was somewhat more active than I am at present, I used frequently to scale the rock three or four times a day without the aid of a rope or a ladder; without any assistance, in fact, whatever. During my late visits I have found it more convenient to ascend and descend by the help of ropes where the track lies up a precipitate cleft, and to throw a plank over those chasms where a false step in leaping across would probably be fatal. On reaching the recess which contains the Persian text of the record, ladders are indispensable in order to examine the upper portion of the tablet; and even with ladders there is considerable risk, for the foot ledge is so narrow, about eighteen inches or at most two feet in breadth, that with a ladder long enough to reach the sculptures sufficient slope cannot be given to enable a person to ascend, and, if the ladder be shortened in order to increase the slope, the upper inscription can only be copied by standing on the topmost step of the ladder, with no other support than steadying the body against the rock with the left arm, while the left hand holds the notebook, and the right hand is employed with the pencil. In this position I copied all the upper inscriptions, and the interest of the occupation entirely did away with any sense of danger.

To reach the recess which contains the Scythic translation of the record of Darius is a matter of far greater difficulty. On the left-hand side of the recess alone is there any foot ledge whatever; on the right-hand, where the recess, which is thrown a few feet farther back, joins the Persian tablet, the face of the rock presents a sheer precipice, and it is necessary therefore to bridge this intervening space between the left-hand of the Persian tablet and the foot ledge on the left-hand of the recess. With ladders of sufficient length, a bridge of this sort can be constructed without difficulty; but my first attempt to cross the chasm was unfortunate, and might have been fatal, for, having previously shortened my only ladder in order to obtain a slope for copying the Persian upper legends, I found, when I came to lay it across to the recess in order to get at the Scythic translation, that it was not sufficiently long to lie flat on the foot ledge beyond. One side of the ladder would alone reach the nearest point of the ledge, and, as it would of course have tilted over if a person had attempted to cross in that position, I changed it from a horizontal to a vertical direction, the upper side resting firmly on the rock at its two ends, and the lower hanging over the precipice, and I prepared to cross, walking on the lower side, and holding to the upper side with my hands. If the ladder had been a compact article, this mode of crossing, although far from comfortable, would have been at any rate practicable; but the Persians merely fit in the bars of their ladders without pretending to clench them outside, and I had hardly accordingly begun to cross over when the vertical pressure forced the bars out of their sockets, and the lower and unsupported side of the ladder thus parted company from the upper, and went crashing down over the precipice. Hanging on to the upper side, which still remained firm in its place, and assisted by my friends, who were anxiously watching the trial, I regained the Persian recess, and did not again attempt to cross until I had made a bridge of comparative stability. Ultimately I took the casts of the Scythic writing . . . by laying one long ladder, in the first instance, horizontally across the chasm, and by then placing another ladder, which rested on the bridge, perpendicularly against the rock.

The Babylonian transcript at Behistun is still more difficult to reach than either the Scythic or the Persian tablets. The writing can be copied by the aid of a good telescope from below, but I long despaired of obtaining a cast of the inscription; for I found it quite beyond my powers of climbing to reach the spot where it was engraved, and the craigsmen of the place, who were accustomed to track the mountain goats over the entire face of the mountain, declared the particular block inscribed with the Babylonian legend to be unapproachable.

At length, however, a wild Kurdish boy, who had come from a distance, volunteered to make the attempt, and I promised him a considerable reward if he succeeded. The mass of rock in question is scarped, and it projects some feet over the Scythic recess, so that it cannot be approached by any of the ordinary means of climbing. The boy's first move was to squeeze himself up a cleft in the rock a short distance to the left of the projecting mass. When he had ascended some distance above it, he drove a wooden peg firmly into the cleft, fastened a rope to this, and then endeavoured to swing himself across to another cleft at some distance on the other side; but in this he failed, owing to the projection of the rock. It then only remained for him to cross over to the cleft by hanging on with his toes and fingers to the slight inequalities on the bare face of the precipice, and in this he succeeded, passing over a distance of twenty feet of almost smooth perpendicular rock in a manner which to a looker-on appeared quite miraculous. When he had reached the second cleft the real difficulties were over. He had brought a rope with him attached to the first peg, and now, driving in a second, he was enabled to swing himself right over the projecting mass of rock. Here, with a short ladder, he formed a swinging seat, like a painter's cradle, and, fixed upon this seat, he took under my direction the paper cast of the Babylonian translation of the records of Darius which is now at the Royal Asiatic Society's rooms, and which is almost of equal value for the interpretation of the Assyrian inscriptions as was the Greek translation on the Rosetta Stone for the intelligence of the hieroglyphic texts of Egypt. I must add, too, that it is of the more importance that this invaluable Babylonian key should have been thus recovered, as the mass of rock on which the inscription is engraved bore every appearance, when I last visited this spot, of being doomed to a speedy destruction, water trickling from above having almost separated the overhanging mass from the rest of the rock, and its own enormous weight thus threatening very shortly to bring it thundering down into the plain, dashed into a thousand fragments. [It is still there, 1967: G.D.]

The method of forming these paper casts is exceedingly simple, nothing more being required than to take a number of sheets of paper without size, spread them on the rock, moisten them, and then beat them into the crevices with a stout brush, adding as many layers of paper as it may be wished to give consistency to the cast. The paper is left there to dry, and on being taken off it exhibits a perfect reversed impression of the writing.

7   *Excavation*

Excavation is of course not the be all and end all of archaeology, but without excavation there could be no systematic development of the subject; so that the development of a systematic discipline of excavation is, in one way, the story of the development of the systematic discipline of archaeology. There were of course excavations long before the nineteenth century, and we have referred to the long-sighted observations of stratigraphy and association made by a seventeenth-century antiquary like Edward Lhwyd or a late-eighteenth-century antiquary like John Frere. We have also quoted from the clear and definite instructions on field archaeology in general set out by Worsaae. In this chapter we shall look at some extracts which show what excavation meant to some people between the middle of the nineteenth century and the middle of the twentieth century—that hundred years during which, slowly and with great difficulty, the modern techniques of excavation were developed. Let us begin with an account of an excavation in 1844. It is from an article by Thomas Wright entitled "Wanderings of an Antiquary: Part VII" and was originally published in *The Gentleman's Magazine* for 1852.

> It was in the latter part of the August of 1844 that I accompanied Lord Albert Conyngham (now Lord Londesborough) on a visit to the Friars at Aylesford, for the purpose of opening a large Roman barrow or sepulchral mound in the adjoining

parish of Snodland . . . the hill is named Hoborough, or Hol-
borough. . . .

Our party at the "digging" consisted of our kind and hospi-
table host and hostess, Mr. and Mrs. Charles Whatman of the
Friars, Lord Albert Conyngham, the Rev. Lambert B. Larking
of Ryarsh, and two or three other ladies and gentlemen from
the neighbourhood. As the barrow was of large dimensions, we
had engaged some twelve or fourteen labourers, and, having determined to cut a trench of about six feet wide through the centre of the barrow from east to west, we commenced both ends
of the trench at the same time, and divided the men between the
two excavations. A rough sketch which I took on the spot, when
the excavation was tolerably advanced on the east side, will give
the reader a tolerable idea of the method on which we went to
work. It was the labour of four long days to cut entirely through
the barrow, but we who were not absolutely diggers contrived to
pass our time to the full satisfaction of all the party. We had
hired one of the boats which are used in this part of the country
for carrying the amateur toxophilists along the Medway to their
archery meetings, and each morning, after an early breakfast,
we were rowed several miles down the river, which is here picturesque and singularly tortuous, to the place of landing. A
plentiful supply of provisions had been procured for picnicking
on the hill, and we remained by the barrow all day, watching
and directing the operations. Unfortunately it was one of those
large barrows which do not repay the labour of cutting through
them; and, although the final result was interesting in itself, we
all felt somewhat of a disappointment as our men laboured hour
after hour, and no sepulchral chamber presented itself, and not
even a burial urn could be found to reward our patience. Two
or three small fragments of broken pottery were all the articles
which occurred in the body of the mound until we came to the
floor on which it had been raised.

We contrived to pass our time, at intervals between digging
and picnicking, in games of various descriptions—not exactly
such as those which the builders of the mound celebrated when
they laid the deceased on his funeral pile—and in other amuse-
ments. The season was fortunately exquisitely fine, and it was

only once or twice that we were visited with a heavy shower
from the southwest, when the only shelter near was afforded by
the hole we had ourselves dug on the western side of the mound,
in which we managed so to interlace parasols and umbrellas—
much as the Roman soldiers are said to have joined together their
shields when advancing to the attack of a fortress—as to form
a tolerably impenetrable roof over our heads . . . [Plate 40].

We had uncovered the floor on which the mound was raised
through the whole extent of the trench, and our observations
held out no promise of any further discoveries if we cut into the
mound in other directions. We had therefore determined to proceed no further, when an unexpected accident put a stop to our
labours. The mound was twenty feet high, made of fine mould,
and the workmen had imprudently cut the walls of the trench
perpendicular; the consequence of which was that in the afternoon of the fourth day the upper part of one side fell in, and one
of the labourers escaped narrowly with his life.

. . . it appeared that the barrow had been raised over the
ashes of a funeral pile. A horizontal platform had first been cut
in the chalk of the hill, and on this a very smooth artificial floor
of fine earth, about four inches deep, had been made, on which
the pile had been raised, and which we found covered with a
thin coating of wood ashes. . . . In the floor of ashes were
found scattered a considerable number of very long nails (which
had probably been used to fasten together the framework on
which the body was placed for cremation) with a few pieces of
broken pottery which had evidently experienced the action of
fire. A part of a Roman fibula was also found. My impression is
that this mound was the monument of some person of rank,
whose body, like that of the Emperor Severus, was burnt on the
funeral pile, and his ashes carried home perhaps to Italy. The
barrow was raised on the site of the pile, as a sort of cenotaph
to his memory.

In 1844 the British Archaeological Association was founded; it
was a breakaway from the tradition of a society like the Society of
Antiquaries of London which had all its meetings in London. The
association intended to meet in the country, to visit monuments,

museums, and private collections, and to excavate or at least visit excavations. Its first meeting was held in Canterbury under the presidency of Lord Albert Conyngham, mentioned in the previous excerpt. The following passages from the report of the meeting published in the first volume of *The Archaeological Journal* (1845) show what went on at these meetings, and what was then involved in excavation. The previous digging took four days; here we seem to have many barrows opened in an afternoon.

MONDAY, SEPT. 9

The proceedings of the general meeting were opened at half past three o'clock by an address from the President upon the objects of the Association, and the benefits it was calculated to realize. His lordship remarked that a disposition to cultivate intellectual pursuits was making rapid progress in this country, as well as on the continent, and this growing feeling was especially manifested with regard to archaeology. Most men of cultivated minds were now beginning to take an interest in examining and pondering over the remains of past ages. They were no longer satisfied with taking for truth the baseless vagaries of the human mind; they wished to judge for themselves, and to form theories that would spring from a study of facts, well scrutinized and established by the test of personal examination and severe criticism. Archaeology, thus placed on a sound footing, would go hand in hand with history. The antiquary was no longer an object of ridicule. . . .

Mr. C. Roach Smith, the Secretary, then read the list of papers which were to be brought before the meeting. . . . It having been suggested that owing to a large accumulation of papers it would be desirable at once to bring forward some portion of them, Sir William Betham read from an elaborate paper on the origin of idolatry. . . .

The meeting then adjourned to Barnes's rooms, where a conversazione was held. The tables were covered with an interesting variety of antiquities. . . . Lord Albert Conyngham exhibited some ancient gold ornaments found in Ireland, and a variety of amethystine beads, fibulae, and other objects, chiefly from barrows on Breach Downs opened by his lordship. . . .

Between nine and ten o'clock the members assembled on the Breach Downs to be present at the opening of some barrows, under the superintendance of the noble President. The workmen employed had previously excavated the barrows to within a foot of the place of the presumed deposit. Eight barrows were examined. . . . They are generally of slight elevation above the natural chalky soil, the graves, over which the mounds are heaped, being from two to four feet deep. Most of them contain skeletons, more or less entire, with the remains of weapons in iron, bosses of shields, urns, beads, fibulae, armlets, bones of small animals, and occasionally glass vessels. The graves containing weapons are assigned to males; those with beads, or other ornaments, to females. The correctness of this appropriation seems determined by the fact that these different objects are seldom found in the same grave. The deposit in one of the barrows opened this morning presented the unusual association of beads and an iron knife. All contained the remains of skeletons much decayed; in some, traces of wood were noticed, and vestiges of knives.

After the examination of these barrows, the whole party visited the mansion of the noble President, at Bourne, and having inspected his lordship's interesting collection of antiquities, and partaken of a substantial repast, attended the excavation of two barrows in his lordship's paddock, forming part of the group of which some had been recently opened. . . .

The members met in the theatre at eight o'clock, where Mr. Pettigrew first read an essay on the different kinds of embalmments among the Egyptians, and then proceeded to unroll the mummy which had been obtained from Thebes by Colonel Needham. . . . It measured five feet two inches, and was invested with a considerable quantity of linen bandage, stained of the usual colour by the gum of acacia. . . . Time would not permit of the complete display of the mummy, but the head was fully developed, and the face was found to have been gilt, large portions of gold leaf, upon the removal of the bandages, presenting themselves in most vivid brightness.

Sixty years before these excavations in Kent a large mound had been excavated in Virginia and its stratigraphy and structure studied with care and interpreted analytically by no less a person than Thomas Jefferson, third President of the United States. He left behind him the following inscription intended for his own tomb:

HERE LIES BURIED

THOMAS JEFFERSON

AUTHOR OF THE DECLARATION OF
AMERICAN INDEPENDENCE, OF THE
STATUTE OF VIRGINIA FOR
RELIGIOUS FREEDOM, AND FATHER
OF THE UNIVERSITY OF VIRGINIA

But, as A. F. Chamberlain has said, "these three great achievements by no means summed up his activities. He was extremely interested in the science of his day, natural history in particular. He devoted some time to the consideration of the ethnological problems involved in the history of the Red Man and the Negro in America." [1] In 1784 he excavated a burial mound in Virginia; as the following extract shows, he did so with a purpose—to find out which of the many theories about these mounds was right.

There being one of these in my neighbourhood, I wished to satisfy myself whether any and which of these opinions were just. For this purpose I determined to open and examine it thoroughly. It was situated on the low grounds of the Rivanna, about two miles above its principal fork, and opposite to some hills, on which had been an Indian town. It was of a spheroidical form, of about forty feet diameter at the base, and had been of about twelve feet altitude. . . . I first dug superficially in several parts of it, and came to collections of human bones, at different depths, from six inches to three feet below the surface.

---

[1] Alexander F. Chamberlain, *American Anthropologist*, IX, 1907, p. 499.

. . . I proceeded then to make a perpendicular cut through the body of the barrow, that I might examine its internal structure. This passed about three feet from its centre, was opened to the former surface of the earth, and was wide enough for a man to walk through and examine its sides. At the bottom, that is, on the level of the circumjacent plain, I found bones; above these a few stones, brought from a cliff a quarter of a mile off, and from the river one eighth of a mile off; then a large interval of earth, then a stratum of bones, and so on. At one end of the section were four strata of bones plainly distinguishable; at the other, three; the strata in one part not ranging with those in another. The bones nearest the surface were least decayed. No holes were discovered in any of them as if made with bullets, arrows, or other weapons. I conjectured that in this barrow might have been a thousand skeletons. Everyone will readily seize the circumstances above related, which militate against the opinion that it covered the bones only of persons fallen in battle; and against the tradition, also, which would make it the common sepulchre of a town, in which the bodies were placed upright, and touching each other. Appearances certainly indicate that it has derived both origin and growth from the customary collection of bones, and deposition of them together; that the first collection had been deposited on the common surface of the earth, a few stones put over it, and then a covering of earth, that the second had been laid on this, had covered more or less of it in proportion to the number of bones, and was then also covered with earth; and so on. The following are the particular circumstances which give it this aspect. 1. The number of bones. 2. Their confused position. 3. Their being in different strata. 4. The strata in one part have no correspondence with those in another. 5. The difference in the time of inhumation. 6. The existence of infant bones among them.

The beginnings of excavation in the Near East were as tentative and hurried as they were in western Europe. The first ray of light came with the purposeful work of Auguste Mariette (1821–81), who was sent out to Egypt in 1850 by the Louvre to search for Coptic manuscripts. He became at once more interested in field monuments than in manuscripts and in that same year excavated the Serapeum at Memphis, the great temple of Osiris-Apis, with its cemetery of sacred Apis bulls. Here is an extract from his account of this excavation taken from his *The Monuments of Upper Egypt,* published in 1877.

The Serapeum is one of the edifices of Memphis rendered famous by a frequently quoted passage of Strabo, and by the constant mention made of it on the Greek papyri. It had long been sought for, and we had the good fortune to discover it in 1851.

Strabo, in his description of Memphis, expresses himself thus:

One finds also [at Memphis] a temple of Serapis in a spot so sandy that the wind causes the sand to accumulate in heaps, under which we could see many sphinxes, some of them almost entirely buried, others only partially covered; from which we may conjecture that the route leading to this temple might be attended with danger if one were surprised by a sudden gust of wind.

If Strabo had not written this passage, in all probability the Serapeum would to this day lie buried under the sands of the necropolis at Saḳḳárah. In 1850 I had been commissioned by the French Government to visit the Coptic convents of Egypt, and to make an inventory of such manuscripts in Oriental languages as I should find there. I noticed at Alexandria, in M. Zizinia's garden, several sphinxes. Presently I saw more of these same sphinxes at Cairo, in Clot-Bey's garden. M. Fernandez had also a certain number of such sphinxes at Geezeh. Evidently there must be somewhere an avenue of sphinxes which was being pillaged. One day, attracted to Saḳḳárah by my Egyptological studies, I perceived the head of one of these same sphinxes obtruding itself from the sand. This one had never been touched, and was certainly in its original position. Close by lay a libation table, on which was engraved in hieroglyphs an inscription to Osiris-Apis. The passage in Strabo suddenly occurred to my mind. The avenue which lay at my feet must be the one which led up to that Serapeum so long and so vainly sought for. But I had been sent to Egypt to make an inventory of manuscripts, not to seek for temples. My mind, however, was soon made up. Regardless of all risks, without saying a word, and almost furtively, I gathered together a few workmen, and the excavation began. The first attempts were hard indeed, but, before very long, lions and peacocks and the Grecian statues of the dromos, together with the monumental tablets or *stelae* of the temple of Nectanebo, were drawn out of the sand, and I was able to announce my success to the French Government, informing them, at the same time, that the funds placed at my disposal for the researches after the manuscripts were entirely exhausted, and that a further grant was indispensable. Thus was begun the discovery of the Serapeum.

The work lasted four years. The Serapeum is a temple built without any regular plan, where all was conjecture, and where the ground had to be examined closely, inch by inch. In certain places the sand is, so to speak, fluid, and presents as much difficulty in excavating as if it were water which ever seeks its own level. Besides all this, difficulties arose between the French and the Egyptian governments, which obliged me several times to discharge all my workmen. It was owing to these circumstances (to say nothing of other trials) that the work proved so long, and that I was compelled to spend four years in the desert— four years, however, I can never regret.

Apis, the living image of Osiris revisiting the earth, was a bull who, while he lived, had his temple at Memphis (Mitrahenny) and, when dead, had his tomb at Saḳḳárah. The palace which the bull inhabited in his lifetime was called the *Apieum;* the *Serapeum* was the name given to his tomb.

As far as we can judge by the remains found during our researches, the Serapeum resembled in appearance the other Egyptian temples, even those which were not funereal in their character. An avenue of sphinxes led up to it, and two pylons stood before it, and it was surrounded by the usual enclosure. But what distinguished it from all other temples was that out of one of its chambers opened an inclined passage leading directly into the rock on which the temple was built, and giving access to vast subterranean vaults which were the *Tomb of Apis.*

The Serapeum, properly so called, no longer exists, and where it stood there is now nothing to be seen but a vast plain of sand mingled with fragments of stones scattered about in indescribable confusion. But the most beautiful and interesting part of the subterranean vault can still be visited.

The Tomb of Apis consists of three distinct parts which have no direct communication with one another.

The first and most ancient part carries us back as far as the Eighteenth Dynasty and Amenophis III. It served as the burial place of the sacred bulls up to the end of the Twentieth Dynasty. Here the tombs are separate. Every dead Apis had his own sepulchral chamber hewn here and there, as it were at random, out of the rock. These chambers are now hidden under the sand, and were never possessed of any very great interest.

The second part comprises the tombs of Apis from the time of Sheshonk I (Twenty-second Dynasty) to that of Tahraka (the last king of the Twenty-fifth Dynasty). In this part a new system was adopted. Instead of isolated tombs, a long subterranean gallery was made, on each side of which mortuary chambers were excavated, to be used whenever an Apis expired at Memphis. This gallery is also inaccessible now, the roof having in some places fallen in, and the remainder not being sufficiently secure to allow of its being visited by travellers.

In approaching the entrance to the Tomb of Apis by the ordinary path, one sees to the right, i.e., towards the North, a somewhat large circular hole. Here are to be found the vaults which preceded those we are about to visit. This hole was caused by the falling in of a portion of the stonework. In blowing up the debris with gunpowder, we discovered not an Apis, but a human mummy. A gold mask covered its face, and jewels of every description were arranged on its breast. All the inscriptions were in the name of Rameses' favourite son, who was for a long time governor of Memphis. It may therefore be reasonably supposed that it was here this prince was buried.

The third part is that which is now so well known. Its history begins with Psammetichus I (Twenty-sixth Dynasty), and ends with the later Ptolemies. The same system of a common vault has been followed here as in the second part, only on a much grander scale. These galleries cover an extent of about 350 metres, or 1,150 English feet; and from one end to the other the great gallery measures 195 metres, or about 640 English feet. Moreover, granite sarcophagi have been used here. Their number throughout the whole extent of the galleries is twenty-four. Of these only three bear any inscription, and they contain the names of Amasis (Twenty-sixth Dynasty), Cambyses, and Khebasch (Twenty-seventh Dynasty). A fourth, with cartouches without any name, most probably belongs to one of the last Ptolemies. As to their dimensions, they measure on an average 7 feet 8 inches in breadth, by 13 feet in length, and 11 feet in height; so that, allowing for the vacuum, these monoliths must weigh, one with the other, not less than 65 tons each.

Such are the three parts of the Tomb of Apis.

It is well known that the exploration of this tomb has furnished science with unhoped-for results. For what the traveller now sees of it is merely its skeleton. But the fact is that, although it had been rifled by the early Christians, the tomb, when first discovered, still possessed nearly all that it had ever contained that was not gold or other precious matter. There existed a custom which had especially contributed to enrich the tomb with valuable documents. On certain days in the year, or on the occasion of the death and funeral rites of an Apis, the inhabitants of Memphis came to pay a visit to the god in his burial place. In memory of this act of piety they left a *stela*, i.e. a square-shaped stone, rounded at the top, which was let into one of the walls of the tomb, having been previously inscribed with an homage to the god in the name of his visitor and his family. Now these documents, to the number of about five hundred, were found, for the most part, in their original position . . . and as many of them were dated according to the fashion of the time, that is with the year, month, and day of the reigning king, a comparison of these inscribed tablets must necessarily prove of the greatest importance, especially in fixing chronology.

Mariette's methods of excavation have often been decried; he himself excavated over thirty sites in as many years. Admittedly he was concerned with getting good results and finding splendid things. In 1883 a man who was for a long while to be synonymous with Egyptian exploration and excavation, Sir Flinders Petrie (1853–1942), described how Mariette excavated near the Sphinx, and blasted away with dynamite the fallen ruins of a temple. "Nothing was done," said Petrie, "with any uniform plan; work is begun and left unfinished; no regard is paid to the future requirements of exploration and no civilized or labor-saving appliances are used. It is sickening to see the rate at which everything is being destroyed, and the little regard paid to preservation." Mariette had died in 1880; three years later the Egypt Exploration Fund (later the Egypt Exploration Society) was founded in London and its first field director was W. M. Flinders Petrie. In 1883 he wrote to the secretary of the fund saying, "The prospect of excavating in Egypt is a most fascinating one to me, and I hope the results may justify my undertaking such a work." They did; and in 1892 he was able to publish his *Ten Years' Digging in Egypt*. In 1904 Petrie published his *Methods and Aims in Archaeology*, from which the following extract is taken.

Archaeology is the latest born of the sciences. It has but scarcely struggled into freedom, out of the swaddling clothes of dilettante speculations. It is still attracted by pretty things, rather than by real knowledge. It has to find shelter with the Fine Arts or with History, and not a single home has yet been provided for its real growth. . . . The Science which inquires into all the products and works of our own species, which shows what man has been doing in all ages and under all conditions, which reveals his mind, his thoughts, his tastes, his feelings—such a science touches us more closely than any other.

By this science, of which History forms a part, we trace the nature of man, age after age—his capacities, his abilities; we learn where he succeeds, where he fails, and what his possibilities may be . . . it gives a more truly "liberal education" than any other subject, as at present taught. A complete archaeological training would require a full knowledge of history and art, a fair use of languages, and a working familiarity with many sciences. Archaeology—the knowledge of how man has acquired his present position and powers—is one of the widest studies, best fitted to open the mind and to produce that type of wide interests and toleration which is the highest result of education . . .

We have nothing here to do with the details of the facts discovered; but deal only with the methods and aims, which have been slowly learned in a quarter of a century. . . .

In few kinds of work are the results so directly dependent on the personality of the worker as they are in excavating. The old saying that a man finds what he looks for in a subject is too true; or if he has not enough insight to ensure finding what he looks for, it is at least sadly true that he does not find anything that he does not look for. . . . Of late years the notion of digging merely for profitable spoil, or to yield a new excitement to the jaded, has spread unpleasantly. . . . Gold digging has at least no moral responsibility, beyond the ruin of the speculator; but spoiling the past has an acute moral wrong in it. . . . Let us be quit, in archaeology at least, of the brandy-and-soda young man who manipulates his "expenses," of the adventurous speculator, of those who think that a title or a long purse glorifies any vanity of selfishness. Without the ideal of solid continuous work, certain, accurate, and permanent—archaeology is as futile as any other pursuit. Best of all is the combination of the scholar and the engineer, the man of languages and the man of physics and mathematics, when such can be found. . . .

The spoken language of the country should be fluently acquired for simple purposes, so as to be able to direct workmen, make bargains, and follow what is going on. To be dependent on a cook, a dragoman, or a donkey boy, is very unsafe and prevents that close study of the workmen which is needed for making the best use of them. . . . Not a single living person combines all of the requisite qualities for complete archaeological work. . . .

In the externals of the work an excavator should be always his own best workman. If he be the strongest on the place so much the better; but at all events he should be the most able in all matters of skill and ability. Where anything is found it should be the hands of the master that clear it from the soil; the pick and the knife should be in his hands every day, and his readiness should be shown by the shortness of his fingernails and the toughness of his skin. . . .

To attempt serious work in pretty suits, shiny leggings, or starched collars would be like mountaineering in evening dress, or remind one of the old prints of cricketers batting in chimney-pot hats. The man who cannot enjoy his work without regard to appearances, who will not strip and go into the water, or slither on slimy mud through unknown passages, had better not profess to excavate. . . . To suppose that work can be controlled from a distant hotel, where the master lives in state and luxury completely out of touch with his men, is a fallacy, like playing at farming or at stockbroking: it may be amusing, but it is not business. And whatever is not businesslike in archaeology is a waste of the scanty material which should be left for those who know how to use it. . . .

The question between day pay and piece pay is an open one. . . . When working by the day it is needful to give the signals for beginning and stopping work, and to insist on regular and continuous digging. It is impossible to be known to be away, as then no work will go on effectively. An air of vigilant surprise has to be kept up. A sunk approach to the work behind higher ground is essential; and, if possible, an access to a commanding view without being seen going to and fro. A telescope is very useful to watch if distant work is regular. At Tanis the girls in a big pit were kept by the men walking up and tipping baskets at the top; but the telescope showed that the baskets were all the time empty. The immediate dismissal of fourteen people was the result. A telescope will also show if a boy is put up to watch for the master's coming. Various approaches should be arranged from different directions, and the course of work so planned that no men can give notice to others. In this way a pleasing group of musicians and dancers may be found in the excavations, where picks and baskets are lying idle; and the arrangement is closed by requesting the boys to dance on their own resources, and the transfer of your pay to other pockets. The need of thus acting as mainspring, without which the work goes on at an official pace, is wearing and time-wasting; and it leaves no chance of doing writing, drawing, etc., during work hours.

Working by the piece saves all this trouble, and if the men

are well trained, and the work simple, it goes on automatically
and takes the smallest possible amount of attention. In detached
small sites men may even be left unvisited for two or three days,
merely reporting each evening how far they have worked. In
one case some lads were left to work at a great sarcophagus for
weeks unwatched, and came some miles to report progress, and
say when further attention was wanted. The pay for that was
given by contract, to cut and lift a stone lid under water, for so
many pounds.

Some of this reads curiously today, but sixty years separates us
from 1904, as nearly sixty years separated that moment from
Mariette's excavations of the Serapeum. Flinders Petrie was certainly one of the founders of modern excavation; but in western
Europe the real founder of modern technique was that remarkable
soldier Augustus Lane-Fox, who, when he inherited estates in
Cranborne Chase, had to change his name to Pitt-Rivers (1827–
1900). This was in 1880; he had done some excavation before as
Colonel Lane-Fox, but it was as General Pitt-Rivers that he enters
the history of archaeology with his excavations between 1880 and
1900 at Woodcuts, Rotherley, Woodyates, Wor Barrow, Bokerly
Dyke, and Wansdyke. As the present author has said elsewhere,
"Unlimited by considerations of finance, time or labour, Pitt-
Rivers was able to make these excavations a model of scientific excavation." In four privately printed volumes produced between
1887 and 1898 and entitled *Excavations in Cranborne Chase,* he
published his excavations in detail, and wrote what he thought
about the principles and practice of excavation. The following passages are from those volumes, the first from Volume I (1887).

Having retired from active service on account of ill health,
and being incapable of strong physical exercise, I determined to
devote the remaining portion of my life chiefly to an examination of the antiquities on my own property. Of these there were
a considerable number, especially near Rushmore, consisting of
Romano-British villages, tumuli, and other vestiges of the
Bronze and Stone Ages, most of which were untouched and had
been well preserved. . . .
I had an ample harvest before me, and with the particular

225

tastes that I had cultivated, it almost seemed to me as if some unseen hand had trained me up to be the possessor of such a property, which, up to within a short time of my inheriting it, I had but little reason to expect. I at once set about organizing such a staff of assistants as would enable me to complete the examination of the antiquities on the property within a reasonable time, and to do it with all the thoroughness which I had come to consider necessary for archaeological investigations.

A permanent residence in the district to be explored is almost necessary for a satisfactory investigation of its ancient remains, and it is needless to say that ownership adds greatly to the power of carrying out explorations thoroughly, for although I have found my neighbours at all times most obliging in giving me permission to dig, it requires some assurance so far to trespass on a friend's kindness as to sit down and besiege a place on another man's property more than a year, which is not at all too long a time to spend in the excavation of a British village.

Whilst living at Kensington, I had carefully examined the drift gravels near Acton and Ealing, and by constantly watching the excavations for buildings made at no great distance from my place of abode, I had been able to make the first carefully recorded discovery of palaeolithic implements in association with the remains of extinct animals that had been made in the Thames Valley near London up to that time . . . in Sussex also I had made some more or less lengthy excavations, in camps at Mount Caburn, Cissbury, and other places, dating from the late Celtic period, the value of which would certainly have been much increased if a permanent residence in the neighbourhood had enabled me to devote more time to them. At Thebes, in Egypt, I had discovered palaeolithic implements in the gravels of the Nile Valley embedded in the sides of Egyptian tombs, a discovery the interest of which consisted in finding these implements for the first time *in situ*. But anthropology has no pet periods, all ages have afforded materials of nearly equal value for the history of the human race, and in the region around Rushmore my attention has been drawn more especially to the Romanized Britons, as being the race for whose study the district appears capable of affording the greatest facilities . . .

226

It will, perhaps, be thought by some that I have recorded the excavations of this village [Woodcuts Common] and the finds that have been made in it with unneccessary fullness, and I am aware that I have done it in greater detail than has been customary, but my experience as an excavator has led me to think that investigations of this nature are not generally sufficiently searching, and that much valuable evidence is lost by omitting to record them carefully. That this has been so in the present instance is proved by the fact that this village had before been examined and reported upon in the twenty-fourth volume of the *Journal of the Archaeological Institute,* and not a single pit or skeleton had been found; whilst I have discovered ninety-five pits and fifteen skeletons.

Excavators, as a rule, record only those things which appear to them important at the time, but fresh problems in archaeology and anthropology are constantly arising, and it can hardly fail to have escaped the notice of anthropologists, especially those who, like myself, have been concerned with the morphology of art, that, on turning back to old accounts in search of evidence, the points which would have been most valuable have been passed over from being thought uninteresting at the time. Every detail should, therefore, be recorded in the manner most conducive to facility of reference, and it ought at all times to be the chief object of an excavator to reduce his own personal equation to a minimum.

I have endeavoured to record the results of these excavations in such a way that the whole of the evidence may be available for those who are concerned to go into it, whilst those who confine themselves to an examination of the plates will find each object carefully described on the adjoining page. . . . I have placed all the relics discovered in the ancient villages and tumuli in a museum near the village of Farnham, Dorset, where each object is carefully ticketed and described. Accurate models have been made of the villages, and models on a larger scale of the particular finds. In the case of Rotherley, I have a model of the ground, both before and after excavation, by means of which the results of the exploration are explained in such a way as to require the least possible effort of attention. The museum also includes other objects of husbandry and peasant handicraft, calculated to draw the interest of a purely rural population ten miles distant from any town or railway station, and I am glad to say the interest it has attracted amongst the workingmen of the neighbourhood has exceeded my utmost expectations. On Sunday afternoons the visitors' book often records more than 100 visitors: and on special holidays, between 200 and 300 frequently visit the museum. . . . I have established a pleasure ground and built a temple in the woods, with a private band, . . . where upwards of 1,000 of the villagers and neighbours frequently congregate with their wives and families, between the hours of divine service upon Sunday afternoons.

All the villages and tumuli, after being excavated, have been restored and turfed over, leaving sufficient indication to mark the various parts discovered in the villages, and at the bottoms of the principal excavations I have placed the medallet drawn and described in the adjoining woodcut, to show future explorers that I have been there.

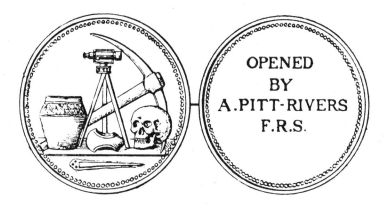

This Medalet (*sic*) was designed for me by Dr. John Evans, Treasurer of the Royal Society, and President of the Society of Antiquaries, to whom I am also indebted for valuable assistance and advice on many occasions. It has been placed near the bottom of the greater number of excavations made by me since 1880, together with a few coppers and other objects, and the date has usually been stamped on it with a punch.

It only remains to say something of the way in which the work has been carried out. I saw clearly that it was more than I could accomplish without assistance in the brief space of time allotted to me at my period of life. I therefore determined to organize a regular staff of assistants, and to train them to their respective functions after establishing a proper division of work. It was necessary they should all have some capacity for drawing in order that the relics discovered might be sketched as soon as found, instead of entrusting the drawings to inexperienced lithographers and artists who had little feeling for the subject. Surveying I was able to teach them myself, having always been fond of field sketching as a soldier. The work of superintending the digging—though I never allowed it to be carried on in my absence, always visiting the excavations at least three times a day, and arranging to be sent for whenever anything of importance was found—was more than I could undertake singlehanded, with the management of a property and other social duties to attend to, and I had by ample experience been taught that no excavation ought ever to be permitted except under the immediate eye of a responsible and trustworthy superintendent. The work of clearing and drawing the skeletons on the ground also required to be done by competent hands, although no skeleton has ever been taken out except under my personal supervision. The calculation of the indices, the classification and sorting of the pottery upon so large a scale, and with the care that I considered necessary, involved an amount of labour that I was not able to devote to it alone. . . .

Reserving, therefore, to my share of the work the entire supervision of everything, the description and arrangement of the plates, the writing of the record, checking the calculations and the measurement of every relic discovered in the diggings, and all the bones, I have, after some changes and preliminary trials been able to engage . . . assistants with suitable salaries. . . . All have from time to time been present at the excavations and have acquired much archaeological experience, which, I trust, may be useful to them in after life.

Mr. Martin, the estate carpenter, has shown much ingenuity

in constructing wooden models of the villages and pits from plans and sections provided for him by the assistants. Some of the workmen of whom I employed from eight to fifteen constantly, have acquired much skill in digging and detecting the relics in the several villages and tumuli that have been examined, so as to entitle them to be regarded as skilled workmen, upon which no small share of the success of an investigation of this kind depends.

The following passage is from the Preface to Volume II (1888).

I have endeavoured to keep up in the present volume the minute attention to detail with which investigation commenced. Much of what is recorded may never prove of further use, but even in the case of such matter, superfluous precision may be regarded as a fault on the right side where the arrangement is such as to facilitate reference and enable a selection to be made. A good deal of the rash and hasty generalization of our time arises from the unreliability of the evidence upon which it is based. It is next to impossible to give a continuous narrative of any archaeological investigation that is entirely free from bias; undue stress will be laid upon facts that seem to have an important bearing upon theories that are current at the time, whilst others that might come to be considered of greater value afterwards are put in the background or not recorded, and posterity is endowed with a legacy of error that can never be rectified. But when fulness and accuracy are made the chief subject of study, this evil is in a great measure avoided. . . .

No excavations have been carried out at any time during my absence . . . all the measurements of skulls and bones, human and animal, as well as of all the objects found in the excavations, have been taken by myself personally. All the descriptions, and the letterpress, have fallen to my share as well as the close direction and supervision of the whole, both indoors and out. Nothing has been delegated to the assistants which has not been personally supervised by me. . . . As a rule I visited the diggings from two to three times a day, regulating my time on the ground by the importance of the work that was going on. The excavations in Winkelbury having been carried on before my assistants were sufficiently trained, I never left the ground during any part of them. One or more of the assistants were always engaged in superintending the workmen upon the ground, and the others were employed in planning the ground, or in drawing the objects, in repairs to the skulls and the pots, and in forming the relic tables, by which means the records have been kept up to date; and it has been found important that, as far as possible, everything should be recorded whilst it was fresh in the memory. . . .

The expense of conducting explorations upon this system is considerable but the wealth available in the country for the purpose is still ample, if only it could be turned into this channel. The number of country gentlemen of means who are at a loss for intelligent occupation beyond hunting and shooting must be considerable; and now that a paternal Government has made a present of their game to their tenants, and bids fair to deprive them of the part that some of them have hitherto taken, most advantageously to the public, in the management of local affairs, it may not perhaps be one of the least useful results of these volumes if they should be the means of directing attention to a new field of activity, for which the owners of land are, beyond all others, favourably situated. It is hardly necessary to insist upon the large amount of evidence of early times that lies buried in the soil upon nearly every large property which is constantly being destroyed through the operations of agriculture, and which scientific anthropologists have seldom the opportunity or the means of examining.

To render all this evidence available for anthropological generalization is well worth the attention of the owners of property, who may thus render great service to an important branch of science, provided always that it is done properly; for to meddle with and destroy antiquities without recording the results carefully would be a work as mischievous as the converse of it would be useful . . .

An almost new branch of inquiry has been added to this volume by the careful measurement of all the bones of domesticated animals, of which a large number have been found in the Romano-British villages; fifteen animals have been killed for comparison as test animals after external measurement, and by this means the size of all the animals whose bones have been found in the villages has been ascertained.

The final extract comes from the Preface of Volume III (1892).

Tedious as it may appear to some to dwell on the discovery of odds and ends that have, no doubt, been thrown away by their owners as rubbish, and to refer to drawings, often repeated, of the same kind of common objects, yet it is by the study of such trivial details that Archaeology is mainly dependent for determining the dates of earthworks; because the chance of finding objects of rarity in the body of a rampart is very remote. The value of relics, viewed as evidence, may on this account be said to be in an inverse ratio to their intrinsic value. The longer I am engaged in these pursuits, the more I become impressed with this fact, the importance of which has, I think, been too much overlooked by Archaeologists. Hereafter it will probably strike future Archaeologists as remarkable that we should have arrived at the state of knowledge we now possess about ancient works of high art and yet have paid so little attention to such questions as when iron nails for woodwork were first introduced into Britain, what kind and quality of pottery was in common use at different periods, when red Samian was first introduced from abroad, at what exact period in the world's history flint flakes ceased to be fabricated and used for any purpose, and other matters of that nature . . .

Next to coins, fragments of pottery afford the most reliable of all evidence, and, on this account, I have elsewhere spoken of pottery as the human fossil, so widely is it distributed. . . . Vessels of pottery in prehistoric and Roman times were subject to breakage, as are now our less fragile and more durable ones; the pieces were not carried away by the dustman, as is now the case, but were scattered and trampled into the soil . . .

A tumulus is easily dug into and the relics obtained from it are of value, whereas the examination of a town or encampment is a costly undertaking and the relics have seldom any intrinsic value, consisting mostly of common objects that have been thrown away by the inhabitants. It is for this reason that our knowledge of prehistoric and early people is derived chiefly from their funeral deposits, and for all we know of their mode of life, excepting such information as has been obtained from lake dwellings, and crannoges, they might as well have been born dead. Yet the everyday life of the people is, beyond all comparison, of more interest than their mortuary customs. . . .

I hope that these excavations, and the models of them that have been deposited in my museum at Farnham, Dorset, if they serve no better purpose, may at least be a means of showing how much the value of a museum may be enhanced by models, and may serve to stimulate research into ancient sites, in preference to mere relic grubbing; not that I wish to be understood to deprecate continued researches into graves and tumuli. . . .

The methods and message of Pitt-Rivers took a very long time to be accepted and practiced. Three years after the publication of Petrie's *Methods and Aims in Archaeology,* and seven years after Pitt-Rivers' death, a young man destined to become very famous in archaeology found himself, completely untrained, in charge of an excavation. Here is Sir Leonard Woolley's (1880–1960) account of his beginnings in archaeology.[1]

I have seldom been more surprised than I was when—it is nearly fifty years ago now—the Warden of New College told me he had decided that I should be an archaeologist. It is true that I had taken a course in Greek sculpture for my degree, but so had lots of other undergraduates. Because of their bearing on Homer I had read Schliemann's romantic account of his discoveries, the treasure of Priam at Troy and the tomb of Agamemnon at Mycenae, and like everyone else I was rather vaguely aware that Flinders Petrie was, year after year, making history in Egypt and that Arthur Evans was unearthing the palace of Minos in Crete; but all this was at best only background knowledge and the idea of making a life study of it had never occurred to me. And I must confess that when the prospect did present itself, not as a mere idea to be played with (for one did not lightly play with the Warden's decisions) but as something definite and settled, I was not altogether happy about it. For

[1] *Spadework,* 1953.

me, and I think for the Warden too, archaeology meant a life spent inside a museum, whereas I preferred the open air and was more interested in my fellow men than in dead-and-gone things; I could never have guessed that after a short—and invaluable— apprenticeship in the Ashmolean Museum at Oxford, all my work was to be out of doors . . . and I had yet to learn that the real end of archaeology is, through the dead-and-gone things, to get at the history and the minds of dead-and-gone men. . . .

My first experience of digging was at Corbridge in Northumberland, and I know only too well that the work there would have scandalized, and rightly scandalized, any British archaeologist of today. It was however typical of what was done forty-five years ago, when field archaeology was, comparatively speaking, in its infancy and few diggers in this country thought it necessary to follow the example of that great pioneer Pitt-Rivers. *The Northumberland County History* was being written and the writers wanted to know more about the Roman station at Corbridge, so [they] proposed a small-scale dig to settle the character of the site. The committee naturally appealed to Professor Haverfield as the leading authority on Roman Britain, and he, as he had intended to take a holiday on the Roman Wall, agreed to supervise the excavations. Somebody, of course, had to be put in charge of the work, and because I was an Assistant Keeper in the Ashmolean Museum, my qualifications were, in the eyes of an Oxford professor, *ipso facto* satisfactory. Haverfield arranged with Sir Arthur Evans, the Keeper, that I should go to Corbridge. In point of fact, I had never so much as seen an excavation, I had never studied archaeological methods even from books (there were none at the time dealing with the subject), and I had not any idea of how to make a survey or a ground plan; apart from being used to handling antiquities in a museum, and that only for a few months, I had no qualifications at all. I was very anxious to learn, and it was a disappointment to me that Haverfield only looked in at the excavations one day in the week and then was concerned only to know what had been found—I don't think that he ever criticized or corrected anything. Fortunately it had been arranged that the plans should be done by W. H. Knowles, an architect with very wide archaeological experience, and he not only relieved me of an impossible responsibility but gave me practical lessons in planning and surveying, the only lessons on the subject that I have ever had, and I am proportionately grateful to him.

My other helpers were amateurs like myself. Admittedly the first season was but experimental; it lasted for no more than five weeks and at no time did we employ more than nine labourers; but it was so far successful that a committee was formed to carry on the excavations with a view to the complete uncovering of the site. In 1907, therefore, I found myself in charge of a really important dig, being still, of course, quite unfitted for the task, and again my helpers, apart from Mr. Knowles, were as inexperienced as I. But the work went very merrily, I had beginner's luck, which pleased everyone, and we were all, I think, happily unconscious of the low standard of our performance, nor did anyone from outside suggest that it might have been better; actually, of course, it did improve with time, as both we and our workmen learned our job.

The most dramatic discovery was that of the Corbridge Lion. We had found a stone cistern attached to a large Roman building and in the course of the morning had cleared about half of the earth filling. It happened to be a Saturday and after my lunch I went to the bank to draw money for the men's wages, and as I was kept waiting for some while, the interval was over and work had started again before I got back to the site. As I came near I saw all the men crowded closely together by the side of the cistern, and wondered what had happened; only when I was close up did they separate this way and that, and between the two groups of them I saw the stone lion grinning over the fallen stag. They had lifted it out of the cistern (which of course was wrong of them) and had deliberately staged a surprise for me, and a fine surprise it was, but what struck me at once was that the men were even more excited than I was. The actual finder, who was not Tyneside but a "foreigner," an East Anglian curiously unlike his fellow miners, a big fellow with a round fair face and a fair round belly, was shaking as if with an ague and quite incoherent; when he recovered enough to speak at all in answer to my question "Did *you* find that?" he could only stammer, "Yes, sir, and you'll never believe me, but it's God's own truth, when I first saw that there lion he had a blooming orange in 'is mouth."

Such were the beginnings in excavation of one who was destined to be a great excavator himself; a short account of one of his most important and meticulous discoveries is included in chapter 6. Leonard Woolley was not, of course, right in saying that no books existed on excavational technique when he was posted to Corbridge. Petrie's *Methods and Aims* had been out for several years—but then perhaps if he had read that book he would have arrived at Corbridge with a telescope and dug a sunken approach to the site and kept up "an air of vigilant surprise." Who knows? All we do know is that he soon learned and also soon appreciated the methods and principles of General Pitt-Rivers.

Eight years after Woolley had found himself in charge of a major excavation, J. P. Droop wrote a book entitled *Archaeological Excavation* (1915) in the Cambridge Archaeological and Ethnological Series. The following passages come from this book of half a century ago.

The time has perhaps gone by when it was necessary, if it ever were, to put forward a defence of the pleasant practice of digging, a defence of it, that is to say, not as a harmless recreation of the idle rich, but as a serious business for a reasonable man. In all ages the maker of history and the recorder of history have alike received due honour. Today a place is found, not equal, of course, in glory but in the same hierarchy, for the reverent discoverer of the dry bones of history; and on Clio's roll of honour next to Homer and Agamemnon there is now a place for Schliemann. . . .

In Greece, at least, and in Egypt it was unavoidably, but none the less deplorably, the case that the great men of the past lacked the experience that is now ours. Excavation, like surgery, is an art, but, unlike the surgeon, the excavator has no unlimited supply of new subjects ready to benefit by his growing skill. The number of sites that have been spoiled will not bear thinking of, sites that bring a vicarious remorse to the mind that remembers by what ignorance they were very lovingly but very shamefully mishandled, so that their secrets, instead of being gathered up, were spilled and lost. The pity of it is that in the old days excavation was not recognized as an art; the excavator took a spade and dug and what he found he found; what could be more simple or more satisfying? . . .

I believe that to be able to dig a stratified site well is to have attained to the highest and most remunerative skill in this particular work. . . . If time and money were of no account there is no doubt that for a productive site the best digging tool would be a kind of bread knife without a point. The use of such a weapon goes nearest to insure the fewest possible breakages, for it is light, and the blunt end does not provide the same strong temptation as a point to use premature leverage. . . .

The keeping of an excavation daybook is sometimes thought advisable. . . . In practice however it happens that reference is seldom made to the daybook, each man preferring to refer to his own notes, and what is felt to be the useless labour of writing it up every night becomes a great burden. The better plan would seem to keep such a book for entering once a week or once a fortnight not the details of every day, which are safe enough elsewhere, but the general trend of the excavation, and the broad conclusions drawn from the work accomplished to date. . . .

Meticulous care directed by common sense along the lines laid down by past experience, that is the essence of good digging; yet the ideal man to have charge of an excavation would be a very versatile person. . . . He should have tact and social charm both for dealing with his staff, for an unhappy dig is an inefficient dig, and for negotiating any difficulties that may arise. He should have a good temper, but a stiff jaw. . . .

I may perhaps venture a short word on the question much discussed in certain quarters, whether in the work of excavation it is a good thing to have co-operation between men and women. I have no intention of discussing whether or no women possess the qualities best suited for such work; opinions, I believe, vary on the point, but I have never seen a trained lady excavator at work, so that my view if expressed would be valueless. Of a mixed dig however I have seen something, and it is an experiment that I would be reluctant to try again; I would grant if need be that women are admirably fitted for the work, yet I would uphold that they should undertake it by themselves.

My reasons are twofold and chiefly personal. In the first place, there are the proprieties: I have never had a very reverent care for these abstractions, but I think it is not everywhere sufficiently realized that the proprieties that have to be considered are not only those that rule in England or America, but those of the lands where it is proposed to dig; the view to be considered is the view of the inhabitants, Greek, Turk, or Egyptian. My chief reasons, I said, were personal, but I hasten to add that they have nothing to do with the particular ladies with whom I was associated; should these lines meet their eyes I hope they will believe me when I say that before and after the excavation I thought them charming; during it, however, because they, or we, were in the wrong place, their charm was not seen. My objection lies in this, that the work of an excavation on the dig and off it lays on those who share in it a bond of closer daily intercourse than is conceivable, except perhaps in the Navy where privacy is said to be unobtainable, except for a captain; with the right men that is one of the charms of the life, but between men and women, except in chance cases, I do not believe that such close and unavoidable companionship can ever be other than a source of irritation; at any rate I believe that, however it may affect women, the ordinary male at least cannot stand it. . . . Marriage apart, and I can imagine a man conducting a small excavation very happily with his wife, mixed digging I think means loss of easiness in the atmosphere and consequent loss of efficiency. A minor, and yet to my mind weighty, objection lies in one particular form of constraint entailed by the presence of ladies, it must add to all the strains of excavation, and there are many, the further strain of politeness and self-restraints in moments of stress, moments that will occur on the best-regulated dig, when you want to say just what you think without translation, which before ladies, whatever their feelings about it, cannot be done.

This last passage from Droop is a historical one in studying archaeology. It reminds one of the prohibition on ladies' attending lectures in geology in London in the early nineteenth century because it was a dangerous subject, and contrasts remarkably with what J. H. Parker said in his Oxford lecture of 1870. Droop could hardly know, or he would not have so written, that one of the fascinating features of twentieth-century excavation would be the presence of women on most digs and the emergence of a number of remarkable women in charge of excavations; in reading, a half-century later, Droop's misgivings and gloomy forebodings, we should remember the names of, among others, Gertrude Bell, Winifred Lamb, Gertrude Caton Thompson, Dorothy Garrod, Kathleen Kenyon, Suzanne de Saint-Mathurin, and Germaine Henri-Martin.

There was one person who certainly did not share Droop's views, namely Sir Mortimer Wheeler, a junior contemporary of Leonard Woolley's. He began excavating before the 1914–18 war, but the first excavations of his own were at the end of and immediately after the war. In his autobiography *Still Digging* (1955), he has described how he deliberately and consciously went back to the work of Pitt-Rivers for inspiration and for detailed instruction. With all his firmness and protestations, Flinders Petrie had not been the constant vigilant observer that General Pitt-Rivers was. Although Wheeler had, as we all have, a great admiration for the work and inspiration of Flinders Petrie, he said, "My pen melts as I transcribe those words," [2] when he quoted the famous sentence, "In detached small sites men may even be left unvisited for two or three days, merely reporting each evening how far they have worked." Wheeler went on to quote a sentence from the *Manuel de recherches préhistoriques* published in 1929 by the Société Préhistorique Française (*"The best way to ensure your workmen is not to leave them a minute"*—it was printed in italics), and the passage from W. F. Badé's *A Manual of Excavation in the Near East* (Chicago, 1934), in which the author describes how the foreman "receives general instructions from the director for each day's work, picks men for special tasks, . . .

[2] *Archaeology from the Earth*, 1954, p. 15.

sees to it that regulations are carried out, . . . usually stands on some high point from which he can oversee the excavations. . . . Of course it would be very unwise for a director to leave him or any overseers of gangs to their own devices for long, since their understanding of methods is mechanical." Half a century after Petrie's *Methods and Aims,* Wheeler wrote his instruction book in field archaeology, based on his Rhind lectures of 1951 and entitled *Archaeology from the Earth* (1954), and the following extracts are from this book.

There is no right way of digging but there are many wrong ways. Amongst the latter our successors will no doubt include ways which we regard today as relatively right, in accordance with the natural principle whereby every generation is liable to belittle the achievement of its predecessors. This attitude is often enough unjust. . . . But there is much, far too much, in more recent archaeological excavation that falls short of the highest available standards and therefore deserves the lash. At the best, excavation is destruction; and destruction unmitigated by all the resources of contemporary knowledge and accumulated experience cannot be too rigorously impugned. . . .

The average standard of field archaeology in Great Britain itself during the past half-century has been unsurpassed, if approached, by that of any other country. That statement is made with no insular prejudice. In Holland, Dr. van Giffen and others have evolved methods of excavation which mark a new standard of finesse, and certain of the German excavators, notably Dr. Gerhard Bersu, need no commendation from me. Since its inauguration in 1890, the German *Limes* Commission, though often technically below the General Pitt Rivers standard, has produced admirably co-ordinated work, particularly valuable in its attention to small finds. But in the very limited area of the British Isles, rich in remains of differentiated cultures, with the General's example behind them, field archaeologists have worked within close range of one another and under the fire of constant and even fierce mutual criticism. Bad work has been done, but rarely with impunity. . . .

. . . in much of our archaeology fixed time-points are intermittent and chancy. More usually, the archaeologist must be content to establish the *relative sequence* of his evidence, to ensure that, however ill-focused, his perspective is essentially correct. Therein lies his primary duty: to secure beyond doubt the orderly succession of the vestiges with which he deals, even though, in any given phase of research, he may be compelled to leave finer adjustment and interpretation to his successors. To come at once to the core of the matter, his first task as an excavator is with *stratification*. . . .

Today the digger must learn to read his sections, or he should be constrained from digging. In practice, the identification and correlation of the strata or layers which represent the successive phases in the archaeological "history" of a site is one of the principal tasks of the excavator and will occupy the major portion of his time. . . . The task is one which involves clear and logical thinking reinforced by experience and infinite patience. . . . The reading of a section is the reading of a language that can only be learned by demonstration and experience. A word of advice to the student. However practised, do not read too hastily. Be your own devil's advocate before passing judgement. And, wherever possible, discuss your diagnosis with others—with colleagues, with pupils, with your foreman. ("The testimony of one person is no testimony," declares Hywel Dda, the wise Welsh lawgiver.) Be humble. Do not ignore the opinion of the uninstructed. "Everyone knows as much as the savant. The walls of rude minds are scrawled all over with facts, with thoughts." Emerson said so, and he was right. Even if you do not accept the views of those you question, the mere act of questioning is at the same time a restraint and a stimulus. . . .

Reference must be made to a method of recording that not long ago was widespread in the East and may in fact still survive there. If so, it is the survival of a fantastic and monstrous device evolved in the alluvial plains of the great river valleys of Egypt and Mesopotamia as a substitute for exact observation in ill-controlled "mass excavations." Its origin is probably to be found in Petrie's belief that on an Egyptian town site it was possible to equate the accumulation of material with a specific time-scale. The validity of this "principle" was doubtful and dangerous enough in its original specialized context; it has no place whatsoever in the general technique of modern field archaeology. Yet in India, for example, as recently as 1944 it was still the only method known.

Briefly, it consisted of the mechanical recording of every object and structure in relation to a fixed bench level. Thus in the excavations at the great prehistoric city of Mohenjo-daro in the Indus Valley, in 1927–31, the records were prepared from bench levels, in one area "178.7 ft. above the mean sea level" and in another "180.9 ft. above sea level," the assumption being that all objects and structures at the same level below (or above) datum line were in the same "stratum," i.e. contemporary with one another! I have described this system as "incredible" and I repeat the description. So incredible is it, and yet so widespread, that the excavator's own proud account of it may be repeated. He says:

"In order that our deep digging might be satisfactorily carried out, an extensive system of levelling was necessary. The levels of every building and of every wall were therefore taken, especial attention being paid to doorsills and pavements as being for purposes of stratification the most important parts of a building. In addition, both the locus and level of every object found, whether it was regarded at the time as important or not, were noted in order not only to correlate each object with the building in which it was found, but also to facilitate the study of the development of art and technique. As some thousands of objects were unearthed in the sections that we excavated, it may be thought that this procedure was unnecessarily laborious. This, however, was not the case. The levelling instruments were set up early in the morning and remained in position all day; and it was quite a simple matter to take the level of each object directly it appeared."

It was, however, admitted that this method was not wholly free from complexity; that there were "limitations to the deductions to be drawn from the levels at which objects are found. For instance, if a jar or a seal lies either below or at some distance above a pavement or doorsill, it is difficult to decide to what period it belongs. We, therefore, adopted the rule that all objects found in or near the foundations of a building be assigned to the period of that building rather than to the previous phase, unless they actually rested on the remains of a pavement of earlier date; for it is more than probable that they were dropped or left behind when the foundations were being made.''

The chapters on the pottery and other finds in the excavator's subsequent report include page after page of elaborate but insignificant tables based on this procedure.

In other words, be it repeated, the so-called stratification of the Indus Valley civilization, one of the major civilizations of the ancient world, was dominated, not by local observation, but by the level of the sea nearly 300 miles away! This mechanical classification can only be categorized as the very parody of scientific method. It bears little more relationship to scientific archaeology than astrology bears to astronomy.

To appreciate its utter absurdity, we need only recall that except perhaps at the earliest level of a site (hardly ever adequately explored), an ancient city of the East is never level. Very rarely is a city completely destroyed and completely rebuilt at one moment and at one horizon. Normally, a house is reconstructed or replaced as it decays, or at the whim of its owner. The town as a whole is constantly in a state of differential destruction and construction. Individual building sites rise above their neighbours; the town site itself rises and assumes the contour of a hill; buildings on its slopes are contemporary with buildings on its summit. A doorway or a potsherd may be found at one spot ten feet below a doorway or potsherd of precisely the same date at another spot. Such differences, of vital importance to the scientific interpretation of the site, are ironed out and obliterated by the bench level. If it be necessary to illustrate further the grievous fallacy of this method, two diagrams may serve. They are self-explanatory (see p. 244).

Yet, for all the obvious absurdity of the datum-line system just described, the substitution of so-called levels—whether abstract building levels or purely arbitrary depth lines—for factual stratification, dies hard. It recurs, for example, in a revised edition (1950) of *A Manual of Archaeological Field Methods* prepared by a leading American university. There, as sturdily as ever, thrives the old outworn system, with its mechanical "unit-levels," governed not by changes of soil, but by "the length of the shovel-blade (six to twelve inches)." True the word "stratification" is not unknown to the authors. It represents a phenomenon, they admit, which "may be visible in the walls of the excavation"; but, we are assured, "any stratigraphy of artifact types and animal bones will appear after a study has been made and need not bother the excavator in the field" (*sic*). The notion of peeling off the successive strata in conformity with their proper bed-lines, and thus ensuring the accurate isolation of structural phases and relevant artifacts, is not even considered.

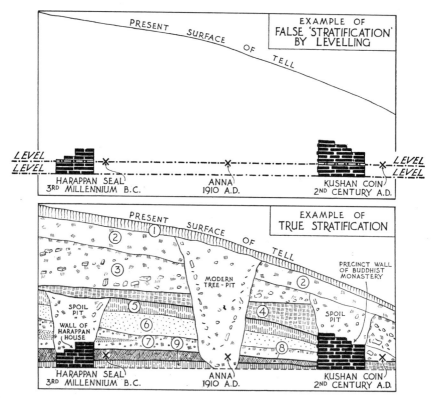

The diagrams reproduced here, which are found in Wheeler's *Archaeology from the Earth* (first published, Oxford, 1954; Penguin, 1956), originally appeared in an article written by Sir Mortimer Wheeler in *Ancient India*, 1947, no. 3, p. 146. Professor Piggott returns to this theme of false stratification in an article on "Archaeological Draughtsmanship: Principle and Practice," in *Antiquity*, 1965, and we quote a paragraph from this article.

There has perhaps been a tendency towards wishful thinking on the part of archaeologists who would like to be classed as "scientific" because of the element of social and academic prestige believed by them to be associated with this now almost meaningless word. In the New World much labour has been directed towards the construction of systems which will so far as possible eliminate the personal factor, not only for reasons of being thought respectable because "scientific," but of being more democratic and egalitarian by minimizing the variables of human knowledge, experience, skill, and (dirty words!) flair and genius. Such systems have been described as "anthropologically oriented," and the observation of archaeological stratification written off as "at best so difficult that even the most experienced excavators fall into error" in its interpretation. But in such a context "interpretation" is a dirty word too: the excavators in this instance, and in the year 1951, "decided to use a system of artificial levels that would serve to control the stratigraphic sequence of our ceramic sample and so offset the difficulties involved in other systems." In other words it was just made easier: no application of thought was now necessary.

Piggott was quoting from W. A. Fairservis's *Excavations in the Quetta Valley, West Pakistan* (1956, p. 203), and Sir Mortimer Wheeler's reference was to the second, revised (1950) edition of R. F. Heizer's *A Manual of Archaeological Field Methods,* first published in 1948. It is to be remembered, as Wheeler reminds us in a footnote, that mechanical foot levels were used by William Pengelly in 1865 when he was beginning the re-excavation of Kent's Cavern, Torquay. "It is sad," comments Wheeler, "to find the same outworn method advocated by a distinguished University in 1950."

And now a further extract from Wheeler's *Archaeology from the Earth,* in which he discusses horizontal and vertical excavation.

From time to time the question arises: shall stress be laid (in some particular programme of work) upon horizontal or upon vertical excavation? By "horizontal excavation" is meant the uncovering of the whole or a large part of a specific phase in the occupation of an ancient site, in order to reveal fully its layout and function. By "vertical excavation" is meant the excavation of a restricted area *in depth,* with a view to ascertaining the succession of cultures or of phases and so producing a time-scale or culture-scale for the site. The two procedures are of course complementary, not antagonistic, and the excavator may be expected to attempt, if rarely to achieve, both methods of approach. But in a great majority of instances, a priority has to be determined, having regard to the state of current knowledge and the resources available. . . .

Vertical excavation alone, whilst supplying a key to the length of an occupation, to its continuity or intermittency, and to some part of its cultural equipment, cannot be expected to reveal save in the most scrappy fashion the significant environment—economic, religious, administrative—of a human society. In other words, it leaves us in the dark as to those very factors which fit a past culture or civilization into the story of human endeavour and so make its recovery worth while. It is the railway timetable without a train. On the other hand, the extensive horizontal excavations which were in effect the normal practice before stratification was adequately understood generally produced an abstraction—often a very confused and misleading abstraction—unrelated with any sort of precision to the sequence of human development. They were trains without a timetable. The trains sometimes ran vigorously enough, but we knew not when they were running or where they started, or their intermediate stopping places, or their destination.

At certain stages of research both these incomplete methods may have a substantive value; indeed, they are themselves stages in the progress of research. I am not, for example, of those who scorn the horizontal excavation (in the nineties) of the Roman town of Silchester. True, it was dug like potatoes, without a shadow of the scientific nicety of the contemporary excavations in Cranborne Chase; and the resultant plan is the uncritical synthesis of a varying urban development through more than three centuries. But it gave at once, and with a rough accuracy, the general impression of a Romano-British town such as fifty years of subsequent and often more careful work have failed to equal. More exact vertical and horizontal digging on both this and other similar sites has indeed begun to reveal the sociological evolution essential to our historical perspective; but who amongst these later and wiser excavators has not constantly referred back with profit to the crude primitive assemblage of Silchester?

So also elsewhere. The Glastonbury lake village, excavated uncritically with results that are often infuriatingly baffling, has nevertheless given us the complete layout of a small Early Iron Age settlement and so enabled us to assess in broad terms the social and economic significance of such a settlement as no exacting and partial probing could have rendered possible. For that, even in moments when the evidence in detail completely fails us, we may be properly thankful. And let us for a moment look further afield. One of the most dramatic and revealing of all excavated cities is prehistoric Mohenjo-daro, beside the Indus in Pakistan. Technically the methods adopted by a succession of excavators there became almost an international scandal, and neither Professor Piggott nor I have been at pains to spare the lash. But the primary marvel of the great Indus city is not that it did (or did not) develop in such-and-such a fashion between, let us say, 2500 and 1500 B.C., *but that it existed at all* in the remarkable form that extensive, if disproportionately summary, excavation has revealed to us. Its house walls, towering accumulatively above our heads, its long straight streets, its lanes, its elaborate drainage system, its citadel—these and other things in bulk re-create a whole phase of human society even though in detail they fail to analyze it for us. Analysis—by careful vertical digging—should, of course, have accompanied all this summary horizontal clearance; but there can be no question that Mohenjo-daro takes its place as the representative of one of the greatest civilizations of the ancient world in some measure by virtue of the crimes of its explorers. . . .

It must not be inferred that horizontal excavation is necessarily summary and unscientific! Ideally, the excavation of a town site would begin with vertical digging, sufficient to establish the time- or culture-sequence, and would proceed to the careful horizontal digging of successive phases, one at a time. . . . Careful horizontal digging can alone, in the long run, give us the full information that we ideally want. Vertical digging will, by itself, serve a valuable purpose in establishing the geographical distribution of a culture and its time relationship with other cultures from place to place; but this evidence still derives its ultimate significance from a knowledge of the social environment of the cultures concerned.

These passages from Wheeler's *Archaeology from the Earth* may be taken not only as a statement of faith and doctrine but as a summary of a lifetime of practice. We can perhaps do no better than bring this chapter to an end with some sentences from Wheeler's preface to his book.

It cannot be affirmed too often that bad scholarship in the field generally involved the fruitless and final obliteration of evidence, and bad scholarship is still all too prevalent there. . . . If there be a connecting theme in the following pages, it is this: an insistence that the archaeologist is digging up, not *things,* but *people*. Unless the bits and pieces with which he deals be alive to him, unless he have himself the common touch, he had better seek out other disciplines for his exercise. . . . I would make it clear at once that here is an earthy book, inapt to clerkly hands. Not for an instant, of course, is it pretended that the spade is mightier than the pen; they are twin instruments; but in this matter of digging, the controlling mind must have in a developed degree that robust three-dimensional quality which is less immediately essential to some other inquiries. In a simple direct sense, archaeology is a science that must be lived, must be "seasoned with humanity." Dead archaeology is the driest dust that blows.

8 The Mature Science

The Three-Age system of the Scandinavian archaeologists was, in a modified form, the basis of the framework of prehistory in the nineteenth century and for at least the first quarter of the twentieth century. Joseph Déchelette in his *Manuel d'archéologie préhistorique* (1908) described it as "the basis of prehistory," and R. A. S. Macalister in his *Textbook of European Archaeology* (1921) called it "the cornerstone of modern archaeology." The Three-Age system had become a Four-Age system when Lubbock in 1865 proposed the division of the Stone Age into a Paleolithic or Old Stone Age, and a Neolithic or New Stone Age. The following year in a lecture to the Anthropological Society, Hodder M. Westropp proposed to distinguish prehistoric stone artifacts by the following terms: Paleolithic, Mesolithic, and Kainolithic—and by this last word he meant the recent Stone Age. In 1872 Westropp published his *Prehistoric Phases, or Introductory Essays on Prehistoric Archaeology*. By now the Kainolithic had gone but the Mesolithic was firmly in, and during the next fifty years became an established part of archaeological nomenclature.

The Five-Age system was the structure of prehistoric archaeology in the early twentieth century and it seemed to many that the methodological development of the subject was the division of the five ages into further smaller compartments. Thus the Iron Age was very properly divided into an Early Iron Age (or pre-Roman Iron Age) and the Historic Iron Age, the Paleolithic was divided into various periods, and so were the Neolithic and the Bronze Age. In France Gabriel de Mortillet was the great advocate of these subdivisions. He saw prehistory as a kind of classificatory exercise; the archaeologist was faced with an enormous chest of drawers, and his task was just to put the artifacts into the right drawer.

But gradually it was being realized that the vertical chest of drawers was not the simple answer to archaeological methodology. As archaeologists began to work in different parts of the world, different successions of drawers were required, and, what was more shattering still, it was discovered that some of the epochs into which prehistoric time had been divided were contemporary with each other: in fact, they were not epochs at all but different patterns of material culture. The anthropologists and the human geographers had for some while been discussing the idea of "culture," and "a culture." Soon it was seen that the archaeologist was not collecting subdivisions of a Five-Age system but cultures which could be grouped for technological convenience into the five great divisions. Here is an interesting early definition of the idea of culture, from James Mackinnon's *Culture in Early Scotland,* published in 1892.

I use the word culture in a general sense. It embraces the mental condition of man and its modes of expression—whatever, in short, is of interest and importance in the condition of a people. It refers to its intellectual and moral state, its sense of art or its manual skill, its customs and social institutions, etc., as far as these may be inferred, or have been handed down by written record. The term is usually applied to denote intellectual acquisition or refinement, and viewed in this sense may appear entirely out of its element in conjunction with the words barbarian or savage. It may seem, at first sight, to be degrading gold with a coating of tin. But culture need not be the equivalent for high intellectual refinement or attainment, though it has come to have this special meaning in literary phraseology. The history of the race, as of the individual, is a history of development, and every stage of civilization indicates a grade of culture, however low it may be. There is such a thing, then, as primitive culture, and the manner in which the primitive man thinks and acts is truly a phase of that growth by which the highly refined man has reached maturity. The culture of today rests indeed on that of primeval ages, and it is not difficult to find in the customs, the traditions that have survived from the remote past, the traces of its presence and its influence. . . . We may feel a vast gulf between ourselves and our primeval ancestors, who lived in caves and hunted with the flint arrowhead, and in many respects we cannot be said to be related by any bond of sympathy. The influences which shape our thoughts are largely different, for instance; still there is the race connection, there is the human spirit, in whose workings a real though rude soul reflects itself. Genius there may not be in our sense of the term, but reason certainly, and we must be shortsighted and supercilious to a degree if we can perceive no trace of our likeness in the reflection.

As the idea of culture grew in archaeological usage, the Five-Age system began to be seen as less relevant. In 1924 Professor H. J. Fleure wrote, "While we are permanently indebted to the archaeologists who first made a chronological scheme of Old Stone, New Stone, Bronze and Early Iron Ages, we are getting beyond that classification as some of the pioneers foresaw that we should." [1] The real trouble was that divisions of his valuable system were being made to serve in all sorts of classificatory ways in archaeology. In 1943 the present writer said in his *The Three Ages*:

The simple system of the three ages has now become elaborated into a complicated succession of Eolithic, Paleolithic, Mesolithic, Neolithic, Chalcolithic, Bronze Age, Early Iron Age, Historic Iron Age, merging, one supposes, into an age of steel: and our textbooks of prehistoric archaeology are full of forbidding tables based on subdivisions of this succession. The existence of such elaborate tables does prove beyond all cavil, were such proof needed here, that the concept of the three ages does indeed form the "cornerstone of modern archaeology" as Macalister said; but sometimes, looking at such tables or listen-

[1] *Archaeologia Cambrensis*, 1924, p. 241.

ing to archaeologists talking easily of Mesolithic II or Neolithic IV or Early Bronze Age B or La Tène IA, it is a little difficult to recognize the simple division into industrial stages which Thomsen and Worsaae propounded. The complexity and formality of some of these tables makes one forget the simplicity of the idea of the three ages which underlies them. But it is not only the simplicity of the idea of the three ages which has been lost in the elaboration of these tables: in many cases the idea itself has vanished. The simple division has been so systematized and elaborated, so garnished with subdivisions and loaded with names, that it is no longer possible to see the wood for the trees. It is inevitable that any scientific idea should be elaborated and developed, but in the case of the three ages of Thomsen the change has not merely been one of elaboration; for the three ages have now been given different connotations—cultural, chronological, racial, diffusionist, functional, economic—and they are no longer the simple industrial and technological stages which they were originally conceived to be.

What first had to be realized was that the Thomsen-Worsaae system was not an absolute truth but a model of the past, a working hypothesis. This was a technological model and it had served its purpose brilliantly as a working hypothesis of the past in the nineteenth century: it could, and still can, serve as a general model, and terms like the Upper Paleolithic and the Middle Bronze Age will go on being used for a very long time. But what was not clearly realized at first was that the names and the subdivisions of this system were being used not simply as a technological model, but as providing names for artifacts and cultures and even for chronology. Let us here take the first point first and see what Professor Stuart Piggott has to say on the use of models in archaeology. This passage is from his *Approach to Archaeology,* first published in 1959.

The past being what it is, accessible to us only at second hand through historical or archaeological sources, its study naturally involves constructing some sort of a picture of what the historian thinks it looked like. He can never be sure, because he can never go back in time to make his investigations on the spot, so what he must do is to try to put together, from all the available sources, something which will be consistent with the evidence he uses, and account for all the phenomena he has observed as convincingly as possible. Now this is really the same sort of approach to a problem as that made by the scientist investigating natural phenomena. He makes a number of strictly controlled observations, or uses those made by other scientists, he looks for the underlying connections between them, and then tries to devise some hypothesis or theory which will account for the observed phenomena in the most satisfactory manner. In scientific language, he will construct a *model,* a mental creation expressing the relationships and arrangements—perhaps in a mathematical formula—which will best account for all the observations he has made. The model will be a "true" one in so far as it does satisfactorily account for the phenomena, but you can have more than one model at a time, all "true," and the devising of a new model does not mean that all the others have to be scrapped, though some may have to be abandoned or drastically modified in the light of new thought.

Ever since man started thinking about his past, and so trying to contruct history, he has in fact been making models (in the sense we have just discussed) of the past of mankind, just as the geologists and physicists have made similar models of the past of the world and the universe before the advent of man, or before life existed at all on this planet. . . .

. . . let us look at the models of prehistory that were constructed over the past three hundred or so years in Britain. We must remember, in the first place, that the idea of there being a remote past for mankind without any written documentation was impossible so long as the Biblical narrative had to provide the framework for all thinking about the human past—in other words so long as a theological model of history (and prehistory) was believed to be valid. With this, too, there came from the Middle Ages a mythological model for pre-Roman Britain, based on invented "histories" of Brutus and other nonexistent heroes. But by Elizabethan times, scholars were beginning to look at what we would now call archaeological evidence objectively. . . .

Two new models were now constructed, or at least sketched out, of which the first was really based not on archaeological evidence, but on that of written history, and interpreted prehistoric remains in terms of groups of peoples with racial names —Celts, Iberians, and so on. This racial, or ethnic, model went on in use well into the last century, and one still sometimes hears it being used today (though fortunately not by archaeologists). . . .

The other model was one developed in the nineteenth century to such a degree that for a time it superseded all others. This was the model based on a classification of the substance and form of prehistoric tools and weapons, and the techniques of their manufacture: it also involved a theory of simple evolution from one type to another. Basically this was a technological model, and is still with us, for it was the famous division of prehistory into Three Ages, those of Stone, Bronze and Iron. It is a very good model, taken side by side with others, but like all of them it has its limitations and drawbacks. . . .

You can see it from another angle if you consider alternative models which have been constructed in more recent times in response to the greater and more varied body of information made available by increased refinements in archaeological techniques. Chief of these is one based on the subsistence economics of groups of peoples—whether they are living by hunting and food gathering, for instance, or whether they were settled agriculturists growing a crop of corn. If you use this, you make what looks like a very significant division in the Stone Age, what used to be called the New Stone Age being an agricultural economy, while the Middle and Old Stone Ages which preceded it in Northern Europe were based on hunting and fishing as a means of obtaining food. But in the Near East, people who were not certainly food producers with an agricultural economy seem likely to have lived on occasion in settled villages, which in an alternative model based on social evolution had been thought to be characteristic only of agriculturists with cereal crops.

The truth is that none of our archaeological models of the past, inherited or recently devised, seems capable of providing a wholly convincing picture of prehistory on its own; there does not seem to be what a scientist would call a general theory covering all aspects. Perhaps this is no bad thing. The more facets of the past we can perceive, the more likely we are to have a view approximating to a general truth. On the whole, the tendency among most archaeologists today is to try to construct for the prehistoric (or very slightly literate) past a model which comes as near to a historical framework as the differing source material will admit. . . .

The view of the past which one can form is conditioned by the evidence from which this view is constructed, especially as meaningful arrangements of the phenomena observed can only be made within the framework of some sort of conceptual model which will permit of their interpretation. The models used when dealing with archaeological evidence have to be largely technological, evolutionary, and economic, because it is these aspects of history which are reflected in the material culture which forms the archaeologist's subject matter, and in the absence of historical documents archaeological evidence on its own will necessarily tend to produce a materialist view of the past, simply owing to the nature of the evidence available within this particular discipline.

We will revert to the idea of alternative models later in this chapter. Now let us turn to the second and major difficulty of the development of the Three-Age system, namely that it was being made to do everything—describe artifacts, name cultures, describe time, and describe major stages of cultural development. Thus in the twenties and thirties it was easy to find archaeologists writing and talking about a Neolithic ax head, or the Early Neolithic culture of a country, or saying that some object or monument or culture "dated" to the Neolithic, or discussing "the Neolithic" as a phase of culture in man's history; Gordon Childe as we shall see later was even prepared to label one of the very great and fundamental changes in human history as "the Neolithic Revolution." No one has analyzed so clearly the nature and necessities of ar-

255

chaeological nomenclature and terminology as Professor Robert J. Braidwood in his paper "Terminology in Prehistory," published in 1946 in *Human Origins: An Introductory General Course in Anthropology: Selected Readings Series II* (University of Chicago Press), and the following extract is from this paper.

For the purpose of setting forth the problems involved, let us suppose that an artifact be found. What can we say of it?

1. We can give the location of the find and deduce (more or less successfully depending on the circumstances of the find) that the makers of the artifact either lived in, traveled over, or traded into the area where the find was made. (Factor of *locality*)

2. We can give a description of the artifact itself, in terms of its material, form, and technique of manufacture. We may also (depending on the circumstances of the find) be able to describe something of the assemblage—both artifactual and nonartifactual—in which our artifact has immediate context. We may be able to place it in some classificatory scheme. (Factor of *primary archaeological description*)

3. We may be able (depending on the circumstances of the find) to assess the approximate time in which the artifact had use. The evidence for this assessment may be geochronological . . . or it may be historical (based on the artifact's being associated with written records of some kind). If neither geochronological nor historical evidence is available, we shall have to assess the time element as best we can, in a *relative* way, by means of typological seriation, archaeological stratigraphy, and "Synchronism." (Factor of *time*)

4. We may make use of the artifact, and of the notions implied in each of the three foregoing factors, to draw interpretations as to the cultural achievements of the people who produced the artifact. (Factor of *archaeological interpretation*)

Not being concerned here with the artifact's possible museum value, we could say that what is encompassed by the four factors listed above includes everything which could possibly concern us as archaeologists. . . .

Of the four factors listed above, one need not change—*local-*

ity. As *time* changes, *description* and *interpretation* will presently change. . . . There are only two ways of reckoning *real* time in the archaeological sense; by geochronology and by direct historical (written) evidence. . . . We have three general types of chronology: historical chronology, geochronology, and the various types of relative chronologies. Only the first two imply dates which are in any sense *real,* and how real these dates are depends on the amount and quality of evidence available for the area under concern. Dates applied to the relative chronologies are mainly "guess dates"; they may be useful, but they should best be accompanied by an expression of tolerance which is in itself often only an intelligent guess. . . .

. . . to assume that we have "dated" Mount Carmel by calling it simply "Levalloiso-Mousterian" is meaningless, as the latter is not a term with primarily chronological meaning.

The Factor of Archaeological Description. Here our interest is to consider what kinds of terms may have validity, which are derived from the actual indicators of human activity—the artifacts, the nonartifactual materials, and the contexts. But, at this point, our interest differs from that . . . which considered the individual artifacts and classes of the same type of artifact, with the intention of classification. What we need now are terms in the purely descriptive sense . . . which can be applied to the total bulk of available materials from a given time in a given site or locality. The literature generally makes use of such terms as "culture" to imply what we mean, but "culture" is a troublesome word, with many meanings, and we would do well to drop it from the terminology of prehistoric archaeology . . .

The system we advocate for the basic descriptive usages could be summarized as in the table on the following page.

The Factor of Interpretation. . . . If, in view of the limitations of the archaeological record we can interpret little but food gathering until at least 7000 B.C.±1000, then our first interpretative term might well be "food gathering." . . . We certainly can recognize a "food-producing stage" archaeologically, and the stage also persists at present over the greatest proportion of the inhabited area of the world; the "industrialized stage" appears in pockets on a map of the contemporary

A PRIMARY TERMINOLOGY FOR ARCHAEOLOGICAL DESCRIPTION
(with special emphasis on Old World Prehistory)

Technologico-typological considerations alone	*Context, with technologico-typological considerations secondary*
TRADITION Preparation traditions in flint (etc.) tools: Core, Flake, Blade, "Chopper-chopping tool"	AGGREGATION * A collection of tools (in one or more traditions) which appears in nonarchaeological contexts
	INDUSTRY * A collection of tools of one category of materials (in one or more traditions) which appears in archaeological contexts, or in certain very specialized (untransported) geological contexts
FACIES * An especially detailed type of tool preparation appearing in some one of the traditions	ASSEMBLAGE * A variety of categories of artifacts and nonartifactual materials which appear in archaeological context

* Terms which may be particularized by prefixing a site name.

food-producing area. . . . As representational art and writing appear, we may presently forsake the archaeological terminology for an historical one. With sufficient descriptive material in literature, and with a variety of tangible forms of artistic expression available, we may begin to employ the words "culture" and "civilization" in ways which make sense. . . .

This brings to an end the system we suggest for a primary archaeological terminology. Many of the terms we suggest are not original, and some of the implications of the terms are already in use. Yet we have so far dodged using such terms as "Paleolithic" or "Iron Age" or "Acheulean culture," and we believe we can give a comprehensible and fairly brief archaeological ticket to almost any given material and not use these old and controversial terms. Essentially, what we have done can be charted, thus:

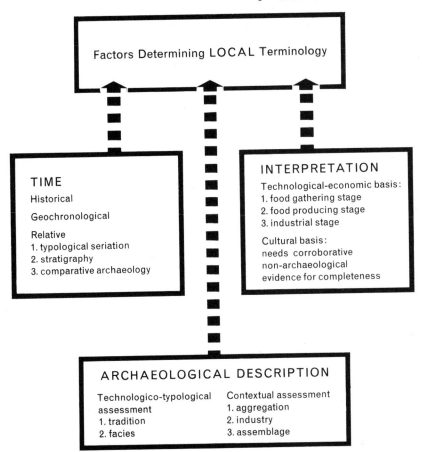

If we were to attempt to illustrate our terminology in several random cases, it might be as follows:

1. Somme Valley (France); Günz-Mindel interglacial; Core tradition (plus ?), Abbevillian aggregation; Food-gathering stage.

2. Choukoutien (Peking, China); Mid-Pleistocene (Choukoutien beds); Chopper-chopping tradition, Locality I industry; Food-gathering stage.

3. Mount Carmel (Palestine); time ? (Riss 2–Würm); Flake tradition, incl. Acheulean facies, Tabun Ed industry; Food-gathering stage.

4. Arpachiyah (Mosul, Iraq: 4000 B.C.±250 years; al-Ubaid assemblage (north Tigris variant); Food-producing

stage (mode 1). Put in its entirety, the system takes more words than are usually expended, but the reward in explicitness would seem worth the penalty. In practice, much of the wordage seems to disappear as the terms fall into place once, and need not be repeated.

In this account Braidwood presents for us what he calls "A Trinomial System of Terminology," but it is really a quadrinomial or four-part terminology. There are five things required in archaeological terminology relating to place, type of artifact, assemblage of artifacts in a real geographical and chronological context, date, and over-all historical interpretation. The first thing—place—as Braidwood says, has its own name and requires nothing from us. What we then have to do is give names to artifacts and to groups of artifacts in real geographical and chronological contexts, to date the artifacts and groups or assemblages, and to have suitable names for the over-all historical interpretations we can make. In all aspects of this four-part terminology, it is now clear that any divisions of the Three-Age system can no longer be used. In this respect archaeology has grown up, and in any clear, thoughtful analysis of methodology, such as that we have just quoted from Braidwood, they do not appear. We need and are now getting objective names for artifacts; words like Passage-Grave and Palstave, if defined, are accurate classificatory terms. They are parts of the taxonomy of archaeology.

We may disgress for a° moment here to comment on the fact that in most archaeological textbooks there is hardly any mention of taxonomy; the word typology is used extensively in the last forty years and indeed in the extract we have just quoted Braidwood is talking about "technologico-typological assessment" when he merely means the classification, the taxonomy of an artifact. The word typology—which has other and very different connotations—came into archaeology late, and while the Oxford English Dictionary is prepared to define it as "the classification of remains and specimens according to the type they exhibit and its evolution," this is really including taxonomy and typology *sensu stricto* in one heading. The classification of remains and specimens according to the type they exhibit is the taxonomic aspect of archaeology, and has no implications of a cultural or chronological kind. The classification of remains and specimens according to the type *and its evolution* is immediately a subjective activity with implications of a cultural and chronological kind. This was made clear by Gordon Childe (1892–1957) in the preface to *The Danube in Prehistory* (1929) when he wrote: "Where stratigraphical or geological evidence is lacking, we must have recourse to typology. This depends on the assumption that types evolved (or degenerated) regularly."

In a word typology is, when carefully used, an aid to the relative chronology of artifacts; it is an interpretative chronological device, not part of the necessary fourfold terminology of archaeology.

The third of the four elements was date, and this has been for a very long time one of the great impediments to the progress of archaeology. Within their limits the divisions of the Three-Age system did give some relative chronology, and indeed without that relative chronology archaeology could not have come into being in the early nineteenth century. The evidence of stratigraphy provided other clear evidence of relative chronology, and, as Childe said in the passage we have just quoted, in the absence of sound stratigraphical or geological evidence, it was possible to have recourse to typology.

But what was wanted was an absolute chronology so that the archaeologist could speak in terms of years. Man-made chronology only goes back to 3000 B.C. in Egypt and the Near East, and the problem of the archaeologist was to extend this human chronology from areas like the ancient Near East to areas outside like India and Europe and Africa where there was no writing, and secondly to get some dates behind the historical limits. The technique of extension was done by cross-dating; Sir Austin Layard provided an account of what was perhaps the oldest example of this technique, which was then developed by Flinders Petrie, Montelius, Childe and others to enable some dates after 3000 B.C. to be suggested for the barbarian societies of Europe. But this was all a very hazardous business and many of the dates were guesswork, and as we know now, were wrong guesses.

What was wanted was a technique of dating independent of

man, a geochronological technique which produced dates from natural events. The first of these geochronological techniques to be developed was that of endrochronology, or dating by tree-ring counts. Its value was appreciated as early as the second quarter of the nineteenth century.

But the real revolution in the problem of dating in archaeology took place when Professor Willard F. Libby, then of the University of Chicago, discovered the existence of carbon-14 as well as carbon-12 in organic matters, and realized that this radioactive isotope, decaying at a fixed rate, could be used to date material in archaeological contexts. Here at last was a geochronological device that really dated the past. Let us hear an account of the discovery of this technique from Libby himself in association with Anderson and Arnold.[2]

Some time ago the occurrence of radiocarbon in living matter and dissolved ocean carbonate was reported (see references 1, 2, 4, 5) as a result of researches on sewage methane gas from the city of Baltimore. The postulated origin (see reference 5)—cosmic ray neutrons reacting with atmospheric nitrogen to give radiocarbon at high altitudes—clearly predicted that all material in the life cycle and all material exchangeable with atmospheric carbon dioxide, such as carbonate dissolved in sea water, would be radioactive. The long half-life of radiocarbon, 5,720±47 (see reference 3), further seemed to ensure that the mixing processes would have ample time to distribute the radiocarbon uniformly throughout the world.

Since completing the first tests using isotopic enrichment with Dr. Grosse and his associates, an improvement in counting technique has enabled us to investigate materials without enrichment to about 5–10 per cent error. The samples are counted in the form of elementary carbon in a screen wall counter (see reference 6). Six grams of carbon are spread uniformly over an area of 300 cm², to give an "infinitely thick" layer; about 5.9 per cent of the disintegrations register in this arrangement. The background of the counter has been reduced from 150 cpm

[2] Reprinted from an article by Libby, Anderson, and Arnold in *Science,* 109, 2827, March 4, 1949, 277ff.

(when shielded by 2 inches of lead) to 10 cpm by means of anti-coincidence shielding and the addition of a 4-inch iron liner inside the lead shield. The technique will be described in detail elsewhere. A world-wide assay has been completed, and the uniformity apparently established. The data are presented in Table 1.

Table 1. WORLD-WIDE ASSAY OF RADIOCARBON

Samples	Assay (cpm/gm of carbon)
Baltimore sewage methane (1, 2)	10.5 ± 1.0
Ironwood from Marshall Islands	11.5 ± 0.6
Ironwood from Marshall Islands	12.6 ± 1.0
Elmwood, Chicago Campus	12.7 ± 0.8
Elmwood, Chicago Campus	11.9 ± 0.7
Pine, Mt. Wilson, New Mexico (10,000′ altitude)	12.5 ± 0.6
Bolivian wood	13.5 ± 0.6
Bolivian wood	11.3 ± 0.8
Ceylon wood	12.5 ± 0.7
Tierra del Fuego wood	12.8 ± 0.5
Panamanian wood	13.0 ± 0.5
Palestinian wood	12.4 ± 0.4
Swedish wood	12.6 ± 0.5
New South Wales wood	13.3 ± 0.4
North African wood	11.9 ± 0.4
WEIGHTED AVERAGE	12.5 ± 0.2
Sea shell, Florida west coast	13.3 ± 0.5
Sea shell, Florida west coast	14.9 ± 0.7
Sea shell, Florida west coast	14.6 ± 0.5
WEIGHTED AVERAGE	14.1 ± 0.3
Seal oil, Antarctic	10.4 ± 0.7

The numbers quoted are intended to be absolute disintegration rates per gram of carbon. It must be said, however, that our absolute calibration of the counters used may have as much as 10 per cent error. We hope to improve this in the near future. Since all the samples were measured with the same technique, the relative comparison does not involve this point. With the exception of the Antarctic seal sample, which has been run only once to date, the uniformity is well within experimental error. Since one expects the arctic samples if anything to be high, because the neutron intensity is lowest at the equator and rises toward the poles (see reference 9), and since the deviation of the seal oil from the mean is not much larger than the error of the measurement, it is believed that further measurements will show this sample to be normal also. The result on the sea shell sample is interesting. It has been shown (see references 7 and 8) that C^{13} occurs in higher abundance in carbonates than in organic material. The result we find for radiocarbon in sea shells versus wood and other organic material is in line with this earlier finding for C^{13}. It is true, however, that the difference may be somewhat larger in our case than that predicted from the earlier results, though the error of our measurement is so large at present as to well overlap the predicted value.

AGE DETERMINATION

Having established the world-wide uniformity of the radiocarbon assay at the present time, it seems a logical assumption that this would have been true in ancient times. Assuming this, and using the half-life of radiocarbon, $5,720 \pm 47$ years (see reference 2), one can calculate the specific activity to be expected after any given time interval elapsed since the removal of any carbonaceous material from equilibrium with the life cycle. For living materials this probably coincides with the time of death; for carbonates it would correspond to the time of crystallization (assuming no further interchange with the solution or atmospheric carbon dioxide to occur). On this basis we have undertaken examination of wood samples of well-established age from the ancient Egyptian tombs. Two such samples were used, one from the tomb of Sneferu at Meydum (furnished by Froelich Rainey, of the University of Pennsylvania Museum, Philadelphia), which was $4,575 \pm 75$ years old; the other from the tomb of Zoser at Sakkara (furnished by Ambrose Lansing, of the Metropolitan Museum of New York), which was $4,650 \pm 75$ years old. The former sample is cypress wood; the latter is acacia. John Wilson, of the Oriental Institute of the University of Chicago, has given the dates quoted, at the behest of a committee of the American Anthropological Association, consisting of Frederick Johnson, chairman, Froelich Rainey, and Donald Collier. The expected assay for 4,600-year material is easily calculated to be 7.15±0.15 cpm/gm of carbon on the basis of the present assay and the half-life. Table 2 presents the data obtained on these materials.

Table 2. AGE DETERMINATION ON THE ANCIENT EGYPTIAN SAMPLES

Samples	Specific activity found (cpm/gm of carbon)
Zoser	7.88 ± 0.74
Zoser	7.36 ± 0.53
Sneferu	6.95 ± 0.40
Sneferu	7.42 ± 0.38
Sneferu	6.26 ± 0.41
WEIGHTED AVERAGE (both samples)	7.04 ± 0.20
Expected value	7.15 ± 0.15

The data on both samples were averaged since the error in ages almost overlaps the difference, and the weighting was taken according to the error quoted in each run. The errors quoted here and in Table 1 also are standard deviations determined strictly from the statistical counting error, and, since the data agree within these errors, we believe that no other appreciable error is involved in the measurement. It is gratifying that the mean of the determinations agrees with the expected value within 1 standard deviation unit. An error of 0.4 cpm/gm in the specific activity corresponds to an error of 450 years in a 4,600-year-old sample.

On this basis we feel encouraged to proceed with further tests on younger samples of known age. This work is now in progress. It is hoped that certain unknowns can be measured in the near future. A large thermal diffusion column similar to the one used by Dr. Grosse and his associates has been installed in the laboratory and a considerable increase in accuracy should result, permitting the measurement of samples as old as 20,000 to 25,000 years.

REFERENCES

1. E. C. Anderson, W. F. Libby, S. Weinhouse, A. F. Reid, A. D. Kirshenbaum, and A. V. Grosse, *Phys. Rev.,* 1947, 72, p. 931.
2. E. C. Anderson, W. F. Libby, S. Weinhouse, A. F. Reid, A. D. Kirshenbaum, and A. V. Grosse, *Science,* 1947, 105, p. 576.
3. A. G. Engelkemeir, W. H. Hamill, M. G. Inghram, and W. F. Libby (to be published).
4. A. V. Grosse and W. F. Libby, *Science,* 1947, 106, p. 88.
5. W. F. Libby, *Phys. Rev.,* 1946, 69, p. 671.
6. W. F. Libby and D. D. Lee, *Phys. Rev.,* 1939, 55, p. 245.
7. B. F. Murphey and A. O. Nier, *Phys. Rev.,* 1941, 59, p. 771.
8. A. O. Nier and E. A. Gulbransen, *J. Amer. Chem. Soc.,* 1939, 61, p. 697.
9. J. A. Simpson, Jr., *Phys. Rev.,* 1948, 73, p. 1277.

It is no exaggeration to say that the discovery of radiocarbon dating is the most important development in archaeology since the discovery of the antiquity of man and the acceptance of a system of three technological ages. The work described in this book in chapters 3 and 4 brought archaeology as a scientific discipline into existence instead of the fog about the past of which Rasmus Nyerup complained. It brought relative chronological depth to a subject floundering among Ancient Britons and Gauls, all of whom seemed to have no more history than they were prehistoric. There have been of course difficulties and problems in the early years of the publication of radiocarbon dates, but now with more than fifty laboratories all over the world engaged in this work, and almost all archaeological problems becoming illuminated by a series of dates—for one carbon-14 date no more makes history than one swallow makes a summer—the archaeological chronological revolution is taking place.

There are three main obvious ways in which carbon-14 dating has affected archaeology: first, it has taken back exact dates in years long before 3000 B.C. and given us, for example, dates for the Upper Paleolithic industries and before. It is now no longer guesswork to refer, as the Abbé Breuil did in his *Four Hundred Centuries of Cave Art* (1952), to a style that began between 40,000 and 30,000 years ago.

Secondly, absolute chronology has been extended not only backward to the food-gathering stage in Europe, which was the main object of Paleolithic studies from 1850 onward, but to peoples in the food-gathering and food-producing stages in areas outside the areas of Europe and the Near East. To an archaeologist like the present writer, trained in his discipline in pre-Libby days, the most exciting result of carbon-14 dating is the fact that artifacts, industries, assemblages, cultures—call them what you will—from the prehistory of America, Africa, Asia, Australia, and Polynesia can now be accurately dated. And in the third place, the dubious and tenuous links in the chains of cross-dating that bound Europe from 3000 B.C. to the Roman conquest of Britain and the Greek colonization of France and Spain to the Aegean and the most ancient Near East can now be reforged with a truer metal. Gordon Childe once said that there were no certain dates in European prehistory before 1400 B.C. Before that was guesswork, and as we now see from the steady accumulation of carbon-14 dates, many of those guesses were wrong—pardonably and understandably, but nevertheless wrong.

If the discovery of the antiquity of man and the invention and proof of the Three-Age technological system produced a science of archaeology with a relative chronology, the Libby revolution produced archaeology as a historical science with an absolute chronology. It has brought us to within range of our ultimate goal, the writing of human history in terms of exact dates.

As the decades of the mid-twentieth century develop, we certainly will no longer have need of any relative chronological devices to date the past. Many people had been trying to side-step the divisions of the Three-Age system in their chronological misuse even before Libby. Gordon Childe, always experimenting with ideas and techniques, did not use the divisions of the Three-Age system when he came to write his *Prehistoric Communities of the British Isles* in 1940 but a system of periods. There were nine of them, and in the end they were some sort of way of making the relative chronology of the succession of cultures in prehistoric Britain into an apparently objective framework. This Childe system was not much used: the present writer tried to use it in his *Prehistoric Chamber Tombs of England and Wales* (1950), published five years after Libby's discovery but before carbon-14 dates had begun to pour in. What all this amounted to was that these "periods" were only a substitute for history with accurate dates. The great virtue of Childe's book and the reason why it is a landmark in the history of the growth of archaeology is that it was not principally organized on the Three-Age divisions. From the moment his book appeared in 1940, it was clear that the use of terms like Neolithic, Chalcolithic, Early Bronze Age, etc., in a chronological sense was really over. The first person to take the plunge and deliberately eschew the chronological use of these technological subdivisions was Professor R. J. C. Atkinson in his *Stonehenge* (1956), and the following passage from his section on the dating of the sequence at Stonehenge must be quoted. Although it is only ten years old, it is a document in the history of archaeology.

Until recently archaeologists have been in the habit of dating their prehistoric material by *periods,* to which names are given such as "Late Neolithic" or "Middle Bronze Age" or "Early Iron Age." This practice is symptomatic, of course, of the relative vagueness of archaeological chronologies; and though it has the merit of honesty, in that it does not claim to be any more precise than the nature of the evidence warrants, it has the disadvantage that except to the expert it conveys very little about the actual periods involved, measured in years. Moreover, it must be realized that names like "Early Bronze Age" are not really labels for periods of past time, but names for stages in the technological development of human societies. And since such development does not take place uniformly, even in an area as small as Britain, it is inevitable that at one and the same time there will be a community, say, in Wessex which, in virtue of the possession of certain diagnostic types of bronze weapons, must be assigned to the Middle Bronze Age, while another in northern England, less advanced, belongs to the Early Bronze Age, and a third in northern Scotland, retarded through geographical isolation, will still be in the Late Stone Age.

Our increased understanding of the regional differences in the rate of technological progress has made this kind of absurdity a commonplace. For this reason archaeologists are now beginning to abandon the use of terms like "Middle Bronze Age," at any rate to distinguish *periods of time,* and are being driven to give dates in actual years, or at any rate in centuries B.C. This is all to the good, if only because the use of a common system of chronology emphasizes that prehistory is nothing more than the backwards extension of history, and that the aims of the archaeologist and the historian are ultimately identical. Moreover, the use of absolute dates is becoming increasingly justified by the dates in actual years now being provided by techniques such as the radioactive carbon estimations. . . .

But it must not be assumed, of course, that the use of a common system of dating implies a common standard of accuracy. To say that St. Paul's Cathedral was built in the seventeenth century A.D. means something very different, in terms of accuracy of statement, from saying that Stonehenge II was built in the seventeenth century B.C. So long as the archaeologist has to deal with societies that are neither literate themselves, nor in close contact with literate communities elsewhere, there must inevitably be a sizeable margin of uncertainty in his dates; and the size of this margin will increase, roughly speaking, in proportion to the distance, measured in time and in space, of the community in question from other communities whose chronologies are either recorded directly, or can be reconstructed with the aid of documents, coins, or inscriptions.

The reader is therefore warned that in what follows the dates are very rough ones, and cannot be treated as if they were dates A.D. For the earlier of them at least, the margin of uncertainty may be as much as two centuries either way. . . .

The Stonehenge sequence may thus be set out in the form of a table, with very approximate dates:

1900–1700 B.C. *Stonehenge I* Construction of the bank, ditch, and Aubrey Holes. Erection of the Heel Stone, stones D and E, and the timber structure A. Inception and use of the cremation cemetery.

1700–1600 B.C. *Stonehenge II* Transport of the bluestones from Pembrokeshire. Erection of the double circle in the Q and R holes. Filling up of the east end of the ditch at the causeway. Digging and filling of the Heel Stone ditch. Construction of the Avenue. Dismantling of stones D and E and timber structure A. Possible erection of stones B and C.

1500 B.C. *Stonehenge IIIa* Transport of the sarsen stones

from near Marlborough. Dismantling of the double circle of bluestones. Erection of the sarsen trilithons, circle, Station Stones, and the Slaughter Stone and its companion. Carvings executed on the stones.

1500–1400 B.C. *Stonehenge IIIb* Tooling and erection of stones of the dressed bluestone setting. Digging and abandonment of the Y and Z holes.

1400 B.C. *Stonehenge IIIc* Dismantling of the dressed bluestone setting. Re-erection of these and the remaining bluestones in the present circle and horseshoe.

A.D. 50–400. Possibly some deliberate destruction of the stones.

It could be said that with the arrival of an absolute chronology through carbon-14 dating, archaeology was fully grown. The story of the development of environmental archaeology and of all manner of scientific aids to archaeology is the story of current archaeology and has no place here in an account of origins and growth which might properly have stopped in the thirties but had to include Libby and carbon-14 dating. Nor have we need here to discuss all the different historical interpretations of the archaeological material which, with the discrediting of the extravagant hyperdiffusionist model, have been current—the Marxist interpretation of many Soviet and east European archaeologists, for example. We will content ourselves with one extract which shows just one of the intriguing ways in which the science of archaeology is still growing, and two passages which illustrate the interpretative ideas of the mature science.

Antiquarians had observed crop marks as early as the sixteenth century, as we have seen (p. 25 above), and even before the advent of air photography on a large scale the value of looking at earthworks from a high hill had been appreciated. But it was the development of air photography in the First World War that showed the real potentialities of air archaeology. These were realized by no one so clearly as O. G. S. Crawford (1886–1957), himself an air photographer in that war: as Archaeology Officer of the Ordnance Survey after the war he had a chance to develop this technique with great effect. Here is a passage from the book

Wessex from the Air, which he wrote with Alexander Keiller and published in 1928. It summarized the results of a few months' flying and photography in Wessex, and was, and is, a classic of its kind.

Long before aeroplanes were invented it was confidently hoped that vertical photographs would some day be taken, and it was felt certain that, if so, they would greatly assist archaeology. Major Elsdale was the pioneer of air photography in the British Army. Between about 1880 and 1887 he carried out many experiments from free balloons, and also invented a method of sending up small balloons just large enough to carry a camera which exposed a certain number of plates automatically; then the balloon emptied itself of some of its gas and came down. Some of the results were quite good considering the difficulties. In 1891 Lieutenant C. F. Close (now Colonel Sir Charles Close) suggested to the Surveyor-General of India that the India Office should be asked to send out similar apparatus to photograph from the air the ancient ruined cities round Agra, with the view of constructing a map from the air photographs. The scheme was approved and the apparatus was sent to India, but official difficulties of the usual type supervened. The result was that Agra was cut out of the scheme, a few photographs were taken over Calcutta at an unfavourable season of the year, and the opportunity was lost. After Major Elsdale left the Balloon Establishment in 1888 little or nothing was done at home in this matter; and after 1892 the Survey of India took no more interest in balloon photography. Major Elsdale spent much of his own money on the experiments in question, but ballooning was not much in favor in the eighties, although some progress was made, and he received little or no official support in his balloon-photography experiments.

In 1906 Lieutenant P. H. Sharpe took a vertical and an oblique photograph of Stonehenge from a war balloon; these were published in *Archaeologia* (vol. lx) by Colonel Capper. During several years immediately preceding the [First World] War, Mr. Henry S. Wellcome successfully used large box kites with specially devised automatic-control cameras for photographing his archaeological sites and excavations in the Upper Nile regions of the Anglo-Egyptian Sudan.

During the War, when aeroplane photographs first became common, it might have been expected that archaeological features would have been observed, but in the British sector in France none was seen, so far as I know. The photographs were often taken at a great height, over country which is archaeologically barren, or which was too rankly overgrown to show results. Moreover, the interpretation of air photographs for military purposes was a new art and in itself sufficiently fascinating to oust academic interests for a time. On other fronts time was found for archaeology. Pioneer work in the air was carried out by the Germans in northern Sinai. Dr. Theodor Wiegand was appointed to a special commission (*Denkmalschutzkommando*) which was sent out with the German forces operating in southern Palestine and Sinai. One cannot but admire the scientific enthusiasm of a country which could remember archaeology in the midst of a world war. The results were published by Dr. Wiegand, and his monograph is the first publication containing direct reproductions of archaeological photographs taken from an aeroplane (1920). The first thirty-five pages contain an account of the military operations, written by General Kress von Kressenstein; the remaining hundred and ten pages are by Dr. Wiegand, and contain a valuable description of the wonderful air photographs obtained. There are eight well-reproduced collotype plates, each containing two air photographs, and in the text are five half-tone reproductions of air photographs of ancient sites. In addition, much archaeological material of the ordinary kind is described and illustrated.

The principal air photographs are of El Arish, Ruhebe (Rehoboth), Umm el Keisume, Mishrefe, Sbeita, and Hafir el Aujsha. The results are most remarkable. The plan of each of these now deserted cities can be seen at a glance with astonishing clearness. Streets, churches, courtyards, gardens, and fields are evident, and orderly rows of cairns (for vine-growing, it is stated) are a prominent feature. Most certainly there is a vast and almost unexplored field for archaeology from the air in Arabia.

About the time that the fortunes of war brought German interest in Sinai to an end, Colonel Beazeley, R.E., was discovering ancient sites in Mesopotamia. Others no doubt had observed the streets and public gardens of Eski Baghdad from the air, but Colonel Beazeley was the first to publish an account of them (1919), and indeed his article appeared a year before the German report on Sinai. If, as has been said, the date of an archaeological discovery is the date of its publication, to Colonel Beazeley belongs the credit of being the pioneer of archaeology from an aeroplane. His article in the *Geographical Journal* is illustrated, however, not by actual reproductions of air photographs, but by plans of ancient cities and irrigation works which, to the ground observer, appear formless. Most remarkable perhaps are the four huge circles tangential to each other with a fine pavilion in the centre.

The air photographs were taken, of course, for military purposes, and it was in the course of this work that the ancient city was discovered. "It was," says Colonel Beazeley, "some twenty miles long and anything up to two and a half miles in width. . . . [It was] well planned, with wide main streets or boulevards, from which wide roads branched off. . . . Had I not been in possession of these air photographs, the city would probably have been merely shown [on the map] by meaningless low mounds scattered here and there, for much of the detail was not recognizable on the ground, but was well shown up in the photographs, as the slight difference in the colour of the soil came out with marked effect on the sensitive film, and the larger properties of the nobles and rich merchants could be plainly made out along the banks of the Tigris." Colonel Beazeley continues: "When riding as a passenger in an aeroplane *en route* for survey over enemy territory, I could clearly see on the desert area the outline of a series of detached forts, whereas when walking over them on the ground no trace was visible. Another interesting thing I could plainly see in my flights was the outline of an ancient scientific irrigation system, such as has been introduced in the Punjab only in comparatively recent years. Unfortunately I was shot down and captured before being able to make a detailed survey of the system during a lull in the military operations." . . .

Arabia and the countries bordering it have played a leading

role in the history of this new method of research. Circumstances are largely responsible for this. The ancient sites there are so plain that no special training or interest is required to detect them. In England the ancient sites are sometimes plain enough, but the remains themselves are seldom self-explanatory. Anyone can recognize an ancient city, but even the best-preserved prehistoric earthwork is something of a mystery, at any rate to those unfamiliar with primitive culture. Those, however, whose main interests lay at home had long hoped for that instrument of discovery which the invention of the aeroplane provided. The War, while it promoted the development of flying, delayed its archaeological exploitation. My own interest dates from the time, before flying became at all common, when I used to discuss with Dr. J. P. Williams-Freeman the possibilities of an overhead view. We knew that the low banks and mounds of prehistoric fields, villages, and barrows were plainly revealed at sunset, even to an observer on the ground, for the long shadows then cast made visible even the slightest undulation on the surface of the downs. We knew also that the course of prehistoric boundary ditches could often be seen in the corn when the observer could view them from a distance, on a hill or on the opposite slopes of a valley. We longed for overhead views of Wessex before the first air photograph had been taken. After the War I made one or two attempts to follow up the subject. In March 1919 I made a suggestion to the Earthworks Committee (of the Congress of Archaeological Societies) that they should get in touch with the Royal Air Force, but it was not taken up and an opportunity was thus lost. On the 22nd October 1922 an air photograph was taken of Old Winchester Hill by the R. A. F. School of Photography at Farnborough, at the suggestion of Mr. C. J. P. Cave. On the hill is a prehistoric hill fort and several barrows; one more barrow was revealed by the air photograph, but it is also plainly visible on the ground. The site is about two miles east of Meon Stoke in Hampshire.

The birth of the new study in England may be said to date from 1922 when Air-Commodore Clark Hall observed certain curious marks on R.A.F. air photos taken in Hampshire. With him must be mentioned Flight-Lieutenant Haslam, who took a number of photographs near Winchester showing what turned out to be Celtic fields. Air-Commodore Clark Hall showed these photographs to Dr. Williams-Freeman, who took me to see them. Dr. Williams-Freeman and I had always been hoping for air photographs of English soil, and looking at these we saw that our expectations were fulfilled, and even surpassed, by what was revealed. It was possible from these photographs to make a map of the Celtic field system near Winchester, which was published in the *Geographical Journal* for May 1923, and reprinted in *Air Survey and Archaeology,* 1924 (Ordnance Survey Professional Paper, New Series, No. 7). Many archaeological air photographs have been taken by the School of Army Co-operation at Old Sarum, and by officers of the R.A.F. stations at Farnborough, Calshot, Lee-on-Solent, and Gosport.

Recently the Air Ministry has sanctioned the transfer to the Ordnance Survey Office of all air photographs containing archaeological information which are not required for service purposes. Thus the connexion between air photography and the Royal Engineers, begun about 1880 by Major Elsdale and continued by Colonel Beazeley, has been maintained. Needless to point out, air-photographs are of great use, when checked and supplemented by field work, in revising the archaeological information on the ordnance maps.

This chapter has been called "The Mature Science" because our series of extracts has led us to the moment in the twenties of the present century when archaeology seemed to have become a mature and recognized discipline. Its origins were in the antiquarianism of the sixteenth, seventeenth, and eighteenth centuries. Those origins came to fruition in the nineteenth century when the Three-Age system of the Danes, the geological revolution of the English, and the demonstration of the antiquity of man by the French and English brought archaeology as a subject into existence by the sixties. This is why our chapter 5 was called "Archaeology Comes of Age." Between the sixties of the nineteenth century and the twenties and thirties of the twentieth century it had matured. We ended the last chapter with the mature excavational techniques of Sir Mortimer Wheeler, and we end this chapter and indeed the whole book with the mature interpretational techniques and ideas of Vere Gordon Childe. If, as we look back on the origins and growth of archaeology, we think we can see stages, I suggest that there are these: first, the stage of those who brought archaeology out of antiquarianism, namely Frere and Thomsen and Boucher de Perthes and Worsaae; secondly, the stage of those who consolidated archaeology when it had come of age—men like Lubbock who wrote *Prehistoric Times* and *The Origin of Civilization;* thirdly, the great discoverers and innovators of the last quarter of the nineteenth century—men like Schliemann and Petrie, and Pitt-Rivers; fourthly, the men who, after the First World War, recreated and refurbished the field techniques of the late nineteenth century, developed entirely new techniques, and, with the wealth of factual knowledge then available, produced a new synthesis of man's past.

Here we are now concerned with this last aspect. The mature science now exists, but one of the main persons who made it mature because he set out and popularized the new synthesis of man's past—with a wealth of comparative archaeological knowledge which no one had before, or then, or perhaps ever again—was Gordon Childe. An Australian who came to Oxford as a postgraduate student, he traveled the world and summarized the knowledge of prehistoric Europe in his *Dawn of European Civilization,* first published in 1925. It is in its seventh (1957) edition, a classic of archaeology. Childe had much to say about archaeological method in his famous preface to *The Danube in Prehistory* (1929):

A word or two must . . . be said on archaeological concepts. We find certain types of remains—pots, implements, ornaments, burial rites, house forms—constantly recurring together. Such a complex of regularly associated traits we shall term a "cultural group" or just a "culture." We assume that such a complex is the material expression of what would today be called a "people." Only where the complex in question is regularly and exclusively associated with skeletal remains of a specific physical type would we venture to replace "people" by the term "race."

The same complex may be found with relatively negligible

diminutions or additions over a wide area. In such cases of the total and bodily transference of a complete culture from one place to another we think ourselves justified in assuming a "movement of people." At other times one or more elements of one culture reappear in various places in a more or less different context. In such cases we assume the existence of some sort of "relation" between the respective areas or cultures. . . . The nature of the "relations" subsisting between cultures cannot usually be defined with any precision. But two main types may be distinguished according as the time factor does or does not intervene. In the first case the traits common to different areas may represent survivals from one former culture that has been at different points in its one time territory overlaid by distinct new cultures. . . . Where such survival is excluded . . . we have to invoke "influences." This word has only a minimal connotation. It may mean actual movements and mixings of peoples, intertribal barter, imitation, or some other form of contact. Often it is merely a confession of ignorance, and in no case must it be taken as an explanation. Where any indications are available to guide us, we attempt to give "influence" a precise meaning in concrete cases. It is plain that "influences" do not travel *in vacuo* any more than influenza germs. They denote actual contact between peoples. But that contact may be anything from conquest or federation to friendly visits between neighbouring chiefs or the "silent trade."

However, some things denote a real change in the habits of a people. . . . Influences disclosed in agreements, affecting the whole habits of a people and not obviously dictated by practical motives, are almost certainly to be interpreted in "ethnic" terms, using "ethnic" as the adjective from "people." On the other hand, no such significance need attach to the spread of an obviously superior device (e.g. the cut-and-thrust sword) or a new fashion in hairpin (among people who wore hairpins). Such denote external relations—trade or imitation. External relations are further disclosed by all accidental agreements. We term an accidental agreement the sporadic occurrence in one culture of types proper to another. . . .

Culture . . . is not necessarily a chronological concept. Even in one place a culture might persist for a long time. In any case, the same culture might appear in one place at a given time and reach another place very much later.

This statement of archaeological method, in 1929, is a classic one, and, in a sense, here is the moment to break off any account of the growth of archaeology. Here in the most remarkable preface to *The Danube in Prehistory* is a statement of aims, methods, and limitations which is with us all today and which can and should be reread with profit by everyone at the present day. Childe wrote many books, and will be remembered not least for his masterly attempts at a general synthesis of our knowledge of man's prehistoric past as revealed by archaeology. *Man Makes Himself* was first published in 1936, and was succeeded in 1942 by *What Happened in History*. Although in these volumes Childe made broad generalizations and set out clearly his views of the Neolithic and urban revolutions in human history, as he called them, he was always conscious of the limitations of archaeology. In his *Social Evolution* (1951) he pays particular attention to this problem, and an extract from that book is a fitting end to this collection of extracts that have attempted to outline some of the stages in the origin and growth of archaeology.

In favourable circumstances archaeology can . . . provide considerable evidence for forming a fairly adequate, though always incomplete, picture, not only of the technology but also of the whole economy of a preliterate society. Social institutions are far more elusive. Yet it is precisely these that are of chief concern to sociology. . . . Social institutions have been classified by Hobhouse, Ginsberg and Wheeler [3] under the headings of government, justice, the family, rank, property, and war—to which institutional religion (as opposed to "beliefs") should surely be added. . . . In certain circumstances, and always with reserve, archaeology can provide some indications as to the form of government and of the family, the recognition rank, the distribution of the social product, and the practice of war. It is never likely to be able to tell us anything about the adminis-

[3] *The Material Culture and Social Institutions of Simpler Peoples* (1926).

tration of justice, the penalties used to enforce it, nor the content of any laws, the way in which descent rather than inheritance of property is determined, the effective limitations on the powers of chiefs, or even of the extent of their authority. The content of religious belief and the nature of the prestige conferred by rank are irretrievably lost. Worst of all, negative evidence is worthless; rich graves or palaces may be evidence for the existence of chiefs, but the absence of the evidence cannot be taken as proof that they did not exist. And much of the available evidence is often ambiguous. As to "government," without inscribed documents we can form no idea at all of the extent of the political units. . . . For community of culture, at least in the archaeological sense, need not mean political unity. It would . . . be rash to equate the archaeologist's culture with the ethnographer's tribe, if tribe implies a single government, the exclusion of wars (other than blood feuds), and even recognized rights of intermarriage . . . the most that an archaeologist can mean by "chiefs" is persons who monopolize an appreciable fraction at least of the social surplus. . . . If it is difficult to recognize chiefs with certainty in the archaeological record, to recognize an aristocracy is much harder.

Sources of the Extracts

ANDERSON, E. C., *see* Libby, W. F.
Archaeological Journal, I, 1845, pp. 269–81.
ARNOLD, J. R., *see* Libby, W. F.
ATKINSON, R. J. C., *Stonehenge,* Hamish Hamilton, 1956, pp. 79, 84.
AUBREY, JOHN, *An Essay towards the Description of the North Division of Wiltshire* (put together between 1659 and 1670). The passage in this book is quoted from A. Powell, *John Aubrey and His Friends,* Heinemann, 1963, 3rd ed., pp. 275–77.
BELZONI, GIOVANNI, *Narrative of the Operations and Recent Discoveries within the Pyramids, Temples, Tombs, and Excavations, in Egypt and Nubia,* London, 1820, pp. 155–58, 347–70.
BOUCHER DE PERTHES, *De l'homme antédiluvien et ses oeuvres,* Paris, 1860, pp. 1–18, translated by Stephen Heizer in Heizer, q.v., pp. 83–93.
BRAIDWOOD, ROBERT J., *Archaeologists and What They Do,* Franklin Watts Inc.: New York, 1960, pp. 4–19.
———, "Terminology in Prehistory," *Human Origins: An Introductory General Course in Anthropology: Selected Readings Series II,* University of Chicago Press, 1946, pp. 32–45.
BREUIL, H., *Les Cavernes du Volp,* Paris, 1958, translated by Jacquetta Hawkes in *The World of the Past,* Thames & Hudson, 1964, pp. 203–205.

CARTER, H., and MACE, A. C., *The Tomb of Tut-ankh-Amen*, Cassell, 1923; vol. I, pp. 86–178.

CHAMBERLAIN, ALEXANDER F., "Thomas Jefferson's Ethnological Opinions and Activities," *American Anthropologist*, IX, 1907, p. 499.

CHAMPOLLION, J. F., *"Lettre à M. Dacier à l'alphabet des hiéroglyphes phonétiques,"* 1822, translated from the French by V. M. Conrad in *The World of Archaeology*, edited and introduced by C. W. Ceram, London, 1965, pp. 162–70.

CHILDE, V. G., *The Danube in Prehistory*, Clarendon Press, 1929, pp. v–vii.

———, *Social Evolution*, Watts, 1951, pp. 54–60.

CLARK, GRAHAME, *Archaeology and Society*, 3rd ed., Methuen, 1957, pp. 17, 32–33.

———, *The Study of Prehistory*, Cambridge University Press, 1954, pp. 7–9.

CRAWFORD, O. G. S., and KEILLER, ALEXANDER, *Wessex from the Air*, Oxford University Press, 1928, pp. 3–5.

DANIEL, GLYN, *A Hundred Years of Archaeology*, Duckworth, 1950, pp. 66–67.

———, *The Three Ages*, Cambridge University Press, 1943, pp. 27–28.

DÉCHELETTE, JOSEPH, *Manuel d'archéologie préhistorique, celtique et gallo-romaine*, Paris, 1908, translated by Glyn Daniel, pp. 239–40.

DE LAET, SIGFRIED J., *Archaeology and Its Problems*, Phoenix House, 1957, pp. 13–14.

DENON, D. VIVANT, *Travels in Upper and Lower Egypt during the Campaigns of General Bonaparte*, translated from the French by E. A. Kendal, London, 1802, pp. 37–38.

DROOP, J. P., *Archaeological Excavation*, Cambridge University Press, 1915, pp. vii–ix, 15, 30, 34, 38, 63–64.

ELLESMERE, LORD, *A Guide to Northern Antiquities*, London, 1848, pp. 63–68.

ENGELS, FRIEDRICH, *The Origin of the Family, Private Property and the State*, Moscow, Foreign Languages Publishing House, 1958, pp. 170–84.

EVANS, ARTHUR, *The Monthly Review*, II, March 1901, pp. 115–32.

EVANS, JOAN, *Time and Chance: The Story of Arthur Evans and His Forebears*, Longmans, 1943, pp. 100–102.

FRERE, JOHN, "Account of Flint Weapons discovered at *Hoxne* in *Suffolk*," *Archaeologia*, XIII, 1800, pp. 204–205.

GORDON, ALEXANDER, *Itinerarium Septentrionale*, 1726, Preface.

HAWKES, C. F. C., "British Prehistory Half-way through the Century," *Proceedings of the Prehistoric Society*, XVII, 1951, pp. 1–9.

HEIZER, R. F. (ed.), *Man's Discovery of His Past: Literary Landmarks in Archaeology*, Prentice Hall, 1962, p. 79, *see* Boucher de Perthes and Tournal, M.

JEFFERSON, THOMAS, "Excavation of a Virginia Burial Mound in 1784," *Notes on the State of Virginia, see* Chamberlain, A. F.

LARTET, ÉDOUARD, *Quarterly Journal of the Geological Society of London*, XVI, 1860, pp. 471–79.

LHWYD, EDWARD, *Philosophical Transactions of the Royal Society,* 1712, p. 503; 1713, p. 97.

LIBBY, W. F., ANDERSON, E. C., and ARNOLD, J. R., "Age Determination by Radiocarbon Content: World-Wide Assay of Natural Radiocarbon," *Science*, 109, 2827, 4 March 1949, pp. 227 ff.

LUBBOCK, SIR JOHN (AVEBURY), *Prehistoric Times*, 1865, pp. 1–3, 578–93.

LYELL, SIR CHARLES, *The Geological Evidences of the Antiquity of Man*, London, 1863, pp. 75–79.

MACE, A. C., *see* Carter, H.

MACKINNON, JAMES, *Culture in Early Scotland*, London, 1892, pp. 1–2.

MARIETTE, AUGUSTE, *The Monuments of Upper Egypt*, 1877, translated by Alphonse Mariette, pp. 88–94.

MONTELIUS, OSCAR, *The Civilization of Sweden in Heathen Times*, London, 1888, pp. 1–4, 43–46.

MORGAN, LEWIS H., *Ancient Society or Researches in the Lines of Human Progress from Savagery through Barbarism to Civilization*, 1877, pp. 5–18.

MORLOT, A., *General Views on Archaeology*, Washington, 1861, pp. 1–10, 40, 55, 59.

NILSSON, SVEN, *The Primitive Inhabitants of Scandinavia*, London, 1868, pp. lvii–lxx.

OTTER, THE REVEREND WILLIAM, *The Life and Remains of the Reverend Edward Daniel Clarke*, London, 1818, vol. IV, pp. 618–21.

PARKER, J. H., *The Ashmolean Museum: Its History, Present State and Prospects*, Oxford, 1870, pp. 9–12.

PETRIE, W. N. F., *Methods and Aims in Archaeology*, London, 1904, pp. 171–78.

PHILLIPS, E. D., "The Greek Vision of Prehistory," *Antiquity*, 1964, pp. 171–78.

PIGGOTT, STUART, *Approach to Archaeology*, A. & C. Black and Harvard University Press, 1959, pp. 1–6, 126.

PITT-RIVERS, GENERAL, *Excavations in Cranborne Chase*, 1887–98 (4 vols.), vol. I, 1887, pp. xii–xx, vol. II, 1888, pp. xii–xvi; vol. III, 1892, p. ix.

PRESTWICH, JOSEPH, *Proceedings of the Royal Society of London*, X, 1860, pp. 50–91.

RAWLINSON, SIR HENRY CRESWICKE, "Notes on some Paper Casts of Cuneiform Inscriptions upon the sculptured Rock at Behistun exhibited to the Society of Antiquaries," *Archaeologia*, XXXIV, 1852, pp. 74–76.

ROWLANDS, HENRY, *Mona Antiqua Restaurata*, Dublin, 1723, Preface, and pp. 19–43.

SCHLIEMANN, HEINRICH, *Ilios: The City and Country of the Trojans*, London, 1880, pp. 18–26, 38–43.

STUKELEY, WILLIAM, *Itinerarium Curiosum*, pp. 76–77, 115, 138, and a "Letter to Roger Gale" quoted by S. Piggott, *William Stukeley*, Oxford University Press, 1950, p. 52.

THOMSEN, C. J., *Ledetraad til Nordisk Oldkyndighed*, Copenhagen, 1836, *see* translation by Ellesmere.

TOURNAL, M., *Annales de Chimie et de Physique*, vol. 25, 1833, pp. 161–81. Translated by A. B. Elsasser and reprinted from *Kroeber Anthropological Society Papers*, No. 21, 1959, pp. 6–16 in Heizer, op. cit.

TURNER, MAJOR GENERAL TOMKYNS, *Archaeologia*, XVI, 1812, pp. 212–14.

TYLOR, EDWARD B., *Researches into the Early History of Mankind and the Development of Civilization,* London, 1865, pp. 1–5, 152, 162, 183–84, 193, 370, 373–74.

———, *Anthropology,* London, 1881.

WHEELER, SIR MORTIMER, *Archaeology from the Earth,* Oxford University Press, 1954, pp. v, 1–4, 15, 40, 49–50, 126–29.

WOOLLEY, SIR LEONARD, *Digging Up the Past,* Ernest Benn Ltd., 1930, pp. 118–20.

———, *Spadework,* Lutterworth Press, 1953, pp. 11–12, 14–16.

———, *Ur of the Chaldees,* Ernest Benn Ltd., and W. W. Norton, 1929, pp. 13–14, 33–35, 42–65.

WORSAAE, J. J. A., *Primeval Antiquities of Denmark,* London, 1849, translated by William J. Thoms, pp. 1–9, 76, 105, 124, 126.

WRIGHT, THOMAS, "Wanderings of an Antiquary: Part VII," *The Gentleman's Magazine,* XXXVIII, 1852, pt. 2, pp. 568–70.

Books for Further Reading

There is no good one-volume history of archaeology. A. Michaelis's *A Century of Archaeological Discovery* (London, 1909) takes the story, mainly in terms of classical archaeology, up to the end of the nineteenth century. My own *A Hundred Years of Archaeology* (London, 1950) and *The Idea of Prehistory* (London, 1962) deal with certain periods and aspects of the whole subject. So does C. W. Ceram in his *Gods, Graves and Scholars* (London, 1952) and his *A Picture History of Archaeology* (London, 1958), and readers may find his small book *Archaeology* (Odyssey Library, New York, 1964; London, 1965) a very agreeable and useful introduction to the subject. The long introductory essay to Jacquetta Hawkes's *The World of the Past* (see below) is a most useful summary, and W. H. Boulton's *The Romance of Archaeology* (London, n.d.) can still be read with profit.

For specialist histories the following: for Mesopotamian archaeology, Seton Lloyd's *Foundations in the Dust* (London, 1947), and E. A. W. Budge, *The Rise and Progress of Assyriology* (London, 1925); for European archaeology, Geoffrey Bibby's *The Testimony of the Spade* (London, 1957); and for British archaeology, Sir Thomas Kendrick, *British Antiquity* (London, 1950), H. B. Walters, *The English Antiquaries of the 16th, 17th, and 18th Centuries* (London, 1934), and Stuart Piggott, *William Stukeley* (Oxford, 1950). For the general relation of the origins and growth of archaeology to those of anthropology, see Stanley

Casson, *The Discovery of Man* (London, 1939), and T. K. Penniman, *A Hundred Years of Anthropology* (London, 1932), and Margaret T. Hodgen, *Early Anthropology in the Sixteenth and Seventeenth Centuries* (Philadelphia, 1964).

Anthologies and readers in archaeology have multiplied in the last decade, and there is now no shortage of really good ones. Margaret Wheeler produced her *A Book of Archaeology: Seventeen Stories of Discovery* in 1957, and followed it up with her *A Second Book of Archaeology* in 1959 (London). Leo Deuel's *The Treasures of Time: First-hand Accounts by Famous Archaeologists of Their Work in the Near East* (Cleveland, 1961; London, 1962) is just what its subtitle says, and goes from Belzoni, Mariette, and Layard to Kramer, Lankester Harding, and Ventris. The volume entitled *Archaeology,* edited by Samuel Raport and Helen Wright, in the New York University Library of Science (New York, 1963) is another useful collection of extracts, and ends up by rescuing for us all E. E. Slosson's fine "The Science of the City Dump" which appeared in his *Snapshots of Science* in 1928, and in which the archaeologist is described as "a sort of inverted sexton, who disinters instead of burying, and he sifts the ashes of a city dump with more assiduity than the scavenger." *Physical Anthropology and Archaeology: Selected Readings* (New York and London, 1964), edited by Peter B. Hammond, is also of great value, and so is R. F. Heizer's *The Archaeologist at Work* (New York, 1959). For England there is that amusing, personal collection by Ronald Jessup, *Curiosities of British Archaeology* (London, 1961), more a bedside archaeological anthology than the more formal readers we have been listing so far. Two new archaeological anthologies have appeared as the present collection goes to press. One is by C. W. Ceram and is entitled *The World of Archaeology* (London, 1966). It is subtitled "The Pioneers Tell Their Own Story" but contains much secondhand material. Archaeology here means what it did to Ceram in his *Gods, Graves and Scholars,* and does not include prehistory. The second is Robert Wauchope's *They Found the Buried Cities* (Chicago and London, 1965), an anthology of writings about, as the subtitle has it, "Exploration and Excavation in the American Tropics."

For the last I have reserved two items; the first is R. F. Heizer (ed.), *Man's Discovery of His Past: Literary Landmarks in Archaeology* (Englewood Cliffs, New Jersey, 1962), and the second is Jacquetta Hawkes's *The World of the Past*. Heizer's anthology is particularly valuable in that it includes all sorts of out-of-the-way items; it is not only a reader for the general public, it is a source book for the specialist. *The World of the Past* is a large, two-volume work published in New York and London in 1963; it is really a reference work of extracts, not an anthology that can be read through: it is an essential for all libraries and serious students and, with its wise selection and generous editing, provides, in four inches of shelf space, the essence of two hundred feet of books.

Index